Matters of Time

Modern **F**rench **I**dentities

Edited by Peter Collier

Volume 115

PETER LANG

Oxford · Bern · Berlin · Bruxelles · Frankfurt am Main · New York · Wien

Lisa Jeschke and Adrian May (eds)

Matters of Time

Material Temporalities in
Twentieth-Century French Culture

PETER LANG

Oxford· Bern · Berlin · Bruxelles · Frankfurt am Main · New York · Wien

Bibliographic information published by Die Deutsche Nationalbibliothek
Die Deutsche Nationalbibliothek lists this publication in the Deutsche
Nationalbibliografie; detailed bibliographic data is available on the
Internet at http://dnb.d-nb.de.

A catalogue record for this book is available from the British Library.

Library of Congress Cataloging-in-Publication Data:

Jeschke, Lisa.
  Matters of time : material temporalities in twentieth-century French culture /
Lisa Jeschke and Adrian May.
    pages cm. -- (Modern French identities ; 115)
  Includes bibliographical references and index.
  ISBN 978-3-0343-1796-2 (alk. paper)
  1. French literature--20th century--History and criticism. 2. Time in literature.
3. Time in motion pictures. 4. Materialism--France--History--20th century. 5.
France--Intellectual life--20th century. I. May, Adrian. II. Title.
  PQ307.T56J47 2014
  840.9'384--dc23
                                            2014021895

Cover image: 'Matters of Time draft' © Lisa Jeschke and Adrian May 2014.

ISSN 1422-9005
ISBN 978-3-0343-1796-2 (print)
ISBN 978-3-0353-0656-9 (eBook)

© Peter Lang AG, International Academic Publishers, Bern 2014
Hochfeldstrasse 32, CH-3012 Bern, Switzerland
info@peterlang.com, www.peterlang.com, www.peterlang.net

This publication has been peer reviewed.

Printed in Germany

Contents

Acknowledgments

The editors would like to thank Alice Blackhurst, Richard Riddick, Emma Wilson and Nick White for their help in organizing the 'Matters of Time' conference, 27–28 April 2013; Emmanuel College, Cambridge, for hosting this event; and the French Embassy, London, for their kind sponsorship.

Furthermore, publication of this volume would not have been possible without the support of the French Department and Clare Hall, Cambridge, with thanks also to Jeff Barda for editorial assistance.

LISA JESCHKE AND ADRIAN MAY

Introduction: Materialist Temporalities After the End of History

Finding one of its structural markers in the repeated refrain of *The End of History*, it becomes clear that the twentieth century was never meant to end. From its very beginning, this span of 100 years was shot through with political and aesthetic vanguards seeking to create a *new man* or a *new society* to fulfil the teleological aspirations of progress bequeathed to it from the nineteenth century.

In France, the key figure theorizing these historical developments was Alexandre Kojève. His lecture courses on Hegel's *Phénoménologie d'esprit*, held from 1933 to 1939 and published as *Introduction à la lecture de Hegel* (1947), was attended by, amongst others, Georges Bataille, André Breton, Jacques Lacan, Raymond Aron and Maurice Merleau-Ponty. The profound influence of these seminal lectures spread beyond this generation, stretching at least to Jacques Derrida and Michel Foucault. This is how Kojève conceptualized 'la fin du Temps humain ou de l'Histoire' during the 1930s:

> En fait, la fin du Temps humain ou de l'Histoire, c'est-à-dire l'anéantissement définitif de l'Homme proprement dit ou de l'Individu libre et historique, signifie tout simplement la cessation de l'Action au sens fort du terme. Ce qui veut dire pratiquement: – la disparition des guerres et des révolutions sanglantes. Et encore la disparition de la *Philosophie*; car l'Homme ne changeant plus essentiellement lui-même, il n'y a plus de raison de changer les principes (vrais) qui sont à la base de sa connaissance du Monde et de soi. Mais tout le reste peut se maintenir indéfiniment; l'art, l'amour, le jeu, etc., etc.; bref, tout ce qui rend l'Homme *heureux*.[1]

---

1   Alexandre Kojève, *Introduction à la lecture de Hegel: leçons sur la phénoménologie de l'esprit professées de 1933 à 1939 à l'École des Hautes-Études, réunies et publiées par Raymond Queneau* (Paris: Gallimard, 1947), 435.

Kojève here emphasizes that the end of history involves also 'la disparition de la *Philosophie*' – or, by implication, the end of the work of philosophy;[2] work is replaced by 'l'art, l'amour, le jeu' and 'etc., etc.': 'bref, tout ce qui rend l'Homme *heureux*'. If work and the work of philosophy – hence the work of dialectics – have ceased, then the end of history might be thought of as a systemic realization of a state after dialectics. Referring to Kojève as 'X.', Bataille writes 'X. imaginait proche la solution révolutionnaire du communisme'.[3] Unambiguously, for Kojève in the 1930s dialectics was the motor to bring about the end of history: to bring about communism. Retrospectively, however, Bataille adds that Kojève *wrongly* placed his faith in communism, given 'les vingt ans qui devaient suivre'. Bataille seems to refer both to the distortion of the communist dream in the repressive Stalinist state, and to the National-Socialists' attempt to arrest history – metaphorically for *a thousand years* – by installing a *Tausendjähriges Reich*. The various kinds of horror unleashed by these projects significantly undermined the hopes of the early 1930s.

2   Referring to a trajectory of thought from Kojève through Bataille to Derrida, Christopher Nealon comments critically on what he considers a conflation in French theory of: 1) work in the sense of labour; and 2) work in the sense of the philosophical work of the dialectic. Nealon writes, considering Derrida's Bataille essay 'From Restricted to General Economy: A Hegelianism without Reserve': 'Philosophy, as the essay unfolds, is "work itself" in the sense that it is a set of operations that *compel* work, that force the negative to produce meaning and knowledge, and that bustles about breathlessly as it mistakenly thinks it is achieving "knowledge" in the process. "Philosophy" – that is, Hegelian philosophy, *Aufhebung*, the dialectic – "philosophy", in this allegory, is a bourgeois': Christopher Nealon, *The Matter of Capital: Poetry and Crisis in the American Century* (Cambridge, MA: Harvard University Press, 2011), 12–13. Nealon seems to imply that if philosophy is the bourgeoisie, the reality of actual conflicts of labour are made irrelevant in self-perpetuating deconstructive readings against philosophy. Yet the overlap of work and the work of philosophy – as dialectical forms of mediation with matter – does already seem given in Hegel's master–slave dialectic. The question of whether Bataillean and subsequent post-structuralist oppositions to that system are sufficiently acute in their understanding of the structural politics of capitalism is further addressed below.

3   This is a footnote retrospectively added by Bataille to his 'Lettre à X., chargé d'un cours sur Hegel ...', in Georges Bataille, *Œuvres complètes. V: La Somme athéologique. Tome 1* (Paris: Gallimard, 1973), 369.

The 1950s as the end of discourses of the end of history? Far from it. Chastened by the experience of the war, Bataille endorsed the Marshall Plan, which inaugurated Europe's economic dependence on America,[4] and Kojève transitioned from believing in communist solutions to believing in the solutions of Western liberal democracy, becoming its bureaucratic functionary. He worked for 'the French ministry of foreign economic relations and became an architect of the European Community and the GATT system of liberalized trade'; avoiding radical circles, he 'despised the student rebels of the 1960s'.[5] A witness to the events of May, he would not live to see De Gaulle's restoration and *rappel à l'ordre*: Kojève passed away on 4 June 1968. Yet once over this last eruption of revolutionary *élan*, the liberal capitalism Kojève had helped to construct went from strength to strength, and following the collapse of the USSR from 1989, it finally appeared to know no major obstacles to its global ambitions. Symptomatically, Professor Robert Howse, the source of above account of Kojève's post-war trajectory, is also a 'frequent consultant or adviser to government agencies and international organizations such as the OECD, the World Bank, UNCTAD, the Inter-American Development Bank, the Law Commission of Canada and the UN Office of the High Commissioner for Human Rights', as the biography on his NYU profile states.[6] Kojève's march through the institutions continued apace, and famously was consecrated when in 1992 Francis Fukuyama presented liberal democracy as *The End of History and the Last Man*. Rather than communism, it was free market capitalism that would provide the teleological end of mankind's historical progress and the conditions for global peace. Luckily for us, in Kojève's terms, 'tout ce qui rend l'Homme *heureux*' could now simply be bought! Fukuyama's account obviously smacks of neo-conservative propaganda, especially given his association with the RAND Corporation think-tank, funded in part

4   See Georges Bataille, *La Part maudite: essai d'économie générale*, in Bataille, *Œuvres complètes. VII* (Paris: Gallimard, 1976), 17–179 (esp. 159 ff.).

5   Robert Howse, 'Kojeve's [*sic*] Latin Empire', *Policy Review* 126 (2004) <http://www.hoover.org/publications/policy-review/article/7118> accessed 27 May 2014.

6   See <https://its.law.nyu.edu/facultyprofiles/profile.cfm?section=bio&personID=28550> accessed 27 May 2014.

by the US State department and acting as an official advisor to its armed forces. Yet such triumphalism only articulates crudely and without inhibition the belief that implicitly informs governments across Europe, as well as the EU framework itself: that liberal democracy and free trade capitalism are the best possible systems of global governance, and must *never* be overthrown. Brutal as this seems, it is also a widely shared belief, even amongst the left: as in the oft-cited quotation, it is now 'easier to imagine the end of the world than to imaging the end of capitalism'.[7] *Fin de partie.*

A publication entitled *Matters of Time: Material Temporalities in Twentieth-Century French Culture* makes sense only insofar as it can develop a conceptual understanding of the twentieth century that goes beyond its descriptive demarcation of a particular sequence of years. *The End of History* as the century's refrain conveys simultaneously a strong sense of what was specific to the century and emphasizes that the attempt here is not at all to think of it as a century that is self-contained: it relies heavily on earlier dialectical and teleological trajectories, which made the idea that history could be completed thinkable as such. The centuries preceding it bleed into the twentieth century and, in turn, we might say the twentieth century leaks and bleeds backwards into the centuries preceding it; as history continues, as our lives go on, it is continuously necessary, in a kind of historiographical hermeneutic circle, to re-adjust our understanding not only of what is happening in the present or what could happen in the future, but also of what has happened in the past. To put it polemically: the Holocaust was a massive influence on Darwin. Furthermore, the twentieth century's oscillations between movements of revolutionary enthusiasm and moments of crisis, reaction, terror or stasis were experienced intellectually and aesthetically as well as historically: one need only think of the artistic avant-gardes before the war, and the intellectual 'fellow travellers' such as Sartre after, to gauge the cultural manifestations of such political stakes. This volume attempts, then, to present a 'meteorology of the times',[8] taking the measure of moments of confidence and crisis within the context of the

7   Frederic Jameson, 'Future City', *New Left Review* 21 (2003), 65–79 (73).
8   For a further discussion of this term, see Adrian May's chapter in this volume.

emphatic conception of the twentieth century delineated above. Through the twists and turns of the period, it will explore confluences and contrasts between a series of writers, artists, thinkers and events in the context of the development of late capitalism, and hopefully provide some new orientations for a properly *materialist* thought.

Matters of *time*: in colloquial speech, it is time and *space* which are normally uttered in one breath. So much so that these two parameters are often taken as one undifferentiated unity: we are never without either. Politically, however, one could be tempted to make a crude opposition between the two: time is a key concept for socialist thought, revolutionary eruptions and Hegelian dialectics. As Alexandra Paulin-Booth puts it in the opening chapter here, for the left time is an 'ideological battleground'. On the other hand, in an interview from 2005, Peter Sloterdijk argues, with a tone of woundedness, that in the 'theory landscape' there has been a 'voluntary spatial blindness'. Whilst 'temporal problems were seen as progressive and cool, the questions of space were thought to be old-fashioned and conservative, a matter for old men and shabby imperialists'.[9] Space, then, can come to stand for a certain political conservatism, especially when tied to ideas of the fixity of national borders, the need to protect our eternally green and pleasant lands (Albion, or *la France profonde*), and so in addition the desire to keep *others* at bay. One can see why Sloterdijk is defensive in response to such depictions: his emphasis on rational, calculated self-creation (the self-made man), coupled with a depiction of humans living in small, self-contained immunized *Bubbles* (2011), has led him to be accused of being 'the liberal conservative *enfant terrible* of contemporary German thought'.[10]

Sloterdijk (often nevertheless labelled the 'most French of the German philosophers') also refers explicitly here to the fate of structuralism as a spatial mode of thought that subsequently became associated with repressive, conservative values. In her seminal account of French

9 Peter Sloterdijk, 'Against Gravity', interview with Bettina Funcke <http://www.bookforum.com/archive/feb_05/funcke.html> accessed 30 May 2014.

10 Slavoj Žižek, *Living in the End of Times* (London: Verso, 2010), 236.

culture in the 1950s and 1960s, Kristin Ross polemically argues that rather than providing a radical challenge to contemporary modes of thinking, structuralism retrospectively appears to have been complicit with establishing the hegemonic ideological victory of late capitalism. In her account, '[c]apitalist modernization presents itself as timeless because it dissolves beginning and end, in the historical sense, into an ongoing, naturalized process, one whose uninterrupted rhythm is provided by a regular and unchanging world devoid of class conflict'.[11] Once again, we encounter capitalism as the motor for producing the end of history: in joyfully static movement, we are accelerating our BMWs on our day off. Guy Debord would vigorously agree: rather than a historical, temporal progression, 'pseudo-cyclical time is the time of consumption of modern economic survival'. Preferably, citizens should content themselves with a routine of professional labour and leisurely consumption without end, with the result that 'daily life continues to be deprived of decision and remains bound, no longer to the natural order, but to the pseudo-nature developed in alienated labour'.[12] As Ross continues, at the very moment when France was transitioning into 'American-style mass culture', structuralism was also promoting 'the dissolution of the event and of diachronic agency'.[13] Effacing temporal relations, the spatiality of structuralist thought described things as they have eternally been, without providing for the possibilities of change: 'Rather than theorizing the liquidation of the historical, structuralism enacted and legitimated that liquidation'.[14] No past, no future: structuralism implied an endless capitalist present.

Ross's account provides one confluence, and one contrast, with our account of Kojève's trajectory. She confirms the rise of the *cadre*, the bureaucratic functionary Kojève would become. The transition to

11   Kristin Ross, *Fast Cars, Clean Bodies: Decolonization and the Reordering of French Culture* (Cambridge, MA: MIT Press, 1995), 10.
12   Guy Debord, *The Society of the Spectacle*, trans. Black & Red (London: Notting Hill Editions, 2013), 108.
13   Ross, *Fast Cars*, 10.
14   Ibid. 177.

American liberalism required a new form of management, one predicated on 'the hygienic language of technique and efficiency'.[15] In 1947, the new École nationale d'administration opened its doors, training the new state employee encouraged to think in terms of statistics, targets and regulations: this 'bureaucratic growth' meant that institutions 'no longer put humans first'.[16] The *mess* of daily life was cleansed from the administrative apparatus. Ross compares this technical dematerialization with the theorization of the new 'Structural man', who was nothing but 'a disembodied creature, a set of mental processes': 'Structural man takes the real, decomposes it, then recomposes it in view of creating the general intelligibility underlying the object; he creates the object's simulacrum'.[17] Furthermore, this historical moment was also characterized by a compulsive desire to erase the traces of abject materiality and dirty bodies. Attempting to distance itself from its troubled past, newly modernized France witnessed the ubiquitous display of 'clean bodies' in the avalanche of soap and detergent commercials flooding the media; these were implicitly placed in opposition to the bodies found in the colonies, structurally abjected as dirty, swarthy, dark, black, unclean. Modern France had no room for the complications of its colonial adventures, and its newfound obsession with cleanliness corresponded with a desire to bury the unhygienic traces of its past, censoring the worst coverage of its 'dirty war' in Algeria. Rather than communism or fascism, however, here it had been imperial capitalism that had produced these abjected remainders.

In an intellectual reaction, the 1960s attempted to inject *matter* back into spatial abstractions. Whether dialecticizing transgressive desire to create works provoking a cultural revolution (*Tel Quel*), or assembling micro-political desiring machines to overturn the oedipal territorialization of traditional, conservative values (Deleuze and Guattari), the irruptive potential of matter was pitted against the rigidly conceptual. For a moment, works such as Deleuze and Guattari's *Anti-Œdipe* (1972),

15 Ibid. 176.
16 Ibid. 177.
17 Ibid. 161.

Lyotard's *Économie libidinale* (1974) and Baudrillard's *L'Échange symbolique et la mort* (1976) seemed brimming with revolutionary potential. Concurrently, Henri Lefebvre and Guy Debord were turning to material experiences of urban existence to romanticize and politicize everyday life, and the neo-avant-gardes turned either to the manipulation of materiality against mimetic representation, or to organizing eruptive situations, happenings which would disrupt the causal unfolding of time. Matter, then, had rendered space a field of revolutionary potential, rather than a vacuous and immunological bubble. Yet, just as with structuralism, capitalism soon caught up with this newly material post-structuralism: as Boltanski and Chiapello analyse in *Le Nouvel esprit du capitalisme* (1999), the language of neo-liberal management was taken straight from Delezue and Guattari's toolbox, and the libidinal desires of the newly liberated youth were cleaned up, plastic-wrapped and sold back to them, blunting the radical edge of counter-culture and signalling, once again, the end of avant-garde struggles. In retrospect, capitalism was less shaken than re-enforced by the radical novelty of the 1960s. Its ahistorical celebration of matter now seems hopelessly naïve, Lyotard subsequently calling *Économie libidinale* his 'evil' book.[18] The absence of a genuinely historical or temporal dialecticization of matter proved to be its undoing: the materialism of the 1960s was, put simply, far too joyful, and too little critical. Such a lack is well worth bearing in mind when considering the raft of 'New Materialisms' resurging today, which often take texts from this period as their starting point.[19]

In the 1930s, Bataille had perhaps been more acute. In his incomplete draft letter to Kojève from 1937, Bataille writes: 'J'imagine que ma vie – ou son avortement, mieux encore, la blessure ouverte qu'est ma vie – à elle seule constitue la réfutation du système fermé de Hegel'.[20] The claim is that

---

18   Benjamin Noys, *The Persistence of the Negative: A Critique of Contemporary Continental Theory* (Edinburgh: Edinburgh University Press, 2010), 2. Noy's text provides an excellent account of this period, and the failures of the 'accelerationist' moment of thinkers such as Lyotard and Deleuze.

19   For more on 'New Materialism' see Jennifer Johnson's chapter in this volume.

20   Bataille, 'Lettre à X., chargé d'un cours sur Hegel ...', 369–70.

a singular life, precisely in the singularity of its experience, might in and of itself constitute a refutation of Hegel's closed system. This life is imagined, in and of itself, as its own abortion – 'avortement': lived life is its own waste product. The flesh is not solid, but by virtue of being flesh is always already wounded – and happily insignificant, specifically in the sense that it exceeds symbolic structures of signification:

> En outre, comme la représentation que je me fais de moi-même varie, et qu'il m'arrive d'oublier, comparant ma vie à celle des hommes les plus remarquables, qu'elle pourrait être médiocre, je me suis souvent dit qu'au sommet de l'existence il pourrait ne rien y avoir que de négligeable: personne, en effet, ne pourrait 'reconnaître' un sommet qui serait la nuit. Quelques faits – comme une difficulté exceptionnelle éprouvée à me faire 'reconnaître' (sur le plan simple où les autres sont 'reconnus') – m'ont amené à prendre sérieusement mais gaiement, l'hypothèse d'une insignifiance sans appel. (V, 370)

Yet Bataille's emphasis on the aborted life also appears as veering dangerously towards another kind of ahistoric experientialism, in his case predicated on the abject rather than joyous desire. As Michel Surya explicates, Bataille was hostile to any *'politique de l'utile'*:[21] the social forces of homogenization are those leading to 'l'asphyxie, l'économisme, la police, la terreur de la réduction de tout ce qui est à l'unité'.[22] This makes him the perfect antidote to rational, bureaucratic instrumentalization, but draws him equally away from any political mobilization. Marx is portrayed as a 'puritain' for his disdain for the *lumpenproletariat* and their *'turpitude naturelle'*.[23] Bataille, however, embraces such figures, and in fact privileges anything which is socially heterogeneous:

> les déchets, les excréments, tout ce qui a valeur érotique (non reproductive), les processus inconscients, les parias, les classes guerrières, les individus violents [...] le luxe [...] Tous les phénomènes sociaux marginaux ou improductifs, rebelles ou

21　Michel Surya, *Humanimalités: Matériologies 3, Précédé de L'idiotie de Bataille* (Paris: Éditions Léo Scheer, 2004), 252.

22　Ibid. 200.

23　Michel Surya, 'Figures du rebut humain', *Lignes* 8 (2002), 168–85 (175).

parasites, indifférents ou somptuaires [...] bas et rebutants [...] la honte, la violence, la folie, la démesure et le délire; en bref, tout ce qui a en commun d'être *inassimilable*.[24]

In his trenchant opposition to 'toute forme d'organisation',[25] even a formalized workers' party was too bourgeois for Bataille. As Bataille would be the first to admit, this is all well and good for a personal liberation from social conventions, but does little to construct a program of broad-based political action or resistance.[26]

Nevertheless, his emphasis on the abject importantly keeps in focus the fact that the difficult dialectics between attempts to emancipate something called humanity and enable a good life for all has, in the twentieth century, often led to the rejection of individual bodies that might besmirch this new society. If the abjecting of bodies considered as *unfit* – in all possible senses of the word – committed in the name of the universal social good has constituted and continues to constitute one of the major failures of twentieth- and twenty-first-century statist regimes, then any future materialist and/or revolutionary thought must begin to think itself from the position of the abject social and political body rather than the healthy and clean social and individual body: it would certainly be simplistic to

24   Surya, *Humanimalités*, 200.

25   Francis Marmande, *Georges Bataille politique* (Lyon: Presses universitaires de Lyon, 1985), 40.

26   This emphasis on the complete heterogeneity of the abject would be taken up, in a psychoanalytic but also politicized register, by Julia Kristeva. Notably, as opposed to the 'desire for meaning', she argues that 'what is abject, on the contrary, is radically excluded and draws me toward the place where meaning collapses'. Furthermore as the abject 'lies outside, beyond the set', from this margin it 'does not cease challenging its master'; yet such radical exteriority is also embraced, as the 'abject and abjection are my safeguards. The primers of my culture': Julia Kristeva, *Powers of Horror: An Essay on Abjection*, trans. Leon S. Roudiez (New York: Columbia University Press, 1982), 3. Such a valorization of the abject is often purveyed by critics seeking an ultimate value in absolute marginality, or in more recent discourses whatever 'provides access to' or an 'experience' of 'the Real'. By arguing for an attempt to re-insert the abject into a political dialectic, we are also questioning whether an unchallenged and romanticized assumption of the singular and indescribable power of abjection leaves its association with capitalist production, exploitation and repression unexplored.

think of political organization and the acknowledgement of base matter as necessary oppositions, and it might be possible to think *with* and *against* – hence *beyond* – Bataille at the same time.[27]

As suggested above, whilst fascism and really existing socialism receded throughout the century, it became more and more evident that capitalism, enabled by liberal democracy, would continue rather than arrest the perpetual creation of abjection in the name of progress. The neo-liberal conjuncture has inculcated 'a universal belief in the desirability of growth',[28] yet rarely questions the human cost of this growth. In recent Marxist thought, Keston Sutherland's emphasis on the expenditure of the worker's body itself in the process of work places a focus on abjection back within the cycle of capitalist production, making it a possible axis for a political dialecticization. In 'Marx in Jargon', Sutherland elaborates on Marx's parodic engagement with the terminology of 'Gallerte' when defining 'abstrakt menschliche Arbeit' as a '*bloße Gallerte unterschiedsloser menschlicher Arbeit*'. In *Capital*, this is translated as 'human labour in the abstract' and 'a mere congelation of homogeneous human labour' (Moore and Aveling) or 'merely congealed quantities of homogeneous human labour' (Fowkes), but Sutherland's piece targets precisely the insufficiency of the translation. *Congelation*, he points out, is from the Latin verb *congelare* ('to freeze together') and the Latin noun *gelum* ('frost'). To explain the concrete reality of *Gallerte*, on the other hand, Sutherland quotes from the sixth volume of *Meyers Konversations-Lexicon*, published in Leipzig in 1888:

> *Gallerte* (also *Gállert*, old German *galrat*, middle Latin *galatina*, Italian *gelatina*), the semisolid, tremulous mass gained from cooling a concentrated glue solution. All animal substances that yield glue when boiled can be used in the production of *gallerte*, that is to say, meat, bone, connective tissue, isinglass, stag horns etc. It is easier to preserve *gallerte* by dissolving pure white glue (gelatine) in a sufficient quantity of water and letting it cool there. It is used in various dishes, *q.v.* jelly.

---

27 Crucially, Bataille's conception of this abject man without qualities is the starting point for Martin Crowley's *L'Homme sans*, an attempt to think an open, non-exclusive form of political solidarity that can still articulate a firm resistance to global oppression and exploitation. See below.

28 Ross, *Fast Cars*, 171.

Vegetable *gallerte* of lichen consists of lichen starch or algae slime and water. In particular it is prepared from Carragaheen, Icelandic moss and the like, and is often used, mixed with other medicaments, in medicine. Vegetable *gallerte* made of fleshy, sour fruits consists of pectins and water. Fruit jellies or jams are popular additions to other meals.[29]

This implies that 'Marx's German readers will not only have bought *Gallerte*, they will have eaten it'.[30] Furthermore, not only would they have eaten *Gallerte*, they are it:

> Abstract human labour is, in Marx's words, undifferentiated and *not* homogeneous, because it has a multitude of material origins (many workers contribute to the manufacture of each commodity, as political economy had recognized since Adam Smith's analysis of the division of labour in *The Wealth of Nations*) but these multiple origins cannot be separately distinguished in the commodity which is the product of the aggregate of their activity. All that is meat melts into bone, and vice versa; and no mere act of scrutiny, however analytic or moral, is capable of reversing the industrial process of that deliquescence.[31]

Sutherland's exploration of Marx suggests that far from being radically outside the capitalist system, expenditure is found throughout it, on every level. A Bataillean economy of sacrifice cannot appear as a viable alternative to an economy of accumulation if the spending of the individual worker's body itself forms the very basis of the exploitation of labour to achieve an economy of accumulation. An economics of expenditure is not resistant to, but rather always already integral to an economy of accumulation. Bodily excrescence is indifferently mixed with brute matter during the production process. Capitalism is abjection and abject: a truly materialist approach to a critique of the contemporary means of production needs to account for the accelerating ability of neo-liberalism to integrate those elements usually seen as heterogeneous waste.

29 Keston Sutherland, 'Marx in Jargon', *world picture* 1 (2008) <http://www.worldpicturejournal.com/World%20Picture/WP_1.1/KSutherland.html> accessed 27 May 2014.
30 Ibid.
31 Ibid.

Let us not exaggerate: we are living in an age of alarmingly high structural unemployment, in which more and more humans of working age are being rendered wholly superfluous to the processes of social and economic reproduction. Debord's utopic 'ne travaillez jamais' today seems less like a charm and more like a curse. In its insatiable desire to find new markets to boost economic growth, capitalism's ability to appropriate and market the abject should not be underestimated. It is no coincidence that the best way to encourage industries to 'go green' is via financial incentives: Starbucks will fly executives around the globe to convince you of the environmental credentials of their brand. Furthermore, what better way to deal with those unfortunate externalities of the production process than to monetize them? Carbon trading allows firms to sell off their pollution, and the third world will happily receive the waste of the first, strapped for landfill space, in return for a healthy cash payment: have too much stuff? Sell us your excrescence! No, no, it's no trouble at all. In fact, I *absolutely insist*.

It is the aim of this volume to consider bodies and objects, objectified bodies, bodies that eat and are eaten, production and exhaustion, in order to begin to formulate a materialism of abjection that can take into account the expendability of both workforces and redundant forces. In juxtaposition, the chapters in this book construct broad historical trajectories making possible an understanding of the developments and antagonisms of materialist thought ranging from early twentieth-century socialist programmes to the events of May 1968 to the neo-liberal developments of the early twenty-first century. These trajectories are fractured, testifying to the breaks, interruptions and disillusionments in the movement of history as much as to that movement itself. Not least, this implies that these chapters do not present a unified or holistic position on materialism, Marxism or history. They are concerned with subjects as divergent as the proliferation of French heterodox Marxisms in the twentieth century; the relation between Marxism and fascism; Hegel's influence on French intellectual culture and conversely with anti-teleological or even anti-dialectical revolutionary programmes; materialisms and idealisms infected or disturbed by one another; the politicization of aesthetic forms, from Verlaine through Artaud to Lefebvre; (anti-)Marxist disillusionment and the spread and domination of liberal democracy and late capitalism in the latter half of the twentieth century; the formal and representational experiments with matter as modernist painting emerges, and the manipulation of time in the cinematic neo-avant-garde; and collective histories of urban lifestyle and ecological futurity.

***

The first section of the volume, *Revolution, Work, Time,* is situated within the trajectory encompassing revolutionary mobilizations of temporal progress outlined above. Alexandra Paulin-Booth's 'A Period of Transition: Political Time in the Work of Jean Jaurès' explores the concept of political time at the turn of the century, and demonstrates how, within the left, time was itself an ideological battlefield. How time was conceived was a key factor for orientating the strategies and goals of socialists, Marxists, anarchists and syndicalists. Jaurès' thought wandered a particular tightrope between a Hegelian conception of dialectical progress, in which History was itself a motor of progress, alongside a historical investigation which revealed the important agency of individuals to bring about successive steps in this teleological motion. As Paulin-Booth describes, for Jaurès this led to a particular relationship to the past, present and future: subjective agency in the present was to be guided by the mechanical drive of history through the past, and geared towards human aspirations for the future.

Lisa Jeschke's 'To Refuse to Imagine: Simone Weil's Materialism' suggests that many of Weil's theological conceptions from *La pesanteur et la grâce* are initially developed in the context of the French reception of Hegel in the late 1920s and of her involvement in socialist struggles in the early 1930s. To this extent, her later theological notes can still be read as entirely materialist. And yet, the translation of structurally politicized thought into other domains, such as the conduct of one's personal life, provokes the question as to whether there is not among French thinkers during the war period – Jeschke mentions Bataille alongside Weil – a tendency towards 'inner emigration' not entirely unlike the one observable among German-language writers during the National-Socialist period. Such an expansion of the terminology of 'inner emigration' is to an extent polemical and provocative – but necessarily so in terms of further indication towards the political mutations from what seemed like viable socialist struggles in the 1930s to more conservative or liberal positions dominating after the war. With regard to questions of French modernist aesthetics and politics before, during and after the war, Jeschke's paper is in particularly close dialogue with May's chapter on Bataille and Blanchot, and Grundy's chapter on Artaud.

The final chapter in Part 1, however, moves us towards the rise of the affluent consumer society that would lead to neo-liberalism, ending with Daniel Poitras' 'Time Matters: The *Mouvement du 22 mars* and the Dawn of May '68'. Poitras introduces the work of François Hartog and notably his deployment of the term *régimes d'historicité*.[32] Such a *régime* takes into account both the historical context and the particular political conjunctures within which certain ideas emerge, and also how social actors experienced their own moment of time; the interpretations of past, present, future available to them; and the new conceptualizations, previously occluded, that this particular situation makes realizable. As Poitras argues, the events of May 1968 took such a radical turn because, in the historical conjuncture, grand narratives of human progress and political certainties of the past seemed exhausted and irrelevant to a new generation. Whilst drawing influences from a range of other recent or contemporary struggles (such as the anti-war movement and the Spanish, German and Japanese student movements), the goals of the *enragés*, and the likely consequences of their actions, were unknown and unpredictable. Such a lack of a definite horizon infused the *Mouvement du 22 mars* with a strategic flexibility and an ability to mobilize a wide range of actors behind a program with no defined goal. The surprising results were not just a mass student movement, but the largest strike in French history, with eleven million workers, 22 per cent of the country's workforce, downing tools for up to two weeks. Subsequently, an entire generation of French thinkers were impressed with the irruptive force of an event that has the potential to change everything: from Badiou's militant theory of the Event to the more pessimistic, melancholic adoption by Derrida of a Benjmanian messianism and a democracy to come, one can

---

32 François Hartog, *Régimes d'historicité: présentisme et expériences du temps* (Paris: Seuil, 2003).

certainly see the allure of the unpredictable intrusion of the radically new for a generation trying to escape the straightjackets of either teleological dialectics or structuralism's immutable time.

Whilst the first section is concerned with the appropriations and rejections of Hegelian dialectics, Part 2, *The Politics of Finitude*, seeks to outline further trajectories of Marxist thought in the twentieth century, particularly in terms of existentialist and phenomenological accounts of the experience and duration of a particular life within historical structures. In defining 'temporalization' as the differentiation between past, present and future, George Tomlinson argues that the use of 'time' in *The German Ideology* masks the temporal stakes of Marx and Engel's historical materialism. In tying individual humans to the social totality, the development of mankind over time is conglomerated with the entirety of human history: this risks reducing the conception of temporality to the homogenous, empty time decried by Walter Benjamin in the 'Theses on the Philosophy of History' (1940). Yet, as Tomlinson notes, all philosophies of time begin from the individual experience of temporality. Via Heidegger and Sartre, Tomlinson considers the stakes of re-introducing personal temporality into Marx's thought, arguing that this is the only systematic manner of considering the individual, social and historical relationships to time in their asymmetric yet contiguous simultaneity.

The unaligned French left from the 1950s onwards re-read Marx from a variety of viewpoints, imbricating Heideggarian existential concerns with Freudian analyses of libidinal desire, Saussurian linguistics and Levi-Strauss's anthropological structuralism. The proliferation of theoretical *revues* in this period, and the influence of thinkers such as Georges Bataille and Maurice Blanchot, combined to produce the intellectual ferment that would produce the 'time of theory'[33] in the 1960s. By charting the work and reception of Bataille and Blanchot from the 1930s to the 2010s, Adrian May provides an expansive overview of key shifts in French intellectual culture throughout the period. He displays not only how Bataille and Blanchot effected a focus on transgressive writerliness in French post-structuralist

---

33   See Patrick ffrench, *The Time of Theory* (Oxford: Clarendon Press, 1995).

thought seeking to question dogmatic Marxism, but also how that same post-structuralist thought came to be de-historicized and disqualified as immoral 'French theory' both by right-wing fractions in American academia and by newly liberal French thinkers. Via a detailed reading of *Lignes*, the chapter develops a complex overview of the political alignment of what is now known as 'theory' in its context, carefully attending to the material conditions of the emergence of such thought within France's fertile *revue* culture.

Martin Crowley's chapter 'Existence–Politics/Exposure–Sacrifice' is a further intervention into formations of left-wing thought in the second half of the twentieth century, and a continuation of his considerations begun in *L'Homme sans: politiques de la finitude*, itself published by *Lignes*. In his piece, Crowley continues his debate with Jean-Luc Nancy on whether the finitude injected into philosophy by thinkers such as Heidegger and Sartre is appropriable for an egalitarian politics. Posited on an inevitably exposed, finite and relational conception of being derived from Bataille and Antelme, Crowley both rejects the dismissal of such an ontological focus on destitution proffered by Alain Badiou and Jacques Rancière as requiring a heroic, active agent vocally capable of contesting its repression, but also Nancy's refusal to politicize ontological exposure due to the risks of a fascist politics of inclusion and exclusion, sacrificing those outside the circle of community for those inside; for Crowley, such a reticence cedes ground to political domination, and no political intervention can remain clean and untangled of compromise. Rather than seeing this cleavage as a stark either/or, heroically sacrificing some for a political egalitarian future or giving up on politics to avoid its sacrificial economy, in the face of a global economic exploitation that affects us all, Crowley transforms this binary into a sliding scale, arguing for a minimal appropriation of finitude into a political articulation to avoid a maximal repression.

Part 3, *Abject Matter*, immediately continues Crowley's interrogation into the relation between the state and finite bodies by considering bodies in, or as, abjection. In 'Doing Time: Bastille Martyrs/Modern Saints', Jessica Stacey concludes that Sade's radical position is compromised by its contamination with a religious discourse of saintliness, a pose of holy martyrdom dragging this icon of modernity back towards our medieval past. As Klossowksi famously argued in *Sade, mon prochain* (1947; his title suggesting the extent to which Sade is often seen as a twentieth- as much as an eighteenth-century writer), the transgressive blasphemies of the libertines drew their radical pleasure from denying the existence of a being that, by tying their pleasure to this denied object, only re-enforced its existence and therefore its power. Transgression, then, re-enforces the authority of that which is transgressed, enclosing Sade in a logic that is still fundamentally religious. Bataille and Artaud, amongst others, would still be struggling with God in the wake of Sade and Nietzsche, Artaud ending his life still trying to *finir avec le jugement de Dieu*.

Nevertheless, in 'What's the Matter with Antonin Artaud? Or, Why The Soul is a Pile of Shit', David Grundy argues that Artaud's re-configuration of the Christian soul as shit constitutes not a mere inversion of Catholic thought, but works as politically subversive not least to the extent that it can be aligned with Marx's description of commodity production – according to which the commodity absorbs the body that is expended in the process of production. In the alchemy of commodity production, the commodity is both a 'crystal' and the shit remainder of the 'social substance' of 'human labour power'.[34] The bourgeoisie which eats, eats shit – it is shit that goes into it and comes out of it. Describing capitalism as a cannibalistic cycle in which all bodies are sacrificed and ingested like the body of Christ in Catholic Communion, Grundy's chapter is one of several in this volume testifying to the continuing metamorphoses of Catholic thought in the twentieth century in France. Paulin-Booth's chapter on Jaurès, Jeschke's chapter on Weil, May's chapter on Bataille and Blanchot and Stacey's chapter on Sade and Latude all engage with inversions, perversions, continuations and manifestations of Catholic imagery in non-dogmatic or specifically anti-dogmatic politicized articulations of, or attempts at, social transgression and, importantly, transformation.

But aside from Catholicism – or, at times, in exact conversation with Catholicism – the theatre must also be central to thinking the body in abjection (it certainly is for Artaud). Continuously and transparently

---

34   Karl Marx, *Capital, Vol. 1*, trans. Ben Fowkes [1976] (London: Penguin, 1990), 128.

exposing the fact that it both produces and exhausts itself through human labour, and that does not allow for any thought to be uttered outside of the human body, the theatre *is* shit. Or *shitre*: in the chapter 'Merdre', Rye Holmboe considers the surplus value of the letter -R- in the famous and infamous exclamation 'merdre' at the beginning and throughout Alfred Jarry's *Ubu Roi* (1896). Holmboe argues that the surplus quality of the -R- in 'merdre' effects much more than a mere swearword would: it might be considered as a breakdown of the symbolic order as such, *merdre* forming an instance of absolute concretion, the word pointing purely to itself. In being simultaneously both absolutely concrete and absolutely abstract, Holmboe suggests that 'merdre' works like the money-commodity: it works *as if* it had value, but it is in fact shit. Hence Holmboe initially distances 'merdre' from human bodies, but goes on to suggest that precisely its abstract concretion and concrete abstraction constitute a pile of shit at the very centre of symbolic exchange: one letter, -R-, embodies the centres and limits of our thought and its fictions.

Part 4, *Transformations of Temporality and Materiality*, continues the focus on politicized aesthetics begun in Part 3. Via a discussion of Georges Rouault's *Tête de clown tragique*, Jennifer Johnson demonstrates how primary responses to this work distinguished nothing but the thick, dark paste of material paint on canvas. Yet critical references to 'coal' and 'pitch' place the work within a context of representations of industrial processes, situating it within a cultural heritage including Courbet and Zola. Johnson's reading questions both Clement Greenberg's privileging of the pure presence of non-representational, materially focused painting, and New Materialist conceptions of matter as brute existing fact. Instead, Johnson articulates the temporality of matter as conceived of by both Karl Marx and Judith Butler. Such a temporality involves not just the physical processes of creation and transformation undergone by matter, but its historical dimension that inevitably returns us to the level of signification: the questions of when, how and why these paintings have taken this particular form interrupts interpretations that pretend to restore a pure materiality to the work. Painting is presented as a paradigmatic locus for investigations into the potential saturation of matter with meaning. Pure materiality and immaterial signification are both rejected, in favour of a dense and inseparable imbrication of meaning in matter, or matter as the very possibility of meaning.

As noted by Poitras, the 1960s saw what has been come to be labelled the end of grand narratives, especially those of teleological progress. The political mutations that resulted are noted above, but the invention of cinema also allowed aesthetic representations of a broken temporal succession. Louis Daubresse traces the history of reverse motion techniques over the entire century, from its first appearance in *Démolition d'un mur* (1896) to contemporary music videos, such as Michel Gondry's *Sugar Water* (1996). Daubresse focuses particularly on the relation between forwards and backwards footage and a progressive/regressive binary. Martin Arnold's staccato interruption of filmic progression disrupts televisual and cinematic clichés: a husband returns home to kiss his awaiting wife, but the constant stalling and regression of his motion, followed by the horizontal and vertical inversion of the frames, seems instead to place the couple in a spatial prison, the trap of preconceived actions and dictated gestures. Gondry's magnificently controlled, symmetrical split-screen inversions, on the other hand, come to stand for Epstein's faith in the intelligence and creative potential of a medium such as cinema to transform our perception of time and metamorphose our spatial relations in a utopic embrace of the representative space. A consideration of Mike Hoolboom's *Scaling* concludes, leading Daubresse to figure an isotropic space in which temporalized matter, and materialized time, no longer have strictly defined qualities and opposites, but permeable boundaries in which a genuinely new and disturbing time-space is revealed.

Christina Chalmers's piece meditates on the more regressive signification of such manipulations. By placing Jean Cocteau into dialogue with the American poet Frank O'Hara, Cocteau's reversed footage seems to belong too simplistically to the forwards/backwards binary deconstructed above. Cocteau's extensive use of reversed footage is described as a kind of suture: with an uninterrupted soundtrack, the disturbing distortions of normal temporal succession are rendered comforting, familial, and part of a wider logic of fairy tale resurrections and eternal returns. By contrast, O'Hara's poetry is parodic, performative and crucially ambivalent, rejecting the comfort of suture, instead leaving open the possibilities of joy and despair, recognition and isolation. Chalmer's chapter suggestively notes that Cocteau's clichéd use of what could be a radically disruptive technique could function within a mass-cultural pacification à la Disney, whereas O'Hara remains sceptical in the face of liberal capitalism, despite taking an evident pleasure in its products and cultural icons such as Greta Garbo and Marilyn Monroe.

Part 5, *Topological Writing*, focuses specifically on writing as a phenomenon that might inject materiality into the temporalization of space and the spatialization of time. Andrew Otway suggests that the journalist and poet Horace Bertin's 1877 city portrait *Les Heures Marseillaises* might provide a methodological template for the programme of rhythmanalysis put forth by late twentieth-century heterodox Marxist sociologist Henri Lefebvre. Otway carefully re-sketches Bertin's movement through and observation of Marseilles in the late nineteenth century, providing an image of the rhythms of a city across a duration of twenty-four hours. Lefebvre's emphasis on the rhythms of the Mediterranean articulated as part of a sociological critique of capitalism is currently of special conceptual and methodological significance, given that the Euro-crisis in the wake of the 2008 financial crisis has been largely played out across divides between North-Western Europe and the Mediterranean countries: the fact that differences in forms of production, family structures and wealth distribution might be accounted for not least by questions of rhythm emphasizes the importance of Lefebvre's analysis as a methodology for analysing capitalism with attention to regional structure.

If Otway examines the rhythm of everyday life, In 'A Stitch in Time: Temporal Threads in Jean Genet', Joanne Brueton explores the rhythms of one single life. There is a sense in which a too strenuous attention to matter ends up rendering one acquiescent to the reduction of the human experience, the 'temporalization of man' and 'a humanization of time', to merely 'the time of things'.[35] Just as in Heidegger one is thrown into a particular historical moment, Brueton explores how for Genet the thread that ties one to their birth – one could imagine an umbilical cord to your times – is one that entangles their life to come, an inescapable bond that gives a

---

35   Guy Debord, *The Society of the Spectacle*, 89 and 104.

certain amount of elasticity and agency, but which still circumscribes the space one can give to a life. Genet materializes this thread, representing the *fils* of time less like a line into the future, but a tether continuously drawing one back to one's own past and internal history. Genet's repeated return to certain moments of his life in his writing, especially his childhood, attest to the power of this thread, entangling the subject in a past that never forms a linear narrative but catches the narrator in a labyrinthine process of becoming. Writing is a way of transforming this filial temporality, a material manifestation of the subject's engagement with his own coming to be within time. At birth, we are given seventy years of time: one can leave it empty, drifting through without contemplation, or one can work it, cultivate it into productive matter. Essentially, however, there is no subject, no volumes of work, no Genet, without this time given to us at birth, which Genet's writing ceaselessly attempts to materially figure.

Daniel A. Finch-Race's chapter focuses on the very late nineteenth century, again with implications of a catastrophe which might find further acceleration in the twenty-first century: the environmental crisis. Finch-Race argues that the narrative of disillusionment and the quest for both personal and poetic values permeating Verlaine's 'Ariettes oubliées' belongs to a broader scheme of artistic and societal reflection on time and identity in the nineteenth century. Throughout this key section of the *Romances sans paroles*, ecological and temporal singularities complement the destabilizing effects of Verlaine's subversive versification: particular Ariettes can be interpreted as attuned to the natural elements, highlighting not only the extent to which Verlaine's poetry is linked to his environment, but also the dearth of human complicity with the non-human world in nineteenth-century French society. By investigating how the intricacies of a broader psycho-social enquiry are developed through the indexation of poetic concerns against ecological and temporal particularities in Verlaine's first, third, sixth, eighth and ninth Ariettes, these enigmatic vignettes evoking uncertainty in love and relational anxieties will be elucidated. Each of these five Ariettes ultimately constitutes a nuance to a process of ecopoetic maturation, manifest not only in the increasing virtuosity with which prosodic rules are subverted, but also in the evolving role of ecological phenomena as counterparts to Verlaine's exploration of amorous, sensorial and temporal concerns. Without such a global ecological conscience, it could be the environment, rather than politics, that brings about the end of human history.

Many of the chapters presented here were given as papers at *Matters of Time*, a conference held in Cambridge on 23–24 April 2013. The contributions from Crowley, Jeschke and May are original to this publication.

Selected Bibliography

Bataille, Georges, *Œuvres complètes* (Paris: Gallimard, 1970–88).

Crowley, Martin, *L'homme sans: politiques de la finitude* (Fécamp: Nouvelles Éditions Lignes, 2009).

Debord, Guy, *The Society of the Spectacle*, trans. Black & Red (London: Notting Hill Editions, 2013).

ffrench, Patrick, *The Time of Theory* (Oxford: Clarendon Press, 1995).

Hartog, François, *Régimes d'historicité: présentisme et expériences du temps* (Paris: Seuil, 2003).

Kristeva, Julia, *Powers of Horror: An Essay on Abjection*, trans. Leon S. Roudiez (New York: Columbia University Press, 1982).

Marmande, Francis, *Georges Bataille politique* (Lyon: Presses universitaires de Lyon, 1985).

Marx, Karl, *Capital, Vol. 1*, trans. Ben Fowkes [1976] (London: Penguin, 1990).

Nealon, Christopher, *The Matter of Capital: Poetry and Crisis in the American Century* (Cambridge, MA: Harvard University Press, 2011).

Noys, Benjamin, *The Persistence of the Negative: A Critique of Contemporary Continental Theory* (Edinburgh: Edinburgh University Press, 2010).

Ross, Kristin, *Fast Cars, Clean Bodies: Decolonization and the Reordering of French Culture* (Cambridge, MA: MIT Press, 1995).

Surya, Michel, 'Figures du rebut humain', *Lignes* 8 (2002), 168–85.

——,*Humanimalités: Matériologies 3, Précédé de L'idiotie de Bataille* (Paris: Éditions Léo Scheer, 2004).

Sutherland, Keston 'Marx in Jargon', *world picture* 1 (2008) <http://www.worldpicture-journal.com/World%20Picture/WP_1.1/KSutherland.html> accessed 27 May 2013.

Žižek, Slavoj, *Living in the End of Times* (London: Verso, 2010).

PART I

Revolution, Work, Time

ALEXANDRA PAULIN-BOOTH

A Period of Transition: Political Time in the Work of Jean Jaurès

All attempts to bring about change have the potential to be configured as a fight over the future, but the left-wing thinkers and activists of late nineteenth- and early twentieth-century France had a particular proclivity for representing and understanding their social and political missions in terms of time. That is to say, there was a marked interaction between their political philosophies and how they conceptualized time. The ways in which left-wing thinkers and activists conceptualized time were multifarious, often conflicting and sometimes surprising. Left-wing political groups and individuals espoused differing versions of past, present, future, the relationships between these three categories, and differing versions of how and when social change might be brought about. Time was therefore contested terrain: it was a battleground imbued with specific and loaded political meaning upon which power and influence could be won or lost. Studying the various ways in which time was conceptualized offers a novel method for analysing the ideological fissures between, for example, socialists, Marxists, anarchists, and syndicalists. It can also reveal unexpected areas of confluence, and ultimately allows for a reconfiguration of accepted ideas about left-wing thought, thereby contributing to a fuller understanding of French political culture during this time.

Jean Jaurès provides a particularly interesting case study for the relationship between ideas about time and political beliefs. A significant amount of his writing is highly philosophical and unafraid of broaching abstract issues, such as that of time; indeed, Jaurès studied philosophy and spent time as a teacher of the discipline in a *lycée* (in Albi) and then a university (Toulouse) before embarking upon a career in politics. Jaurès' work, especially his *Études socialistes*, often demonstrates a strong concern with the movement of time and a willingness to interrogate concepts of past and future, and history and

transition. In particular, the explicitly temporal notion of transition was something which obsessed Jaurès during the first years of the twentieth century.[1]

Jaurès' understanding of time had a profound impact on his political
philosophy, and grasping his ideas about time provides an invaluable insight
into the thought of a key socialist thinker and leader, as well as providing
an entry point into the importance of time for left-wing thought more
broadly. This paper aims to establish the conceptualization of time as a
vital, structural aspect of Jaurès' political thought, and to explore in particular three parts of that conceptualization: his philosophy of history, his
insistence on the vital importance of a period of transition and its nature,
and his reflections on socialism's religious potential. Studying these aspects
of Jaurès' thought also allows us to indicate ways in which time could be
at the forefront of ideological disputes or, indeed, engender unexpected
similarities between differing groups and individuals on the left.

Evoking the notion of conceptualization does not simply mean pointing
out the content of ideas about past, present, and future and the relationship
between these three categories; rather, interrogating the conceptualization
of time necessarily means investigating how and why the ideas themselves
were formed. It is this aspect of conceptualization – specifically, *how* Jaurès
thought time progressed, why he thought it progressed in such a way, and
what he thought the categories of past, present, and future represented –
which this paper addresses first and foremost, with the content of ideas
about time providing supporting material. Insistence on conceptualization
rather than simply on the content of ideas ultimately enables us to add a
highly original dimension to the study of Jaurès, and eventually to the left as
a whole: while the nature of the left's future goals is well established, and its
versions of the past (particularly with reference to the French Revolution)
have been analysed with fascinating results, the importance of the conceptualization of time as a whole has been somewhat overlooked.[2]

---

1   Madeleine Rebérioux, 'Présentation', in Jean Jaurès, *Études socialistes* (Paris: Slatkine,
     1979), unnumbered pages.
2   On versions of the past, see for example, Robert Gildea, *The Past in French History*
     (New Haven: Yale University Press, 1994) and Jeremy Jennings, 'Syndicalism and
     the French Revolution', *Journal of Contemporary History* 1 (1991), 71–96. On the

My deliberate use of the phrase 'political time' takes inspiration from Louis Althusser's analysis of the way in which time operated in modern society. He noted that there are various spheres or levels of time: political, social, or economic, for example. These often overlap, but they are distinguished by differing tempos and sometimes by differing versions of what might constitute past, present, or future. In Althusser's words, 'there can be no single *Now* in which all elements of a social formation come into play'.[3] With regard to Jaurès, what this recognition of the plurality of time means is isolating how he understood time in the context of his political mission; even though he often evoked *social* change, this transformation would be effected by *political* means and it was thus the political timeframe which was important. Ultimately, concentrating on political time allows for a more precise focus on the exchange between Jaurès' conceptualization of time and his political philosophy. There is also a second, related, meaning to the phrase political time: time politicized, evoking again the idea of time as ideological battleground.

Jaurès' Philosophy of History

One very important facet of Jaurès' conceptualization of time was his philosophy of history; this philosophy is expressed quite precisely in a fascinating short essay which is revealingly entitled 'La limite du matérialisme historique'.[4] Jaurès had tackled the same subject in a debate with Paul Lafargue in 1901, and it is a theme he continually re-explored throughout

nature of the left's ideas about the future, see for example, Jean-Jacques Becker and Gilles Candar, eds, *Histoire des gauches en France, Volume I: l'héritage du XIXᵉ siècle* (Paris: La Découverte, 2004).

3　Louis Althusser, cited in John R. Hall, 'The Time of History and the History of Times', *History and Theory* 19 (1980), 114.

4　Jean Jaurès, 'La limite du matérialisme historique', in Émile Vandevelde, ed., *Jaurès* (Paris: Librairie Felix Alcan, 1929), 55–68.

his work.[5] His philosophy of history provided the cornerstone for his understanding of how change operated and could be brought about; it was, therefore, crucial for the elaboration of his political program.

At the crux of Jaurès' argument was the assertion that materialism alone could not explain historical development satisfactorily. Instead, he said, idealism and materialism should be seen to work dialectically. The specific use of the word 'dialectic' was a result of the influence of Hegel, who was frequently invoked by Jaurès. Jaurès spoke of a pattern in which mankind continually aspired to justice, and tried to find economic systems which were less and less repugnant to an ever more acute sense of justice. These economic systems, as the environment within which mankind operated, were in turn formative.[6] Aron Noland, who has written persuasively about the centrality of justice in Jaurès' work, succinctly puts it that for Jaurès 'the individual was as important a factor in historical causation as the economic forces described by Marx'.[7] But whereas it is clear that humans had a certain amount of agency, they also seemed to be caught up in a sweeping, teleological (Whiggish, even) history couched in terms of 'necessary evolution' and 'intelligible direction'.[8] This version of history did not admit of anything but improvement: history became entangled with and welded to the ubiquitous nineteenth-century notion of progress, and eventual change for the better was a matter of certainty for Jaurès, as it was for the majority of left-wing thinkers during this time.[9]

5   This debate was reproduced as a pamphlet: Jean Jaurès and Paul Lafargue, *Idéalisme et matérialisme dans la conception de l'histoire* (Lille: P. Lagrange, 1901).

6   Jaurès, 'La limite', 66–7.

7   Aron Noland 'Individualism in Jean Jaurès' Socialist Thought', *Journal of the History of Ideas* 1 (1961), 69.

8   Jaurès, 'La limite', 67.

9   On history understood as progress, see Reinhart Koselleck, *Futures Past: On the Semantics of Historical Time* (New York: Columbia University Press, 2004) and *The Practice of Conceptual History: Timing History, Spacing Concepts* (Stanford: Stanford University Press, 2002). Notable exceptions to this confidence in future change were certain anarchists, for example Zo d'Axa, a prominent anarchist journalist who proclaimed that he fought 'without dreams of a better future': cited in Alexander

Nonetheless, the idea that humans could bend history to their will – even if that will had an innate and inexorable direction – is important when we consider political time in Jaurès' thought, because this notion informed his insistence that societal transformation would have to be created deliberately and methodically, and it rendered some aspects of the future unknowable (namely, the exact nature of the change and when it would happen). Jaurès looked to history and, as a result of his studies, developed a conceptualization of time in which human agency, in combination with the environments which people created for themselves, had a vital role to play. The idea that humans and environments gradually changed and formed one another allows us to understand at least in part Jaurès' unwaveringly reformist attitude, since a sudden revolutionary upheaval bringing social transformation was an anathema to a conceptualization of time in which change could only occur step-by-step. Interestingly, in a letter to Charles Péguy which appears as the introduction to the *Études socialistes*, Jaurès pointed out quite scornfully that human agency and an unpredictable future are totally absent from the *Communist Manifesto*.[10] Here we begin to see that differing conceptualizations of time were often constitutive of ideological disagreements: Jaurès was rejecting the *Manifesto*'s understanding of time as a predefined process which placed the proletariat on a path towards an ineluctable revolution.

Jaurès used a striking and explicitly time-related (if slightly confusing) analogy to illustrate his idea of the relationship between materialism and idealism. He asserted that in the unconscious, automated workings of the brain, the present only took on meaning in terms of the past, in terms of what had gone before. Conversely, at the level of pure and abstract ideas, at the level of active thought, the present was determined by and guided by notions of the future. These two aspects (unconscious cerebral life and the conscious development of thought and ideas) synthesized to create a

---

Varias, *Paris and the Anarchists: Aesthetes and Subversives during the Fin-de-Siècle* (New York: St Martin's Press, 1996), 104.

10 Jean Jaurès, 'Question de méthode' (letter to Péguy, 17 November 1901), *Études socialistes*, xx.

working person. And so it was with history: one had to take into account both the (past) mechanical workings of economics, and humanity's aspiration towards a higher (future) ideal.[11] The time aspect of the analogy indicates that Jaurès thought carefully about the relationship between past and future, how he could characterize these concepts, and perhaps ascribe a value to each of them. The past mechanically propelled mankind forward, while the future represented a shimmering possibility which simultaneously drew it onward. This introduces the idea that acting based solely on the past was related, in Jaurès' mind, to what was unthinking, what was reactionary, whereas the consideration of the future was linked to what was aspirational.

That assumption formed an important aspect of Jaurès' critique of the Catholic socialist movement. He criticized the abbé Garnier (a Catholic militant, essayist and proponent of Christian democracy) of wanting to recreate the past by constantly evoking a bygone era in which the church had created a 'collective patrimony' for the poor. This was lazy, thought Jaurès; it amounted only to repetition. Socialism, on the other hand, appreciated the newness of circumstances and aspired to a collective patrimony in a crucially new form.[12] In Jaurès' critique of the abbé Garnier we have further evidence of ideas about time being at the interface of ideological conflicts, as well as an illustration of the characteristics which Jaurès sometimes attributed to the notions of past and future. These were not merely neutral and descriptive temporal categories: they were politically loaded.

Nevertheless, Jaurès' approach to the French Revolution and its relevance for his own socialist mission points towards an important nuance in his characterization of past and future. He was very consciously attentive to the demands of changed circumstances, but wanted to avoid slipping into a dichotomous way of thinking in which the past was always equated to what was negative whilst the future was universally good. He sought to pinpoint what he called the 'moral value of history' and to learn lessons

---

11   Jaurès, 'La limite', 58–9.
12   Jean Jaurès, 'Néant du catholisme social', *La Dépêche* (27 April 1892), in *Action socialiste* (Paris: G. Bellais, 1899), 147–8.

from 1789 that could be readapted to present circumstances.[13] For example, he saw in the French Revolution a great triumph of secular morality, and he affirmed that any future change would also have to have morality at its core; accordingly, he called for moral (and not merely civic) education in primary schools.[14] It is clear that Jaurès did not always, as might be suggested by his article on social Catholicism, see the use of the past as wholly negative. Rather, it was accepting the past and yearning for it in its unchanged entirety which was damaging; one needed to critically appraise history and select those aspects of it which were fit for use in the future.

A Period of Transition

According to Madeleine Rebérioux, the notion of transition occupied Jaurès' thought in the first years of the twentieth century; his *Études socialistes* are an extended series of reflections on this problem.[15] These studies were originally intended as an introduction to a far vaster piece of work which Jaurès never came to write, and they are as a result sadly truncated.[16] The very fact that the concepts of transition and passage came to occupy such a central place in Jaurès' thought demonstrates the importance of time for understanding his particular political vision. After all, there is a temporal aspect inherent in or at least bound up with the idea of transition: across what timeframe might change be achieved? When might this change begin? Would it be sudden and ruptured, or gradual and smooth?

The nature of the political and social transition Jaurès desired for France is concomitant with his philosophy of history as a process of gradual change. He forcefully rejected as 'puerile' the idea that an economic

13   Jean Jaurès, 'Introduction à l'histoire socialiste' in Vandevelde, ed., *Jaurès*, 78.
14   Jean Jaurès, 'L'instruction morale à l'école' in *Action Socialiste*, 154.
15   Rebérioux, 'Présentation', Jaurès, *Études socialistes*, unnumbered pages.
16   Ibid.

catastrophe would bring about change for the better.[17] Instead, he advocated 'continuous' and gradual movement towards a new society.[18] The idea that a republic announced, prepared for, or even contained socialism would make this process smoother: France was already on the road to socialism.[19] One needed to be constantly attuned to the movement of society in order to perceive where reality came into contact with the 'new idea'; change would be so gradual as to be barely perceptible.[20] Jaurès repeatedly posited the idea of sudden rupture as opposed to that of gradual, continuous, and conscious change as his sorest point of conflict with the Parti ouvrier français, and he thought that the latter left France at the mercy of 'sudden deliverances'.[21] Issues surrounding time, then, appeared at the interface of Jaurès' political battles in an important way, and were not confined to his criticisms of the *Communist Manifesto*.

Jaurès' thought took place between two certainties: the certainty of the need for the transformation of the present, and the certainty that decisive change would one day happen in the future. He firmly asserted that 'political and social evolution [would] end in communism'.[22] Rebérioux highlights this certainty as a striking feature of the *Études*.[23] However, the precise means by which – and the exact moment at which – this change would be to be effected were almost, in Jaurès' words, 'impossible to know': there was a grey area in the form of the period of transition.[24] Unable to predict the future precisely, Jaurès did away with the ruptured upheaval presented by the *Communist Manifesto* and other (mainly Marxist) elements on the left, establishing instead a more flexible, malleable timeframe in which transition would occur. This points towards a conceptualization of time in which the future was seen to

17   Jaurès, 'Question de méthode', in *Études socialistes*, l.
18   Jaurès, 'Préface: république et socialisme', ibid. lxiv.
19   Ibid. lxiv.
20   Jaurès, *Études socialistes*, 14.
21   Ibid. 32.
22   Jaurès, 'Question de méthode', ibid. xii.
23   Rebérioux, 'Présentation', ibid. [unnumbered pages].
24   Jaurès, 'Question de méthode', ibid. xii.

develop gradually out of the present as a result of diligent work, rather than appearing or landing suddenly.

It is interesting, at this point, to reconsider the extent to which Jaurès thought that history could be shaped by individuals or composites of individuals. The transitionary period of the future could not be envisaged or described exactly by Jaurès precisely because he thought that a new society needed to be consciously created, rendering it largely dependent on mankind. According to Jaurès, it was futile to follow the Marxists' suggestion that the proletariat should wait for a bourgeois revolution that they could divert; they needed to create a movement with an overwhelming majority and the 'communist ideal' as the 'clear and directive idea'.[25] This being the case, predictions couldn't be made about the exact location in time and the precise nature of societal transformation. In other words, once Jaurès had removed the proletariat from the conveyor belt towards revolution to which Marx had consigned them, the future became far less certain.

In light of this, it could be considered contradictory that Jaurès nonetheless saw the ultimate arrival at a socialist society as a certainty, and this apparent contradiction merits further exploration. At points, Jaurès cast doubt on this certainty. For example, at the beginning of his article 'Organisation socialiste: collectivisme et radicalisme' he stated that describing socialism as inevitable was appealing to a kind of vertigo, creating an abyss into which France could fall.[26] However, the principal aim of the article was to sketch out tomorrow's collectivist society, which Jaurès insinuated lay at the end of all routes toward political and social change.[27] This, coupled with the evidence from *Études socialistes* cited above ('political and social evolution [would] end in communism'), quite clearly presupposed a socialist victory.

Jaurès accounted for this contradiction by stating that those who asked what a changed society might resemble were owed an answer, and

---

25   Ibid. xx–xxi, xxviii, liii. Jaurès focuses on the need for a huge majority in a later section of the *Études* entitled 'Évolution révolutionnaire', 43–4.

26   Jaurès, 'Organisation socialiste: collectivisme et radicalisme', *La Revue socialiste* 21 (1895), 258.

27   Ibid. 262.

elsewhere he spoke of the importance of the socialist movement having a tangible aim.[28] He highlights the French Revolution of 1789 as having a huge advantage over other attempts at drastic change because what its instigators wanted either had a precedent or existed already.[29] Although he was reluctant to lapse into the complacency engendered by certain victory, Jaurès needed to be confident in the possibility of transformation of France's political and social system in order to galvanize others and to demonstrate what the new world would look like. His assertions of certainty can perhaps be read as the use of what he called 'poetic license', which revolutionary theory occasionally needed to make use of in order to convey a greater truth. The example Jaurès cites of this 'poetic license' is that in interpretations of the book of Genesis, a day is widely held to represent several millions of years.[30]

Tension between certainty of victory, on the one hand, and the general unpredictability of the future, on the other, is also found throughout the work of Georges Sorel, author of *Réflexions sur la violence*, and Fernand Pelloutier, the leader of the Fédération des Bourses du Travail.[31] This highlights a similarity between Jaurès and others on the left (of apparently very different political affiliations, Sorel being interested chiefly in Marxism and later in revolutionary syndicalism, while Pelloutier was an anarchosyndicalist) on the basis of their conceptualization of the future. Jaurès could be situated in a broader current of left-wing thought which was wrestling, during the final years of the nineteenth century and the early years of the twentieth, to reclaim the future from what was perceived as a Marxist hegemony, and also from the distant dreams of utopians such as Cabet and St Simon. Thinkers such as Jaurès, Sorel, and Pelloutier all made attempts to recapture the future and make revolution or (in Jaurès' case) profound change possible in the present, or at least the very near future.

28   Ibid. 258.
29   Jaurès, *Études socialistes*, 48.
30   Jaurès, 'Question de méthode', ibid. xxxvii.
31   See for example, Georges Sorel and Jeremy Jennings, eds, *Reflections on Violence* (Cambridge: Cambridge University Press, 1999) and Fernand Pelloutier, 'Textes choisis', in Jacques Julliard, *Fernand Pelloutier et les origines du syndicalisme d'action directe* (Paris: Éditions du Seuil, 1971), 265–518.

All, however, ultimately found that they had to engage with the notion of a knowable distant future in which transformation would definitely occur.

Socialism's Religious Potential

There is a third and final aspect of Jaurès' conceptualization of time which it is worth exploring briefly: his ideas about socialism's religious potential. For someone who trumpeted secular morality and who helped orchestrate the historic separation of church and state in 1905, some of Jaurès' ideas about socialism had strikingly religious overtones, and these in turn have intriguing implications for his ideas about political time. His concern with the relationship between religion and socialism is most obvious in his pamphlet *La Question religieuse et le socialisme*. Written in 1891, ten years before *Études socialistes*, it constitutes quite an early work, hailing as it does from before Jaurès' 'definitive entry' into socialism in 1893.[32] Although his concerns became distanced from religion, it is nonetheless worth illuminating this aspect of Jaurès' thought and noting that he engaged with religious notions of time at least at one point in his career.

Having established that socialism had a clear 'religious promise', Jaurès went on in his pamphlet to explain that positivism had eliminated what was at the heart of religious meaning and what lay 'deepest in the human soul', which was 'the feeling of infinity' [*le sentiment de l'infini*]. In fact, humanity only had value as an 'expression of the infinite'. Jaurès goes on to say that socialism would be able to recapture or reinvigorate the capacity for infinity because of the religious promise it held.[33] It is not necessarily,

---

32   Michel Launay's avant-propos in Jaurès, *La Question religieuse et le socialisme* (Paris: Les Editions de Minuit, 1959), 10. On the dating of Jaurès' text, see Madeleine Rebérioux, 'Socialisme et religion: un inédit de Jaurès, 1891', *Annales: Économies, Sociétés, Civilisations* 16 (1961), 1096–120.

33   Jaurès, *La Question*, 39–43.

as one might expect, the reference to infinity which piques the interest of a historian of time, since by infinity Jaurès seems to have meant 'the divine'; instead, it is the notion of salvation strongly present in socialism which is fascinating.[34] Political time, most usually associated with ideological conflicts and often with practical concerns, was here transposed onto a grand religious or even messianic timeframe; socialism thus acquired a salvational aspect because it could inculcate humanity with this 'feeling of infinity' once more. Evoking the idea of salvation imbues the future with an enormous amount of potential, and transforms political concerns into religious ones with much greater import.

In this respect, Jaurès perhaps had more in common with the Catholic socialists than he would have cared to acknowledge: Marc Sangnier, for example, frequently evoked a grand religious timeframe and spoke about his social mission in relation to eternity (a concept close to that of infinity, but more avowedly religious) and salvation in his review *Le Sillon*, mouthpiece for the Catholic socialist movement of the same name.[35] This in turn allows us to glimpse one of the ways in which studying ideas about time can provide us with a useful tool for realigning traditional left-wing groupings: Jaurès, as mentioned above, was ostensibly hostile to the Catholic socialist and Christian democracy movements, but his thought was at times not so far from theirs.

Conclusion

Jaurès' philosophy of history led him to believe that idealism and materialism combined to produce historical development. History was therefore partly dictated by economic structures, and partly in mankind's hands. This view had important implications for Jaurès' version of the transition from a capitalist to a socialist society: the future was largely unpredictable,

---

34   Rebérioux, 'Socialisme et religion', 1097.
35   See, for example, Marc Sangnier, 'Pour l'espérence', *Almanach du Sillon pour l'année 1904*, 9–12. Sangnier was leader of the *Sillon* movement.

though a degree of certainty in change needed to be present to act as a goal and an incentive. Change, affirmed Jaurès, would need to be gradual and continuous, and consciously effected by a movement attentive to the needs of present society. Finally, Jaurès believed that socialism's religious promise provided an opportunity for salvation which brought him closer to Catholic socialists, though this religious aspect is absent from his later work.

Throughout, we have seen that time – and not only different versions of the past, but ideas about the future and the movement of time – figured as an ideological point of conflict or as a point of congruence between those with ostensibly radically differing views. Take, for example, the way in which Jaurès used time to distinguish his ideas from those of Marx and Engels or Jules Guesde, or the unexpected similarity revealed between Jaurès and Sangnier. A particularly pertinent context for Jaurès' work is the struggle to recapture the distant future and to make revolution meaningful in the present and the very near future, played out in the writings of authors such as Fernand Pelloutier and Georges Sorel. Sorel and Pelloutier, as well as Jaurès, evoked a certain victory in the distant future.

The study of political time in the thought of Jean Jaurès has the potential to open up research into time and the left more broadly. A particularly interesting avenue to pursue is the way in which concepts like salvation, eternity, and eschatology crept into socialist thought and introduced not only a resplendent future which went beyond political and social change, but also a religious element which was outwardly rejected by many socialists.

Selected Bibliography

Becker, Jean-Jacques and Gilles Candar, eds, *Histoire des gauches en France, Volume I: l'héritage du XIXe siècle* (Paris: La Découverte, 2004).

Croix, Alexandre, *Jaurès et ses detracteurs* (Paris: Éditions du Vieux Saint-Ouen, 1967).

Dommanget, Maurice, et al., *Jaurès historien de la Révolution française* (Castres: Centre national et Musée Jean Jaurès, 1989).

Gildea, Robert, *The Past in French History* (New Haven: Yale University Press, 1994).

Goldberg, Harvey, 'Jaurès and the Carmaux Strikes: The Coal Strike of 1892' and 'Jaurès and the Carmaux Strikes: The Glass Strike of 1895', *The American Journal of Economics and Sociology* 2 (1958), 167–78 and 307–19.

Jaurès, Jean, 'Organisation socialiste: collectivisme et radicalisme' and 'Organisation socialiste: l'État socialiste et les fonctionnaires', *La Revue socialiste* 21 (1895), 257–66 and 385–408.

——, *Action socialiste* (Paris: G. Bellais, 1899).

——, *La Question religieuse et le socialisme* (Paris: Les Éditions de Minuit, 1959).

——, *Études socialistes* (Paris: Slatkine, 1979).

—— and Paul Lafargue, *Idéalisme et matérialisme dans la conception de l'histoire* (Lille: P. Lagrange, 1901).

Jennings, Jeremy, 'Syndicalism and the French Revolution', *Journal of Contemporary History* 1 (1991), 71–96.

Koselleck, Reinhart, *Futures Past: On the Semantics of Historical Time* (New York: Columbia University Press, 2004).

——, *The Practice of Conceptual History: Timing History, Spacing Concepts* (Stanford: Stanford University Press, 2002).

Noland, Aaron, 'Individualism in Jean Jaurès' Socialist Thought', *Journal of the History of Ideas* 1 (1961), 63–80.

Pelloutier, Fernand, 'Textes choisi', in Jacques Julliard, ed., *Fernand Pelloutier et les origines du syndicalisme d'action directe* (Paris: Éditions du Seuil, 1971), 265–518.

Rappoport, Charles, *Jean Jaurès: l'homme, le penseur, le socialiste* (Paris: M. Rivière, 1925).

Rebérioux, Madeleine, 'Socialisme et religion: un inédit de Jaurès, 1891', *Annales: Économies, Sociétés, Civilisations*, 16 (1961), 1096–120.

Sangnier, Marc, 'Pour l'espérence', *Almanach du Sillon pour l'année 1904*, 9–12.

Sorel, Georges, *Reflections on Violence*, ed. Jeremy Jennings (Cambridge: Cambridge University Press, 1999).

Vandevelde, Émile, ed., *Jaurès* (Paris: Librairie Felix Alcan, 1929).

Varias, Alexander, *Paris and the Anarchists: Aesthetes and Subversives during the Fin-de-Siècle* (New York: St Martin's Press, 1996).

LISA JESCHKE

To Refuse to Imagine: Simone Weil's Materialism

Critical work on Simone Weil (1909–43) is marked by the tendency to single her out as an exceptional figure, a strategy which seems to highlight her radicalism, but which ultimately pushes that radicalism into a niche, rendering it harmless: nothing is at stake for anyone but one eccentric woman.[1] In her essay 'Simone Weil', Susan Sontag distances herself from Weil by declaring that 'I, for one, do not doubt that the sane view of the world is the true one'.[2] 'I, for one' is rhetorical understatement, for Sontag clearly implies that she is not just 'one' – whereas Weil's ideas seem to her shareable only among few:

I cannot believe that more than a handful of the tens of thousands of readers she has won since the posthumous publication of her books and essays really share her ideas. Nor is it necessary – necessary to share Simone Weil's anguished and unconsummated love affair with the Catholic Church, or accept her gnostic theology of

---

1   Weil is certainly considered as an embarrassing exception not merely as a thinker, but as a woman. Chauvinism marks what is widely held to be a representation of Weil in the character of Lazare in George Bataille's novel *Le Bleu du Ciel* (written in 1935–6, first published in 1957): 'C'était une fille de vingt-cinq ans, laide et visiblement sale (les femmes avec lesquelles je sortais auparavant étaient, au contraire, bien habillées et jolies). Son nom de famille, Lazare, répondait mieux à son aspect macabre que son prénom. Elle était étrange, assez ridicule même. Il était difficile d'expliquer l'intérêt que j'avais pour elle. Il fallait supposer un dérangement mental': Georges Bataille, *Œuvres completes. III* (Paris: Gallimard, 1971), 277–487 (401). In seamless transition, compare poet and essayist Kenneth Rexroth: 'I doubt if she was ever aware of the smell of her own armpits': Kenneth Rexroth, 'Simone Weil', in Bradford Morrow, ed., *World Outside the Window: The Selected Essays of Kenneth Rexroth* (New York: New Directions Publishing, 1987), 35–40 (39).

2   Susan Sontag, 'Simone Weil', in Sontag, *Against Interpretation and Other Essays* (New York, 1961), 49–51 (50).

divine absence, or espouse her ideals of body denial, or concur in her violently unfair hatred of Roman civilization and the Jews.[3]

Sontag's list of 'her [Weil's] ideas' strongly suggests that – without making this transparent – she is referring solely to *La pesanteur et la grâce*. While this is probably Weil's best known 'work', it is in fact a selective editorial construct assembled by Gustave Thibon from the notes Weil left with him in 1942, biased not least by his Catholicism. Thibon first published his/ Weil's collection in 1947. Against the paired tendencies in Weil scholarship first to insulate Weil as a woman/thinker and second to isolate *La pesanteur et la grâce* from the rest of her *œuvre*, I will in this chapter outline the continuity of her thought from her early philosophical and political essays to the notes that were to form *La pesanteur et la grâce* – in particular in terms of dialectical configurations of labour and time as systems of mediation materially resisting processes of the imagination. Key concepts appearing in Weil's theological notes are to be understood as emerging from within French intellectual culture from the 1920s through to the 1940s. In particular, I will seek to trace how the development of her thought is indebted to – and a contribution to – the French reception of Hegel, aesthetic and political modernism and, most urgently, the labour movements of the early 1930s.

Early Philosophical Texts

In her years as a socialist activist in the late 1920s and early 1930s, Weil develops a form of Hegelianism which follows Hegel's dialectical approach to work, albeit with an emphasis on the resistance of the object against the grasp of the human subject that differs markedly from Kojève's more

3   Ibid.

detailed reading of Hegelian dialectics.[4] According to Hegel – according to Kojève – man creates himself[5] as man by means of work: man is, tautologically, man's work. By negating that which is, he can create the future, can act with intention and will, can act:

> *Ce Moi sera ainsi son propre œuvre: il sera (dans l'avenir) ce qu'il est devenu par la négation (dans le présent) de ce qu'il a été (dans le passé), cette négation étant effectuée en vue de ce qu'il deviendra. Dans son être même, ce Moi est devenir intentionnel, évolution voulue, progrès conscient et volontaire. Il est l'acte de transcender le donné qui lui est donné et qu'il est lui-même. Ce Moi est un individu (humain), libre (vis-à-vis du réel donné) et historique (par rapport à soi-même).[6]*

Secondly, it is not only man himself who is – rather tautologically – the creator of man himself, but it is also the fact that he works, and makes works. Consequently, the production of man by himself is inseparably linked to the production of objects from that which is given by nature, and consequently the negation of nature:

> *Le produit du travail est l'œuvre du travailleur. C'est la réalisation de son projet [...]. C'est donc par le travail, et par le travail seulement, que l'homme se réalise objectivement en tant qu'homme. Ce n'est qu'après avoir produit un objet artificiel que l'homme est lui-même réellement et objectivement plus et autre chose qu'un être naturel [...].[7]*

---

4   For an extensive discussion of Hegel's reception in France in the twentieth century, see also Bruce Baugh, *French Hegel* (New York and London: Routledge, 2003). Baugh shows how Kojève's Hegel lectures from 1933 onwards were situated in an already established discursive framework in French intellectual culture regarding Hegel. Baugh's argument finds further confirmation when reading Weil's school essays from the late 1920s and socialist essays from the early 1930s, suffused with Hegelian thought.

5   I have chosen not to alter the male third person singular pronoun – not so as to re-enforce, but so as to acknowledge and expose the gendered language of the historical material discussed in these passages.

6   Alexandre Kojève, *Introduction à la lecture de Hegel: leçons sur la phénoménologie de l'esprit professées de 1933 à 1939 à l'École des Hautes-Études, réunies et publiées par Raymond Queneau* (Paris: Gallimard, 1947), 12–13. In this and all subsequent quotations from Kojève, I am following his own formatting in italicizing his commentary and leaving any direct Hegel translations unitalicized.

7   Ibid. 30.

Man distinguishes himself from the natural world through his work, negotiated here through the vocabulary of the 'projet', or project, later expanded
as follows:

> L'Homme n'est mouvement dialectique ou historique (= libre) révélant l'Être par
> le Discours que parce qu'il vit en fonction de l'*avenir*, qui se présente à lui sous la
> forme d'un *projet* ou d'un 'but' (Zweck) à réaliser par l'action négatrice du donné,
> et parce qu'il n'est lui-même réel en tant qu'Homme que dans la mesure où il se crée
> par cette action comme une *œuvre* (Werk).[8]

Man as a dialectical being is equated with man as a historical being, that
is, a time-based being that can negate and alter the givenness of the found,
or natural, world – by projecting into the future. The animal's immediate
relation to the world is replaced by a relation to time which includes the
possibility or even necessity of a future, and time-based actions of planning
and working. That is, man's relation to nature is mediated. The human
agency involved in such mediation requires the appropriation of space to
the largest extent – that is, of given matter, of objects, and of the world
as a whole: '*L'homme qui travaille reconnaît dans le Monde effectivement
transformé par son travail sa propre œuvre*.'[9] This is certainly an instance of
what has sometimes been perceived as Hegel's totalitarianism; not only can
man, through his labour, create himself and particular objects – rather, in
doing so, he also creates the world as a whole, indeed here capitalized as
Monde. The scope of Hegelian dialectics exposes itself here in its ambition
to comprehend total form: the form and scale of the dialectic is unlim-
ited and total, as is the agency of man by means of work, by means of the
transformation of the natural world into a world that is entirely cultural,
historical and man-made.

And yet, if Hegel develops a kind of total form where the world as a
whole is the creation of man, he also emphasizes the autonomy of the object
in its relation to the slave. Even if the slave negates the object, suppressing
it dialectically, he leaves its autonomy intact:

8   Ibid. 533.
9   Ibid. 31.

> Pris comme Conscience-de-soi, en-tant-que-telle, l'Esclave se rapporte lui-aussi à la chose d'une-manière-négative-ou-négatrice, et il la supprime [*dialectiquement*]. Mais – pour lui – la chose est en même temps autonome.[10]

The slave, by means of his labour, prepares the object for consumption, dialectically transforming it, but not annihilating it.

> A cause de cela, il ne peut pas, par son acte-de-nier, venir à bout de la chose jusqu'à l'anéantissement [*complet de la chose, comme le fait le Maître qui la 'consomme'*]. C'est-à-dire, il ne fait que la transformer-par-le-travail [*il la prépare pour la consommation, mais il ne la consomme pas lui-même*].

And it is this resistance of the object against the grasp of human subjectivity which is emphasized in Weil's reception of Hegel, strongly influenced by Émile-Auguste Chartier (1868–1951), a philosopher, journalist, (her) teacher at the Lycée Henri-IV in Paris, and an intellectual cult figure of sorts in the early 1920s, commonly known to his pupils and the public under the pseudonym of Alain. Before Weil, it is Alain who emphasizes the notion of a world materially resisting the subject – and he, as she will, does so in the terminology of a rejection of the imagination. The French author André Maurois, himself a pupil of Alain's, sketches Alain's position as follows: 'L'imagination est maîtresse d'erreurs et la rêverie toujours dangereuse si on ne lui donne un objet. Le rôle des beaux-arts est de lui assurer des objets réels et stables'.[11] In terms of an aesthetics of production, this might mean that in

> l'imagination du romancier errent des fantômes de romans, mais on n'y peut pas plus compter les chapitres que les colonnes dans l'image du Panthéon. L'artiste a besoin de la résistance de la nature, comme la colombe légère de celle de l'air [...].[12]

What is suggested here is that 'l'imagination' can be exposed as unreal – and that means as not having a physical correlative in the outside world – as soon as an attempt is made to give an exact account of what it is one is thinking

---

10   Ibid. 23.
11   André Maurois, *Alain* (Paris: Domat, 1950), 93.
12   Ibid. 94.

of. Hence something which is purely imaginary implies a level of instability which makes it unaccountable, and it is only through the resistance of one's physical environment, of 'la nature', that countability and consequently accountability are established. What is at stake here is not merely an ethical sense of accountability. Rather, the comparison with the necessity of 'air' for the flight of a 'colombe' suggests that the resistance of material nature is in fact the very condition for the possibility of making art. Consequently, the limits imposed upon the artist by the material world are not experienced as limiting limits, but rather as limits that enable the artist to make art in the first place. This implies a re-evaluation of human agency, a model in which 'la nature est le maître des maîtres',[13] an implicit challenge to the master-slave dialectic, as well as to the idea that the artist as creator could submit nature to his genius; on the contrary, the artist is submitted to the objects he works with and does not possess full sovereignty over the process of production.

Nor does any other producer – or worker, we might add – something which will become central to Weil's critique of capitalism, in some ways indicating an early environmentalist approach to Marxism. Unlike Alain, Weil is not specifically concerned with art in terms of the resistance to production, but takes up his notion of artistic work to establish a much broader analysis of work processes as well as of the relation between human subjectivity and its physical environment. In her notes around her 1929 essay 'De la perception ou l'aventure de Protée', Weil develops a gradual scale of different kinds of imagination. Acknowledging that 'l'imagination est nécessairement conservée en toute perception', she states that 'l'on peut distinguer des degrés dans la perception selon que l'imagination y est plus ou moins surmontée':

> une série peut être ainsi formée, dont le premier terme sera l'imagination pure, ou rêve, le seconde terme, l'imagination réglée, qui constitue ce que l'on peut appeler perception vulgaire; le troisième terme est la parfaite perception, où l'imagination est absolument surmontée.[14]

13   Ibid.
14   Simone Weil, 'De la perception ou l'aventure de Protée' [Notes], in Weil, Œuvres complètes, Tome I, Vol. 1: premiers écrits philosophiques (Paris: Gallimard, 1988), 121–39.

What is suggested is a relation to the world that does not overwhelm the world with an aggrandized sense of subjectivity. Such a self-aggrandization would be problematic in terms of the ethical relation of a subject to itself – by suggesting that its scope of action is greater than it actually is, creating a false sense of one's own possibilities. What is more, it would constitute a relation of a subject to the world which would involve imbuing impersonal objects with a sense of human spirit that does not do justice to the dead materiality of the outside world. For Weil, the 'objet est nécessairement muet' (*OC* 1:1, 131) and will hence only ever respond by reflecting back a subject's emotions. In this sense, imagination might be called an extended pathetic fallacy, a thought process that does not see a thing for what it is, a thing: 'Au penseur qui laisse son corps livré au monde, l'objet répond en lui renvoyant pour ainsi dire ses propres émotions' (*OC* 1:1, 131). Hence the emotionally projective thought turns the world into a subject's dream of the world and inflates the subject, thinking he can incorporate the outside into his inside, eat the world – a spatially disproportionate way of thinking. For if the scope of any one individual is enlarged beyond its limits, the outside world is no longer seen as a world of its own proportions, but is appropriated into a respective self. Such a fallacious idea of one's own property and proportion might be overcome by a kind of athletic training of the mind, as Weil goes on to suggest: 'Mais au penseur déjà athlète, et qui sait rester immobile, l'objet ne répond rien, devenant une sorte de sphinx qui finit par dévorer la pensée' (*OC* 1:1, 131).[15] Paradoxically, Weil asks for an athleticism of stillness, as if the sport of thinking consisted of becoming as 'immobile' as the object one is looking at. For only this kind of immobility gives the object that is 'muet' the space to remain 'muet', to not have to respond to thought, to devour thought.

Weil employs Proteus as an allegorical figure representing the way imagination can mould the outside world into constantly changing shapes

---

First published in *Livres Propos* 5 (1929). Weil's *Œuvres complètes* will henceforth be referred to as *OC*, and volume and page numbers will be given in the text.

15 For a similar analogy, see Antonin Artaud's conception of an 'athlétisme affectif' in *Le théâtre et son double* (Paris: Editions Flammarion, 1973).

according to whatever one's own state of thought at any particular point might be. Against Proteus,

> il faut admirer l'homme qui [...] a empoignée Protée, l'a dépouillé, et a trouvé, sous ce manteau d'émotions, la pure étendue, toujours extérieure à soi, matière de nos travaux, qui ne parle, ne pense ni ne veut. (*OC* 1:1, 137)

This quotation also points towards an access to the physical world surrounding us which is, for Weil, an alternative to the imagination, and that is the access through work. Hence she emphasizes the fact that work makes an objective and impersonal demand on those who exercise it, a demand that deletes the role of the will, the self and one's imagination:

> dire que pour agir je dois travailler, c'est dire que les changements produits par moi sont sans affinité avec mes désirs et mes projets, ne portent point le sceau de ma volonté, et se faut comme ils se feraient s'ils étaient produits par toute autre cause. (*OC* 1:1, 137)

Note her employment of the vocabulary of the 'projet', which we have already encountered as a Hegelian notion; while Kojève would stress the agency and will of man, Weil emphasizes the fact that the changes produced by man in work have nothing to do with subjective desires, projects or will; she proposes an anti-subjectivist and impersonal philosophy of work. The following might clarify what she means:

> L'idée d'une matière commence avec le travail, commence quand, par exemple, je grimpe sur le talus où est la rose, faisant avec mes jambes des mouvements qui n'ont aucun rapport avec l'admiration que m'inspire la rose. (*OC* 1:1, 247)

The movements which it is necessary to perform in order to reach the rose stand in no relation to one's actual motivation to perform this action – that is, one would have to perform the same sequence of movements regardless of whether the motive is admiration or the wish to destroy the rose. In this sense, the slope, and the rose on the slope, make certain objective demands in terms of which subjective desires or projects are wholly irrelevant. Weil uses the rose as an object to illustrate a materialist definition of work as that which resists the subjective dream of the world.

Aside from the materiality of the object I am dealing with, there is a second aspect of material resistance in terms of work, as Weil points out, and that is the aspect of time, as understood through the French-Hegelian notion of the 'projet'. Time is a form of mediation that lies between who I am and who I want to be, as well as between what I have not yet made and want to make. It now emerges that the imagination would delete the time necessary to unfold a 'projet'; it is immediate, not mediated, and hence leaves us in the position of a slave:

> Les impressions, les émotions, les imaginations ne nous donnent pas le temps; elles appartiennent au royaume de l'immédiat. Nous sommes, par elles, absolument esclaves à chaque instant, sans que rien ne nous sépare de nous-mêmes [...]. (*OC* 1:1, 150)

For example, it is 'aussi facile de penser dix ou dix mille pas; mais le coureur sentirait la différence' (*OC* 1:1, 154). Similarly, I could imagine turning this into a 10,000- or a 20,000-word essay, but – in writing or reading – the difference between these numbers can only be felt in the execution of either of these lengths and their corresponding duration, and hence only through temporal mediation.

In terms of the modernist context of the late 1920s and early 1930s in Paris, it should be added that both Weil and Kojève's already divergent emphases in the reception of Hegel find a more radically antagonistic counter-trajectory in Breton's Surrealist conception of what might be called a dreamer's or a magician's sense of the possibility of the immediate transformation of an object. Strikingly, Breton also uses the example of the rose:

> For us it was necessary, if one will allow me this parenthesis, to take 'the rose' through a profitable movement of less benign contradictions, where it would be successively the rose which comes from a garden, a rose which has a particular place in a dream, a rose that can't be abstracted from the 'optical bouquet', one which can totally change its properties in entering into automatic writing, one that has no more of the rose than what the painter whished in a surrealist painting, and finally, the one which, totally different from itself, returns to the garden.[16]

16   Quoted from Baugh, 56.

According to Breton, a 'principle of perpetual mutation has taken over both things and ideas, leading to their total deliverance, and man's as well'.[17] While the Surrealists at this point identified as Communist, such a position is openly undialectical. For the deletion of time that takes place in the immediate transformation of the object is ultimately a deletion of the mediation of time which is, in Hegel's and in Weil's sense, work. It is the position of the master, who consumes and annihilates the object in a relation that is not time-based but immediate: *'Tout l'effort étant fait par l'Esclave, le Maître n'a plus qu'à jouir de la chose que l'Esclave a préparée pour lui, et de la "nier", de la détruire, en la "consommant"'*.[18] In Hegel's logic, it is the slave who, by means of his dialectical relation, ultimately forms a revolutionary demand and a real relation to the world. In Kojève's words:

> *L'homme intégral, absolument libre [...], sera l'Esclave qui a 'supprimé' sa servitude. Si la Maîtrise oisive est une impasse, la Servitude laborieuse est au contraire la source de tout progrès humain, social, historique. L'Histoire est l'histoire de l'Esclave travailleur.*[19]

If the Surrealists sought to ally themselves with communist thought, then their revolutionary programme certainly presents a radical departure from Hegelian-Marxist thought, and their revolutionary thought seems to veer towards a consumptive rather than productive relation to the world. Their focus on the dream and on immediacy, their very dreams of immediacy, their relationship to the object world as a relation of direct transformability, seems perhaps utopian in terms of gesturing towards the possibility of

---

17 Ibid.
18 Kojève, *Introduction à la lecture de Hegel*, 23.
19 Ibid. 26. While 'Arbeit macht frei', the metal inscription above several National-Socialist concentration camps, among them Oranienburg, Dachau and Auschwitz, is usually ascribed to Lorenz Diefenbach's 1873 narrative, *Arbeit macht frei*, 'in which gamblers and fraudsters discover the path to virtue through hard work' (Kate Connolly, 'Poland declares state of emergency after "Arbeit macht frei" stolen from Auschwitz', *The Guardian* (18 December 2009) <http://www.theguardian.com/world/2009/dec/18/auschwitz-arbeit-macht-frei-sign> accessed 2 April 2014), it also seems to constitute a mocking echo mouthing the liberatory claim of the master–slave dialectic.

a work-less society. Utopian socialism, however, is not to be equated with dialectical socialism, and diving into an apparent purity of immediacy risks ignoring rather than abolishing the struggle of work.

Socialist Essays

A critique of the deletion of time is where Simone Weil's critique of industrial labour in the early 1930s finds a starting point. According to her, what is lost in industrial labour is first a sense of the resistance of whichever material one is working with and second a sense of the mediation of time as experienced through work. As an example of these losses, she describes how in the recent history of mining, a machine of compressed air had replaced 'le pic' (OC 2:1, 96); unlike the pick-axe, the machine is not part of the human body, but rather subordinates the human body to its constant vibrations:

> Auparavant, il [l'ouvrier] adaptait la forme et la marche de l'outil à la forme et à la durée naturelle de ses mouvements; le pic était pour lui comme un membre supplémentaire qui faisait corps avec lui, qui amplifiait le mouvement de ses bras. À présent c'est lui qui fait corps avec la machine, qui s'ajoute à elle comme un rouage supplémentaire et vibre de sa trépidation incessante. (*OC* 2:1, 97)

Weil here develops what might be called an early theory of the cyborg in her political analysis and critique of the workplace: the transition from the (artisanal) tool to the (industrial) machine, so she argues, involves a transition from man that incorporates the tool as an extension of his limbs to man that is incorporated into the machine, becoming an extension of the workings of the machine. This also explains why, during this period of time, she repeatedly draws up an idealized and nostalgic image of artisanal labour:

> L'artisan qui possède ses propres outils, sa propre matière première, est roi dans son travail. [...] Être vivant et pensant, il dispose librement ses choses inertes qui subissent son action. Son intelligence domine la matière. (*OC* 2:1, 92)

By contrast, the new relation between worker and materials obfuscates the relation between 'projet' and 'œuvre'. Submitted to the machine she is working with, an individual worker will no longer have an overview of the work and its duration as a whole. This problem is caused not only by the proliferation of machines, but also by an extreme form of the separation of labour that has led to the reduction of each worker's tasks to a simple, repetitive gesture. Consequently, Weil notes, the link between the coordination and the execution of any particular 'projet' has been cut:

> à présent un régleur se charge de disposer une certaine quantité de machines selon les exigences du travail à exécuter et le travail est accompli sous ses ordres par des manœuvres spécialisés, capables seulement de faire fonctionner un type de machine et un seul par des gestes toujours identiques et auxquels l'intelligence n'a aucune part. (*OC* 2:1, 269)

Specialization has thus made it impossible for any individual worker to oversee the whole, and it is Weil's earlier thoughts on time which exposes the whole scale of the problem. For the cut between 'projet' and 'œuvre' has not only radically changed the nature of work, but also the nature of time; that is, time as a form of mediation has been erased and replaced by a kind of hellish eternity in which, from the perspective of any one worker, development from A to B is reduced to the infinite repetition of A.

This problem of the modern workplace, so Weil argues, is not particular to capitalist society, but is practised in equal measures in the USA and the Soviet Union. Disagreeing with Trotsky's notion that the Soviet Union is a bureaucratic deformation of socialist ideals, she argues that what is being practised in the Soviet Union is in fact a whole new form of oppression – 'l'oppression exercée au nom de la fonction' (*OC* 2:1, 268), a bureaucracy of 'les cadres' (*OC* 2:2, 9) both in terms of the organization of particular factories and in terms of the organization and co-ordination of the state as a whole. Hence while the opposition between those who buy work and those who sell work has been abolished, this has not automatically led to an abolishment of the distinction between those who dispose of the machine and those of whom the machine disposes.

But Weil does not only seek to point out the flaws in the structure of political entities which have proclaimed themselves as socialist, such as the Soviet Union; she also criticizes flaws in the theory of socialism from Marx onwards. One of her main focal points in this respect is the rhetorical function of the word 'revolution'. In her long essay 'Réflexion sur les causes de la liberté et de l'oppression sociale' (1934), she argues that

> 'L'étape supérieure du communisme' considérée par Marx comme le dernier terme de l'évolution sociale est, en somme, une utopie absolument analogue à celle du mouvement perpétuel. Et c'est au nom de cette utopie que les révolutionnaires ont versé leur sang. (*OC* 2:2, 45)

Her distress at the death of those who fight for a utopian revolution deferred to tomorrow again stems from the critique of a flawed perception of temporal relations. Death occurs in the present; the revolution is anticipated for the future; hence there is no direct link between a death that really occurs and a revolution which is, for the present moment, imaginary. Consequently, the word 'revolution' is pure form without content: 'Le mot de révolution est un mot pour lequel on tue, pour lequel on meurt, pour lequel on envoie les masses populaires à la mort, mais qui n'a aucun contenu' (*OC* 2:2, 45). She goes on to reformulate the link Alain has made between dreams – in this case the dream of liberty – and the imagination to expose communism itself as an instance of a dream: 'Le communisme imaginé par Marx est la forme la plus récente de ce rêve. Ce rêve est toujours demeuré vain, comme tous les rêves, ou, s'il a pu consoler, ce n'est que comme un opium' (*OC* 2:2, 71–2).

Throwing Marx's assertion that religion is the opium of the people back at him is a fiercely polemical attempt to expose and critique those remnants of metaphysics in Marxism which cynically risk the expenditure of human life in the name of uncertain higher ideals. But Weil emphasizes in the same essay that 'rien au monde ne peut empêcher l'homme de se sentir né pour la liberté' (*OC*, 2:2, 71) and that this striving is the source of revolutionary thought. Hence her critique of the revolution and communism at this point should not be taken as absolute, but rather as an attempt to erase reverie and subjective inflation from political thought, against the waste of real lives; nevertheless, the essay seems to anticipate a gradual distancing from socialist activism.

Her distance to fascism was always absolute. Two years earlier, in 1932, Weil had argued in 'L'Allemange en attente', that fascism finds its opium in the construction of force:

> En réalité, ce qui les [les ouvriers hitlériens, my insertion] attire au mouvement national-socialiste, c'est, tout comme pour les intellectuels et les petits-bourgeois, qu'ils y sentent une force. Ils ne se rendent pas compte que cette force n'apparaît si puissante que parce qu'elle n'est pas leur force, parce qu'elle est la force de la classe dominante, leur ennemi capital; et ils comptent sur cette force pour suppléer à leur propre faiblesse, et réaliser, ils ne savent comment, leurs rêves confus. (*OC* 2:1, 126)

Force appears as a supplement to a weak individual and seems to lead towards a kind of future, but is really an entity of the present – again a temporal misconception:

> Ce qui unit les membres du mouvement hitlérien, c'est tout d'abord l'avenir que celui-ci leur promet. Quel avenir? Un avenir qui n'est pas décrit, ou l'est du plusieurs manières contradictoires, et peut être ainsi pour chacun de la couleur de ses rêves. Mais, ce dont on est sûr, c'est que ce sera un système neuf, un 'troisième Reich', quelque chose qui ne ressemblera ni au passé ni surtout au présent. Et ce qui attire, vers cet avenir confus, intellectuels, petits-bourgeois, employés, chômeurs, c'est qu'ils sentent, dans le parti qui le leur promet, une force. Cette force éclate partout, dans les défilés en uniforme, dans les attentats, dans les avions employés pour la propagande; et tous ces faibles vont vers cette force comme des mouches vers la flamme. Ils ne savent pas que, si cette force apparaît comme si puissante, c'est qu'elle est la force, non de ceux qui préparent l'avenir, mais de ceux qui règnent sur le présent. (*OC* 2:1, 150–1)

La pesanteur et la grâce

It is at this point of political confusion between present and future that the jump may be made to *La pesanteur et la grâce*. The following passage indicates a direct continuity from above quote from 'L'Allemagne en attente':

> Perdre quelqu'un: on souffre que le mort, l'absent soit devenu de l'imaginaire, du faux. Mais le désir qu'on a de lui n'est pas imaginaire. [...] Faim: on imagine des

nourritures, mais la faim elle-même est réelle: se saisir de la faim. La présence du mort est imaginaire mais son absence est bien réelle; elle est désormais sa manière d'apparaître.[20]

In this case, the temporal confusion is not one between present and future, but between past and present. If someone has died, that is, has been present in the past but is absent in the present, it is this present mode of absence we need to focus on. Considering these kinds of maxims in the context of Weil's previous development of thought suggests that they are the logical conclusions of a consistent politics of anti-illusionism, now applied to individual thought. This might be understood either as a marker of Weil's increasing depoliticization, perhaps prepared for in her critique of communism as an opium for the people, or as a radical politicization of personal behaviour – or, indeed, as both at once.

The definition of 'la pesanteur' is continually reformulated in the notes that were to form the body of *La pesanteur et la grâce*, but essentially seems to encompass two notions. On the one hand, 'pesanteur' is described as a 'force "déifuge"' (*PG*, 82), as a force that signifies our removal from God as a result of the act of creation. By making it possible for us to exist, God has decreated himself, leaving the necessary space for our existence. Otherwise, 'tout serait Dieu' (*PG*, 82). On the other hand, 'gravity' refers to all kinds of human activities which are employed by the human imagination to make up for the absence of God, or more generally for any sense of emptiness or hurt. As an example, Weil returns several times to the extremely strong headaches she experienced throughout her life:

Ne pas oublier qu'à certains moments de mes maux de tête, quand la crise montait, j'avais un désir intense de faire souffrir un autre être humain, en le frappant précisément au même endroit du front.

Désirs analogues, très fréquents parmi les hommes.

Plusieurs fois dans cet état, j'ai cédé du moins à la tentation de dire des mots blessants.

Obéissance à la pesanteur. Le plus grand péché. (*PG*, 43)

20   Simone Weil, *La pesanteur et la grâce* [1947] (Paris: Pocket, 1991), 69. All following references will refer to this edition; page numbers will be given in the text (*PG*).

Gravity is here considered as a force of structural analogy, a force which tempts an individual to pass their suffering on. Weil outlines what could be called an economics of equilibrium, and it is this economic dimension which distinguishes the notion of 'gravity' from that of 'imagination'. Nevertheless, there is a strong sense of overlap in that 'imagination' is involved in the very economic processes constituting 'gravity': 'La recherche de l'équilibre est mauvaise parce qu'elle est imaginaire. La vengeance. Même si en fait on tue ou torture son ennemi c'est, en un sens, imaginaire' (*PG*, 48–9). The notion presented here might be difficult to comprehend if the hedging insertion of 'en un sens' is not paid sufficient attention to. What 'en un sens' implies is that even if our enemy is actually killed by us, the act of committing this crime is nevertheless imaginary to the extent that we, as the perpetrator, are more invested in our own personal equilibrium than in the objective condition of our enemy; this is exactly why we are capable of killing him – because we do not actually think about him. A similar point is made in terms of positive rewards:

> Une récompense purement imaginaire (un sourire de Louis XIV) est l'équivalent exact de ce qu'on a dépensé, car elle a exactement la valeur de ce qu'on dépense – contrairement aux récompenses réelles qui, comme telles, sont au-dessus ou au-dessous. *Aussi les avantages imaginaires* seuls fournissent l'énergie pour des efforts illimités. Mais il faut que Louis XIV sourit vraiment; s'il ne sourit pas, privation indicible. Un roi ne peut payer que des récompenses la plupart du temps imaginaires [...]. (*PG*, 51–2)

Again, the reason why Louis XIV really smiling is an imaginary reward only makes sense with the previous notion of imagination as the subjective appropriation of objective and impersonal facts in mind. Things or actions which are *also* real, are invested with personal subjectivity to an extent that they must *also* be called imaginary – what is significant to the courtier is the reward she receives, not the objective materiality of Louis XIV's smile, and to this extent she perceives it in an imaginary way.

It is exactly this kind of economic imagination – imposed on us by the force of gravity – through which our common notion of God is channelled, so Weil argues, giving *La pesanteur et la grâce* a theological aspect not present in her early writings: 'Equivalent dans la religion à un certain niveau. Faute de recevoir le sourire de Louis XIV, on se fabrique un Dieu qui nous sourit' (*PG*, 52). What is the notion of Christianity that is developed here? Another brief recourse to Alain's body of thought – again formulated through his disciple Maurier's reception – might help introduce her notion of Christianity:

> 'De quoi sont nées les religions? De ceci que nous cherchons nos propres émotions, nos espoirs et nos craintes dans l'image du monde qui ne peut répondre'. C'est de là que nous formons cette présence cachée et embusquée qui nous fait croire que tout est plein de dieux. Mais les dieux refusent de paraître; et c'est par ce miracle qui ne se fait jamais que la religion se développe en temples, statues et sacrifices [...].[21]

Hence religious sites, rites and objects are supplements which stand in for the absence of the Gods, to create a world that is not silent but will respond to human 'espoirs' and 'craintes'. This criticism of idolatry stems from the traditions of Christianity, as Maurier continues to explain: 'Dans le Bible, au début, il n'y a rien et l'esprit crée comme on pense. Les faux dieux sont immolés; il reste le vide du désert et la formidable absence, partout présente'.[22] This is an account of Christianity as a religion that has killed the Gods on earth, and left only 'le vide du désert' and 'la formidable absence' as what is present. *La pesanteur et la grâce* is a further

---

21　Maurier, 107–8. The critique of idolatry articulated by Alain and Weil points not least to the overlap of their thought with early twentieth-century artistic modernism in terms of its rejection of figuration in favour of abstraction. The representation of 'nothing' in Kazimir Malevich's *Black Suprematic Square* (1915) has, not least by the artist himself, been considered to point to realms of the sacred. At the same time, it constitutes an absolute assertion of materiality, hence, like Weil's thought, opening up a simultaneity of materialism and metaphysics. Nevertheless, the metaphysical aspect is certainly something which must remain dubious to materialist understandings of both; this becomes especially obvious in the case of Malevich, given that the *ersatz* religion 'art' is institutionally charged; assigning metaphysical meaning to works exhibited in such an environment seems unconscious of the conditions of its possibility. See also Brian O'Doherty, *Inside the White Cube* [1976] (Berkeley: University of California Press, 1999); see also Jennifer Johnson's chapter in this volume, in which she argues that the apparently ungiving matter of Georges Rouault's paintings is in fact saturated with signification, not least in terms of processes of industrialization.

22　Ibid. 118.

elaboration of these ideas. A world that is 'muet', a world of impersonal objecthood, it becomes clear at this point, is not only a world that should not be appropriated into one's own subjective processes of imagination, and not only a world to which the only adequate response is the response of work; it is also a world marked by the non-existence of God. With a humorous sense of aggression, Weil writes: 'Cas de contradictions vrais. Dieu existe, Dieu n'existe pas. Où est la problème?' (*PG*, 188). The contradiction is not considered as a problem as it stems from what might almost be a sardonic realism in terms of the absence of God, the everyday observation that God is not present on earth: '"Notre Père, celui des cieux." Il y a là une sorte d'humour. C'est votre Père, mais essayez d'aller chercher là-haut! Nous sommes exactement aussi incapables de nous décoller qu'un ver de terre' (*PG*, 166).

The binary opposition between 'cieux' and 'terre' is an opposition frequently employed in *La pesanteur et la grâce*, not least finding an echo in the title itself. The physical resistance of the outside world appears as a metaphor for the limits of thought in terms of the thinkability of God. God is not thinkable, and in this sense can only appear as an absence, as nothing to human thought: 'Dieu ne peut être présent dans la création que sous la forme de l'absence' (*PG*, 182). This is the pronouncement, all at once, of an anti-materialist materialism and an anti-metaphysical metaphysics.

For Weil, this anti-materialist materialism/anti-metaphysical metaphysics corresponds exactly to the incarnation of Jesus; in the same way that Jesus is incarnate, and acknowledges his absolute abandonment from God, so humans equally should acknowledge the fact that they are incarnate: 'L'homme doit faire l'acte de s'incarner, car il est désincarné par l'imagination' (*PG*, 110). In terms of man's fleshly materiality, he is always already incarnate; but he constantly employs imagination in order to ignore this impersonal reality and consequently chooses to forget the fact that he is abandoned by God. As a consequence, Weil demands the stripping of one's imagination, demands that one make the self nothing, for only in this process of decreation of the self is it possible to give back to God the space that one occupies through one's own will, desire and imagination. It is at this point that the notion of 'grâce' comes in:

Dieu envoie le malheur indistinctement aux méchants comme aux bons, ainsi que la pluie'et le soleil. Il n'a pas réservé la croix du Christ. Il n'entre en contact avec l'individu humain comme tel que par la grâce purement spirituelle qui répond au regard tourné vers lui, c'est-à-dire dans la mesure exacte où l'individu cesse d'en être un. Aucun événement n'est une faveur de Dieu, la grâce seule. (*PG*, 186)

Weil here uses an economic term, 'faveur', reminiscent of the smile of Louis XIV to describe the mechanisms of grace. While the person who seeks a king's benevolent smile, however, has a sense of inflated self-importance, the key to grace is to make the self nothing, to undo, decreate the self – it can only occur when an individual ceases to be an individual and is to that extent not something which can be manufactured through an individual's agency.

Weil defines decreation as follows:

Décréation: faire passer du créé dans l'incréé.
[...]
Dieu renonce – en un sens – à être tout. Nous devons renoncer à être quelque chose. C'est le seul bien pour nous. (*PG*, 81–2)

Weil's notion of the decreation of the self in her theological notes risks translating the reduction of subjectivity as a socialist aim of making more equality possible between everyone (geometrically by giving the masses more space, individually and collectively, by reducing the space of those in power) into a Christian idealization of the state of absolute worthlessness (an idealization that manifests itself in the aim of giving the world and its inhabitants no space so as to cede to God the very space of the world). Her theological notes still carry and articulate rigorous moral demands deriving from her earlier socialist thought, but at times risk becoming anti-emancipatory where they substitute their solidarity with the abject with an embrace of exactly the – inner and outer – poverty socialism would struggle against.

Hence tracing Weil's work from her school essays to her theological notes shows that her work is marked by absolute continuity in terms of her critique of the imagination. Yet her materialism transforms from an objectivist and impersonalist materialism to what is, to her, the true contradiction of an anti-materialist materialism, an anti-metaphysical metaphysics. By translating political concepts into an intensely personalized theological rigour, the notes that were to form *La pesanteur et la grâce* stretch the field of politics into the analysis of personal behaviour according to structurally politicized markers. The verb 'to stretch' is meant in both senses of the word. For any political activist struggling with the acute difficulties of political antagonism, it would be a stretch to accept that a set of theological notes could be considered as politically relevant, and not rather a form of inner emigration under the duress of the rise of fascism;[23] and yet, to stretch the field of politics to a point where individual thinking and acting might be judged according to political and economic criteria, is to sharpen a radically critical understanding of individual and social behaviour.

Selected Bibliography

Artaud, Antonin, *Le théâtre et son double*. (Paris: Editions Flammarion, 1973).
Baugh, Bruce, *French Hegel* (New York: Routledge, 2003).
Hill, Leslie, *Bataille. Klossowski. Blanchot: Writing at the Limit* (Oxford: Oxford University Press, 2001).

23   The term inner emigration is borrowed from German literature studies, where it is applied to authors who did not emigrate from Germany or openly resist the National Socialist regime, instead emigrating into years of concealment and interiority; given that Weil, as a non-German, a Jew and a Socialist did emigrate and went on to work for the French Resistance in London, it seems initially false or even historically perverse to relate this term to her. Yet, Weil's intellectual trajectory could be considered as part of an overdue evaluation of the terminology of inner emigration in relation to French intellectual history in the late 1930s and early 1940s. For example, Georges Bataille, whom we have already seen in oppositional proximity to Weil in the early 1930s, in the early 1940s went through a shift towards mysticism similar to that of Weil, working mostly in the countryside and writing prolifically – producing, among others, *L'Expérience intérieure*, *Le Coupable* and *Sur Nietzsche*. See Leslie Hill, *Bataille. Klossowski. Blanchot: Writing at the Limit* (Oxford: Oxford University Press, 2001), 4.

Kojève, Alexandre, *Introduction à la lecture de Hegel: leçons sur la phénoménologie de l'esprit professées de 1933 à 1939 à l'École des Hautes-Études, réunies et publiées par Raymond Queneau* (Paris: Gallimard, 1947).

Maurois, André, *Alain* (Paris: Domat, 1950).

Weil, Simone, *Œuvres complètes*, ed. André A. Devaux and Florence de Lussy (Paris: Gallimard, 1988).

——, *La pesanteur et la grâce* [1947] (Paris: Pocket, 1991).

DANIEL POITRAS

Time Matters: The *Mouvement du 22 mars* and the Dawn of May '68

The voluminous literature on the causes of May '68 in France and elsewhere can hardly be summarized in a few lines. Nonetheless, we can identify one bias that continues to structure many interpretations: the use of an *ideological grid*. Through such lenses, the sudden surge of creativity and utopic thought and practices of the late 1960s is contextualized within a period characterized by: the constitution of a French 'New Left'; the influence of fashionable intellectuals like Herbert Marcuse; a vague and encompassing *Zeitgeist* (spirit of the times); the imitative behaviour of histrionic students living in an obsolete, imaginary revolutionary world; and the influence of events (like the Berkeley students' revolt in 1964) or philosophies (the variants of Marxism, the *Situationist International*). The list could go on. Despite being repeatedly declared obsolete throughout the twentieth century, the ideological grid is still used to label some *things*, generally to emphasize their 'disconnectedness' with an implicit 'reality'. As David A. Snow and Scott C. Byrd have written, 'ideology' becomes a 'cover term for the values, beliefs, and goals associated with a movement or a broader, encompassing social entity'.[1]

The extended life of the ideological grid is even more visible in new fields of research, such as the one currently turning its attention to student movements. This is no coincidence: the long sixties, identified with the rise (and almost the death) of so many student movements around the world, was an age in which ideology was as intensely contested at it was used. Marxism was still hot: the reality of China under Mao Tse-tung was largely unknown, and Che Guevara, killed in 1967 and 'forever young'

---

1   David A. Snow and Scott C. Byrd, 'Ideology, Framing Processes, and Islamic Terrorist Movements', *Mobilization: An International Journal* 12 (2007), 120.

(according to Bob Marley) was an inspiration for the new generation. But as some have pointed out, many students did not adhere to 'ideologies'; they instead used their own symbols, memories and references to seek alternatives to the bourgeois world.

Alternative conceptions to 'ideology' have been proposed, but they are often subject to the same problems. For example, the term 'master frame' has been used to identify the dominant (seen as the most realistic) representations of a political context at a certain time.[2] Although more subtle – it tries to include the changing of representations over time rather than relating them directly to an inflexible supra-structure (ideology) – a 'master frame' still does not explain *why* representations change, and how we go from one master frame to another. Or, are such transformations included (as variations) into one over-arching master frame? As part of the 'framing perspective' popularized during the 1990s, the 'master frame' tends, in turn, to reify experiences of time by amplifying the rationality of actors. It formalizes their horizon of expectations as a series of goals, some more easily reachable and 'realistic' than others. But how to determine what is 'realistic'?

A popular May '68 slogan ('Soyez réaliste, demandez l'impossible') reminds us that labelling something 'realistic' is necessarily an *a posteriori* process which draws in our own experience, and is more precisely framed within our own horizon of expectation. What is experienced as impossible now often orientates our judgements as to what was unrealistic is the past. Social movement theories have long assumed that 'strategic choice' is 'simply a matter of objective opportunities and organizational efficiency'.[3] In fact, strategies also rely upon multiple cultural elements. Since the 'discursive

---

2   See for example Mario Diani, 'Linking Mobilization Frames and Political Opportunities: Insights from Regional Populism in Italy', *American Sociological Review* 61 (1996), 1053–69. Snow and Benford also use the concept of 'master frames' in their article on cycles of protest: 'Master Frames and Cycles of Protest', in A. Morris and C. McClurg Mueller, eds, *Frontiers of Social Movement Theory* (New Haven: Yale University Press, 1992), 133–55.

3   Myra Marx Ferree, 'Resonance and Radicalism: Feminist Framing in the Abortion Debates of the United States and Germany', *American Journal of Sociology* 109 (2003), 304.

turn' of the 1980s, plenty of proposals have been made to explore how social movements, culture and temporality are interlinked.[4] We intend to contribute to these studies by showing the intertwinement of two different scales of temporality: the narrative building of a student group (the *mouvement du 22 mars*) just before May 1968, and the *régime d'historicité* of the period.[5] This latter term is drawn from François Hartog's *Régimes d'historicité: présentisme et expériences du temps*. As the title of the book suggests, such a *régime* describes not just the historical context of a given period, but also the factors that influenced how contemporaries of that period articulated their own subjective accounts of the past, present and future: in other words, how people experience their own moment in history, and the horizons of expectation, interpretation and possibilities available to them.

The Beginning

There was not much political activity inside French universities before the academic year of 1967–8. Why was it at the Faculty of Letters, Nanterre, that some students broke the status quo? Despite its desolated location (a slum), and its overcrowded classrooms (12,000 students for a capacity of 10,000), the recently created Faculty was not particularly backwards, traditional or authoritarian. But Nanterre quickly came to symbolize what the American students of Berkeley had denounced a few years previously as a *multiversity*: a pluralistic but anonymous, impersonal and cold institution at the service of powers beyond it. Moreover, because of the deficiencies of the educational system, the universities in France were functioning as a

---

4   For an insightful overview, see Doug McAdam and D.A. Snow, eds, *Readings on Social Movements: Origins, Dynamics and Outcomes* (New York: Oxford University Press, 2010).

5   On historicity, see Reinhart Koselleck, *Future Pasts: On the Semantics of Historical Time* (Cambridge, MA: MIT Press, 1985).

'gigantesque machine à sélectionner et à éliminer'.[6] *Selection* was the key-word: roughly 70 per cent of the students were eliminated by the exams. And for the surviving few, the future was no brighter: the new generation of sociologists and psychologists were destined to help regulate and moni-tor a society celebrated as functional, integrated, and productive. After all, managerial staff were needed to appease the anxieties and doubts of the workers. The refusal by some students of this predestined role as 'lackeys of the system' considerably informed the discourse and actions of the *mouve-ment du 22 mars* after its birth in March 1968.

If we go back in time a little, we discover that life on Nanterre's campus was already unstable, at least sufficiently so to allow the feeble Union Nationale des Étudiants de France (UNEF), with only a handful of members at Nanterre, to successfully organize a strike (17–25 November 1967). On this occasion, a pamphlet was produced by the 'Groupe des étudiants fantômes' (GEF), affiliated with the CLJA (Comité de Liaison des Jeunes Anarchistes), in which two future *enragés* of the *mouvement du 22 mars* participated, Daniel Cohn-Bendit and Jean-Pierre Duteuil. In the pamphlet, the GEF deplored the traditional claims and methods of the UNEF, which focused on technical aspects of the university's administra-tion and the students' conditions. Considering the situation, were these claims and methods not signs that the student associations were stuck in the same patterns of accommodation as the workers' unions? Was this not the proof that they were integrated, pacified? Ending their pamphlet with an open question ('*Que faire?*'), the group tried to open another horizon of possibilities. Their suggestions called for actions outside of the box:

> *Il faudrait* (mais personne ne le fera) expulser les flics du campus.
> *Il faudrait* (mais personne ne le fera) [...] veiller à ce que ces comités ne soient pas prématurément 'coordonnés' par une ou plusieurs organisations politiques.
> *Il faudrait enfin* (mais personne ne le fera non plus) [...] que tout le monde apprenne le karaté, soit casqué et botté afin de ne pas avoir l'air ridicule devant les CRS ou à côté des étudiants japonais.[7]

---

6   Alain Schnapp and Pierre Vidal-Naquet, *Journal de la commune étudiante: textes et documents. Novembre 1967–juin 1968* [1969] (Paris: Seuil, 1988), 101.
7   Schnapp and Vidal-Naquet, *La Commune étudiante*, doc. 13.

The use of the conditional tense shows that the group felt almost pessimistic about these suggestions and their larger implications. But despite their isolation, these 'ghost students' were gradually gaining support and visibility, mostly because of their provocative style of action. In January 1968, the future *enragés* announced that orgies would take place to welcome the minister of youth affairs and sports, François Missoffe. The minister was then confronted rather disrespectfully, being called a 'fascist' by Cohn-Bendit. Around the same time, the *enragés* placarded pictures of the university's disguised policemen around Nanterre before throwing them out of the campus, thus humiliating the dean of the Faculty of Letters, Pierre Grappin. A resistant during the Nazi occupation, the dean was the one who had called the police after students sabotaged an exam. Soon overwhelmed by events, the dean became the subject of mockery in a song (*La Grappignole*) composed by the *enragés*,[8] and very popular during the month of May. It began like this:

> M'sieur Grappin avait résolu (bis)
> De nous faire tomber sur le cul (bis)
> Mais son coup a foiré
> Malgré ses policiers
>
> *Refrain*
> Valsons la *Grappignole*
> C'est la misère ou la colère
> Valsons la *Grappignole*
> C'est la colère
> A Nanterre[9]

The culmination of these events, rarely planned in advance, created an unpredictable situation favourable to experimentation. The *enragés* disrupted exams, occupied an administration building and sprayed graffiti inside and outside of the university, infuriating the dean and most of the professors. On 22 March, rumours spread that one student of Nanterre (Xavier Langlade),

---

8   The *enragés* appeared at the beginning of the year 1968. The word refers to the French Revolution and particularly to the disciples of Jacques Roux, an adversary of Robespierre and an ancestor of socialism.

9   See <http://debordiana.chez.com/francais/enrages.htm> accessed 1 March 2014.

arrested during a protest against the Vietnam War, might have been tortured.[10] During the evening, the *enragés* decided to take action. 'Led' by Daniel Cohn-Bendit, 142 of them stormed and occupied the boardroom of the Faculty in a symbolic gesture, giving birth to the *mouvement du 22 mars*.

Identity and Generation

> Don't trust anyone over 30!
>
> —JERRY RUBIN, *Do It!*

For students, clarifying their role and constructing their identity entails a positioning in time through the experience of belonging to a *new generation*. According to Karl Mannheim, from the age of around seventeen to twenty, such a positioning leads to differentiation from older generations – or not – depending on the student's 'historical consciousness'.[11] Of course, considering that you are *new* in an *old* world is both the burden and the opportunity of most new generations, at least since the eighteenth century. What particularizes the fact of being young at the end of the 1960s was the unprecedented demographic power of fifteen to twenty-five-year-olds resulting from the baby boom, which correlated with the extension of leisure time and youth before entering 'adult life' during this period. Moreover, on a cultural level, we can observe a massive rejection by the youth of the official references and values of their society. These references were attached to a certain grand narrative – and connected to a certain

---

10   On the importance of rumours, see Erich Goode and Nachman Ben-Yahuda, 'Moral Panics: Culture, Politics, and Social Construction', *Annual Review of Sociology* 20 (1994), 149–71.

11   Karl Mannheim, *Essays on the Sociology of Knowledge* (London: Routledge & Kegan Paul, 1952).

'régime d'historicité'[12] – around the idea of Progress. In my doctoral dissertation, I observed the importance of the transition from an experience of a triumphant History promising a golden future at the beginning of the 1960s to the experience of an absent – but still stirring – history without a compass or clear direction at the end of the decade.[13]

This loss of direction was concomitant with the denunciation of De Gaulle's regime, at this point in power for ten years, which was seen as endorsing the so-called objective processes of modernity. The double discovery of the eclipse of history and the fragility of the system accentuated the use of the *new/old* binary by the students.[14] It was no longer about filtering and integrating the old in the present for the sake of a brighter future. Increasingly scrutinized, the *old* came to comprise most adults. The criteria of age differentiation tended to overshadow the traditional ideological associations surrounding class. This explains the strong distrust of students of all adults during May, even those who could have been their 'masters', such as Jean-Paul Sartre or Herbert Marcuse.

This wider, experiential context is necessary to understand how the *mouvement du 22 mars* mobilized the intellectual resources at its disposal. Far from choosing some *maîtres à penser* or some ideological programs in vogue, Nanterre's *enragés* did not bind the movement to a particular influence or tradition. Among a multitude of intellectual influences on the movement, we will mention three. The left-wing journal *Socialisme ou barbarie* (1948–67) inspired a general distrust towards big organizations and bureaucracy. From

---

12   See François Hartog, *Régimes d'historicité: présentisme et expériences du temps* (Paris: Seuil, 2003).

13   Daniel Poitras, 'Régime d'historicité et historiographie en France et au Québec, 1956–75: Michel de Certeau, Fernand Dumont et François Furet', doctoral dissertation, Montréal / Paris, UdM / EHESS, 2013.

14   Many pamphlets and graffiti referred to the old and the new world, for example the following: 'Travailleur: tu as 25 ans mais ton syndicat est de l'autre siècle'. A student named Alexandre recalled: 'Je me souviens de cette inscription qu'on avait mise sur le mur de la poste de la rue des Archives: *"À bas le vieux monde!"*, je la regardais et je croyais que le vieux monde allait disparaître parce qu'on l'avait écrit. On avait une idée biblique de la parole!' Quoted in Nicolas Daum, *Des révolutionnaires dans un village parisien* (Paris: Londreys, 1988), 111.

the young anarchist journal *Noir et Rouge* they adopted an idea of a decentralized system with self-managed entities, which would later be decisive regarding projects of *autogestion* (self-management). Thirdly, from the *International Situationist* (IS), the *enragés* borrowed the denunciation of the University and, more generally, an anxiety regarding the contemporary phenomenon of 'aliénation spatiale' in which 'la société sépare à la racine le sujet et l'activité'.[15]

In fact, during the academic year of 1966–7, students close to the IS in Strasbourg had already started to shake things up. They had taken over the students' association (AFGES) intending to sabotage it, thus contesting what was seen as a symbol of student participation in bourgeois, bureaucratic society. The first widely spread student tract of the period – traces of which can be found in many later slogans, graffiti, texts, and discourses – was written by young members of the IS in Strasbourg in the form of a pamphlet entitled '*De la misère en milieu étudiant*'.[16] As a vehement criticism of student apathy, the pamphlet pointed out how students were *already* integrated into the *société du spectacle*, naively contributing to a consumerism that was alienating them, thus slowly expunging their potential as activists. Later, the idea that the University was not transformable within the actually existing society would contribute to the extension of the larger May movement outside of the campuses.

Born in the Flow of Time

To name itself, the *mouvement du 22 mars* did not choose a label that would identify it as one among the many young, leftist organizations of the time (JCR, UJC(m-l), CLER, etc.). Instead, it chose a *date*, as if it was pointing out that it was born *in* time and shaped *through* events. In doing so, it

15   Guy Debord, *La Société du spectacle* (Paris: Buchet/Chastel, 1967), proposition no. 161.
16   AFGES, November 1966. The complete title in English is: *On the Poverty of Student Life: A Consideration of its Economic, Political, Sexual, Psychological and Notably Intellectual Aspects and of a Few Ways to Cure It.*

emphasized the fact that its existence, present and future, was not the result of some tradition, doctrine or programme. Welcoming militant students from most groups (from anarchists to Leninists), encouraging debates and differences of opinion, the movement took advantage of its plasticity. This trait would come in handy during the May protests, in which the movement got 'the maximum out of those moments when a large conscience constituency is called into existence'.[17]

For the movement, choosing a date for its name meant a projection into the unknown. Their birthdate identity contributed greatly to the *narrative* of the movement. Many social movement theories, in line with models of resource mobilization,[18] have focused on the framing processes of social movements to explain how they use ideas and their cultural context to recruit and mobilize. This approach leads to an emphasis on factors related to rational strategies and actions (planning, organization).[19] For example, Oliver and Johnston consider 'frames' as packages of meaning that can be 'marketed' by movement leaders.[20] Taking into account the 'narrative' dimension of a social movement is useful to outline how it constructs its identity day-by-day without necessarily 'marketing' meanings. In the case of the *mouvement du 22 mars*, we observe the deployment of an enticing plot that would come to resonate with many different protagonists. As Francesca Polletta has shown for the sit-ins during the Civil Rights movement in the United States, social movements rely as much on narrative as on framing processes to mobilize:

> narrative is prominent in such interpretive processes because its temporally configurative capacity equips it to integrate past, present, and future events and to align individuals' and collectives' identities during periods of change. Narrative's reliance

---

17   Randall Collins, 'Social Movements and the Focus of Emotional Attention', in Jeff Goodwin, James M. Jasper and Francesca Polletta, eds, *Passionate Politics: Emotions and Social Movements* (Chicago: University of Chicago Press, 2001), 32.

18   See Doug McAdam, John D. McCarthy and Mayer N. Zald, eds, *Comparative Perspectives on Social Movements* (Cambridge: Cambridge University Press, 1996).

19   For a thorough analysis of the consequences of this line of interpretation, see Daniel Cefaï, *Pourquoi se mobilise-t-on? Les théories de l'action collective* (Paris: La Découverte, 2007).

20   Pamela Oliver and Hank Johnston, 'What a Good Idea! Ideology and Frames in Social Movement Research', *Mobilization* 5 (2000), 37–54.

on emplotment rather than explanation further engages potential activists precisely by its *ambiguity* about the causes of collective action.[21]

Among the components of the narrative of the *mouvement du 22 mars*, we notice a reluctance to place itself within a teleological perspective. Instead of being paralysed, like many groups from the left who were waiting for the *right* conditions – according to Marxist scriptures – for *the* Revolution, the movement continually refused to circumscribe the meanings, means and ends that were associated with it. This resulted in an open-ended narrative. As we will see later, this narrative worked so well because of its timing within their *régime d'historicité*.

Another characteristic of the movement's narrative is the inclusion of events and references outside of France. The focus on a larger context of militancy, obvious with the IS, was shared by many *enragés*. In the texts they produced,[22] we can find four movements that are identified as precursors: the anti-war movement, the Spanish student movement, the German student movement, and the Japanese student movement (Zengakuren). All had a specific function in the building of the *mouvement du 22 mars's* identity and narrative: a) the anti-war movement aligned it to the larger protest against American imperialism; b) the German student movement brought the highly popular concept of the *Université critique*, and a martyr (the Sozialistischer Deutscher Studentenbund (SDS) leader Rudi Dutschke, almost murdered by the neo-Nazi Josef Bachmann on 11 April 1968); c) the Spanish student movement, close to the anarchist movement, was an inspirational case of irreverence towards authorities (on 4 December, celebrating the birthday of the dictator Franco, some Spanish students dared to brandish a poster that said: 'Franco, Murderer, Happy Birthday'); d) the Zengakuren, the communist and anarchist league of Japanese students, offered a strong example of commitment, protest organization and resistance to the police. These movements contributed by inspiring similar actions and widening the students' horizons outside of the usual national references and

---

21   F. Polletta, '"It Was Like a Fever ...": Narrative and Identity in Social Protest', *Social Problems* 45 (1998), 138.

22   See Schnapp and Vidal-Naquet, *Journal de la Commune étudiante*, for example doc. 28–31.

expectations. Although the 'fight against capitalism' was globally used as a leitmotiv at the end of the 1960s, the outcomes of battles were reaching a new degree of unpredictability. A 'proletarian revolution', a 'classless society' or a 'new university' were unknowable entities at the time. The reluctance of the members of the *mouvement du 22 mars* to state precisely what they wanted for a new university or a new society is indicative of their attentiveness towards events that offered the possibility of experiencing and thinking *anew*. To *name* and thus *fix* new experiences and new horizons in an old vocabulary and references seems to be an unreceptive approach to genuine novelty. Instead, like Cohn-Bendit, the *enragés* stressed the (unpredictable) *processes* leading into the future:

> Pour moi, il ne s'agit pas de faire de la métaphysique et de chercher comment se fera 'la révolution'. Je crois, je l'ai dit, que nous allons plutôt vers un changement perpétuel de la société, provoqué, à chaque étape, par des actions révolutionnaires.[23]

Were these actions spontaneous or planned? They were both: tension had to be maintained to avoid both a free-for-all activism losing all gravitas, and a rigid, clannish-like organizational strategy. During March and April 1968, when the 'style' of the movement was gradually incorporated into its narrative, it would become decisive for its mobilizing power and resonance.

Violence and Creativity

Violence was an integral part of May. As David A. Snow mentions, violence in social movements is often the result of an 'actual or threatened intrusion into or violation of culturally defined zones of privacy and control'.[24] This

---

23   'Daniel Cohn-Bendit s'entretient avec Jean-Paul Sartre', in J. Sauvageot et al., *La révolte étudiante: les animateurs parlent* (Paris: Seuil, 1968), 88.

24   D.A. Snow et al., 'Disrupting the "Quotidian": Reconceptualizing the Relationship Between Breakdown and the Emergence of Collective Action', *Mobilization: An International Journal* 3 (1998), 17.

was true both for the *mouvement du 22 mars* itself, and for the Nanterre authorities. The occupation of the boardroom on 22 March by the *enragés* was interpreted (rightly) by Dean Grappin as a threat to the hierarchical structure of the university. But the reaction of the dean, who broke the implicit rule of refraining from police involvement in Nanterre, was felt as a violation of, and thus an invitation to challenge, the rules. The escalation that followed, from the firmly suppressed Sorbonne protest on 6 May to the elevation of barricades a few days later, is well-known. Back in April, this outcome was unpredictable. In fact, the *enragés* were then neither following a precise plan nor indulging, as many commentators have written since, in post-adolescence turbulence.

By antagonizing important protagonists (Nanterre's administration and professors, the media, the Communist Party, the Socialist Party, right-wing youth groups such as Occident, and even fellow student organizations),[25] the movement was keeping itself outside of the tracks of traditional claims, strategies and labels. This defiant attitude contributed to the aura of the movement and enhanced the impact of its narrative on mobilizing. *New* and *unprecedented*, the movement was at the same time *uncompromised* with outside structures and authorities, but *available* to much innovation and change inside its own organizational dynamics. As part of its strategy to stand out, the use of 'violence' was also a way of disparaging the mainstream, structured and respectful protests organized by student organizations like the UNEF.

That being said, this 'violence' needs to be contextualized within the decline of the grand narrative of Progress and the *régime d'historicité* associated with it. At the end of the 1960s, violence was a means for many groups to increase the efficiency of their actions, aiming to expose and disrupt the system. Violence was, and is, a highly ambiguous topic, being seen variously as a temporal accelerator, the ultimate revealer or indicator

---

25   Pierre Beylau of *Fac-West* (newspaper of Corpo-Lettres) was against so-called 'spontaneous' movements, whose goals are 'obscures' and methods 'intolérant'. In brief, he advocated 'que l'ordre soit rétabli' so that rational and planned reforms could be undertaken ('Contre les enragés irresponsables', in Schnapp and Vidal-Naquet, *La Commune étudiante*, doc. 39).

of a major crisis, a necessary means to break old patterns, or as a road to chaos or to new kinds of fascism.[26]

As many scholars have noted, violence is a risky but rewarding step for most social movements.[27] The escalation of violence between the protesters and the CRS (police) during May considerably amplified the unpredictability of the outcomes and, thus, boosted the 'resonance'[28] of the narrative of the *mouvement du 22 mars*. Striving to recreate itself every day, the movement integrated violence as one of the dynamic factors that helped it to avert organizational crystallization, thus propelling the movement forward. On another level, the violence used by the authorities seemed to reveal the inherently authoritarian and repressive structure of society:

> Les actions menées ont accéléré la prise de conscience de certains: plutôt que de 'provocations', il s'agissait *d'obliger l'autoritarisme latent à se manifester*.[29]

There was no such thing as 'free violence', because violence generated effects by fuelling the 'dynamisme du mouvement [qui] modifie, en cours de route, la nature des revendications'.[30] In fact, the starting point of May can be located to 2 May, when the contemporary history course of René Rémond was interrupted by the *enragés* who asked to occupy the amphitheatre, and then threw a chair in front of the class. This irruption led Grappin to suspend classes indefinitely, which channelled the students towards the Sorbonne, where the movement would gain in size and visibility.

Violence helped dramatize the disruption of the everyday life of the university, thus revealing how compromised it was becoming. Before May, it had been less about physical or 'revolutionary' violence – symbolized by the barricades – but about spectacular and shocking actions. *Space* was

---

26   See, for example, Michel de Certeau, who writes that 'violence' tells the world: 'Je ne suis pas une chose', because violence is 'le geste qui récuse toute identification: "J'existe"': *La prise de parole* (Paris: Desclée de Brouwer, 1968), 29.

27   See Charles Tilly et al., *The Politics of Collective Violence* (Cambridge: Cambridge University Press, 2010).

28   See Ferree, 'Resonance and Radicalism'.

29   Schnapp and Vidal-Naquet, *Journal de la Commune étudiante*, doc. 28.

30   Cohn-Bendit, *Les animateurs parlent*, 87.

as important as, and for, *time* in these actions. By targeting Nanterre's distribution and regulation of space, the movement opened possibilities for new actions. As D. Zhao wrote about the 1989 Chinese student protests, at the beginning, when a movement faces 'more uncertainties' and has minimal backing, the 'campus ecology [is] crucial to sustain it.'[31] As early as March 1967, the rush into girls' dorms by a random group of students, including some future *enragés*, had already shaken the regulation of space. Despite its apparently juvenile character, this action was a protest against Nanterre's conservative regulations, and more broadly a contestation of a sexually repressed society.[32]

These actions blurred the boundaries of the functions associated with different spaces. By opening new areas in which to discuss, contest, create or just wander, the *mouvement du 22 mars* took the authorities by surprise. Assuming that students needed some place to express themselves, Grappin magnanimously offered them a small reunion room in which to do so, to which access would be restricted by scheduling conditions.[33] Hardly sufficient, this measure shows how the authorities thought they could bind and control the students' space. Nevertheless, the symbolic landscape was already undergoing a transformation. The excesses and hesitations of the authorities stimulated the *enragés*' imagination. It encouraged them to think of, and deploy, new means of provocation inside, outside and around the university's space. The term *Université critique* encapsulates the intended

31   Dingxin Zhao, 'Ecologies of Social Movements: Student Mobilization During the 1989 Prodemocracy Movement in Beijing', in D. McAdam and D.A. Snow, eds, *Readings on Social Movements: Origins, Dynamics and Outcomes* (Oxford: Oxford University Press, 2010).

32   The *enragé* Jean-Pierre Duteuil had been discussing sexual repression with fellow students since 1967. Among other sources, a text of William Reich published in 1936 and entitled 'The Sexual Revolution' was then highly popular amongst students. In this text, Reich highlighted the links between traditional family structures, capitalism, and sexual repression. The text had been reproduced by the *enragés* months before May.

33   '[...] il faut éviter de disperser les discussions dans les couloirs, il vaut mieux les cristalliser dans certains lieux', in Schnapp and Vidal-Naquet, *Journal de la Commune étudiante*, doc. 26.

restructuration of space before and during May '68 well. Let's pay attention to the causality invoked in this passage from the *Bulletin du Mouvement du 22 mars* – also ironically entitled *Bulletin no. 5 494 (supplément au no. 5 494)* – published 22 April:

> Le déclenchement de discussions 'illégales' à l'intérieur de l'Université entraîne l'appel de la police. Est alors révélé clairement aux étudiants le lien entre l'Université et le 'Pouvoir'. L'Université critique se développe d'abord dans l'Université: les salles sont fermées. Les étudiants transportent alors celle-ci au dehors.[34]

This sequence involves not only the spatial shifting of the university from the inside to the outside; it also stresses the importance of sudden awareness ('est révélé clairement') in the narrative of the movement. In fact, one objective of the *Université critique* was to establish a permanent contestation of the university, its ideologies and the so-called pure knowledge it produced. At the end of the 1960s, the focus on the relativity of knowledge – which contrasts greatly with the positivism of the early 1960s – would weaken the university's status. If knowledge is relative and easily manipulated, then objectivity is a myth and there is no solid ground for *reality*. For many students, knowledge, as an instrument used to promote some truths or grand narratives, needed to be desacralized so that new experiences (and interpretations) of the world could arise. This new awareness inclined the students to seek these experiences *outside* of the old frames and *free* of the fake distinction between what is 'real' (realistic, possible) and what is not.

Spatiality and Uncertainty

The storming of the Parisian streets by protesters, which paralysed the city for weeks, in itself symbolized the contestation of the realistic/unrealistic binary. During May, graffiti, paintings, poems and songs were disseminated

34   Ibid. doc. 29.

on the walls of universities, police stations, government buildings and theatres, or randomly on sidewalks and vehicles. Words were in the streets, inviting people to read the situation differently. This dissemination resonated with a belief largely shared among the militants of the *mouvement du 22 mars* (and beyond): the paths to a new society are not to be found *above*, in some ivory tower, but *on the ground*, and even *underneath* it. As with the inside/outside system binary, the above/(under)ground binary was more than a metaphor. As a *belief*, it irrigated what Wiktor Stoczkowski calls 'cosmologies', conceptual apparatuses through which contemporary subjects articulate ontological, soteriological and etiological perceptions.[35] Based on a spatial representation, this belief was essential both to feed the narrative of the movement, and to facilitate its physical manifestation in more sustained social experimentation. The creation of numerous small *comités d'action* (five to twenty people), deliberating on particular topics, reflected the kind of direct democracy the *mouvement du 22 mars* was hoping for. These *comités d'action*, freely created by students, workers, neighbours, the elderly, shopkeepers, etc., were to prefigure a new society by enhancing a decentralized, grounded and direct debating/decision-making process.

Expressions like 'mobiliser à la base', 'organiser par la base', and 'démocratie à la base' could be heard and read everywhere during May. These mottos were also a testimony to the collapse of the already fissured Promethean society of the 1950s and 1960s, in which certain elites (scientists, economists, engineers, etc.) were mandated to inaugurate a brighter future through rationalization and planning.[36] The radical gradualism embodied by the *comités d'action* corresponded to the flexible framing processes of the *mouvement du 22 mars*. It was intended to avoid the mysticism of abstract ideas (such as Progress, Welfare, Revolution) and to instead

---

35 Wiktor Stoczkowski, *Anthropologies rédemptrices: le monde selon Lévi-Strauss* (Paris: Hermann, 2008).

36 At the beginning of the 1960s, most students were still enthusiastically projecting themselves as a future elite overseeing a *Brave New World*. In *L'Étudiant de France*, the journal of the Union nationale des étudiants de France (UNEF), the key word was *adaptation*, mainly to Progress and the needs of society.

preserve an open-ended narrative. After protesting and talking with some *enragés*, the director of *L'Événement*, Emmanuel d'Astier, summarized the importance of this plasticity well:

> ils sont un mouvement spontané pour provoquer le dialogue, le désordre, l'explosion. Ils ne sont pas là pour un programme, une organisation, une revendication [...] La Révolution – ils n'emploient pas le terme – ne se proclame ni ne se vote, elle se dégage et se fait. Les refrains de Florent sont la rue, la jeunesse, une action, un travail.[37]

Considering this spatial reconfiguration, the students' rather ambiguous success in converting the workers to their cause is not just the echo of a past world resonating with expectations of a classic proletarian revolution. 'Workers' are seen as the victims of the system and as the ones who reside *underneath*, where the fate of revolutionary activity resides. As a symbol, a hope, and a part of the soteriological dimension of the student's cosmology, the 'workers' incited the students to reach out of their campus, thus trying to fulfil one expectation raised by their narrative. Inviting the workers inside the Sorbonne was also an attempt to blur the spatial polarization between manual and intellectual work. As we can see, the kind of practices and messianic hopes that drove the students cannot be understood through any one ideological grid or psycho-social clichés on the inherent nature of 'youth'.

Spatial disruption through uncanny, provocative and/or violent actions exacerbated doubts concerning the social, 'natural' order of capitalism and liberal democracy. On a temporal level, the *mouvement du 22 mars* successfully gained control over temporal succession in two manners: by suspending what *was* actually happening, they broadened the possibilities of what *could* happen. At the end of the 1960s, the experience of the time of modernity – characterized by a dynamic tension between a fast-paced present and an unknown future – still served as a motor to produce different, imagined futures. But this space of experience took place outside

---

37   Emmanuel d'Astier, 'Regard sur l'événement', in *Première histoire de la révolution de mai* (Paris: L'Événement, 1968), 16.

of the aegis of History. For the youth, and particularly for the *enragés*, history was deprived of its capital H, Revolution of its capital R, and the various propagated 'isms' were losing their relevance. In other words, the acceleration of history was still experienced as a leap into the future, but without map, compass or direction.

This particular *régime d'historicité* explains why contemporaries oscillated between fierce optimism and bleak discouragement, as *anything* could happen, either revolution or totalitarianism. Uncertainty was thus highly stimulating. At a time during which praxis seemed *ahead* of theory, references and discourses, the informal search for a new and adequate language was thrilling. The gap between official references and effective practices generated hopes of a reconciliation between ideas and praxis, references and experiences, or intellectual and manual labour. This explains why spontaneous and startling actions were welcomed by students, and surprisingly tolerated by many adults. These actions needed no justification because they were sparks emanating from the in-between of two historical eras. They were leading to something else, and their 'meaning' was suspended in the genesis of new social and cultural forms.

* * *

Cours camarade, le vieux monde est derrière toi.
—A slogan in May

The *mouvement du 22 mars* generated such a dynamism and influence for May '68 because it took place in a *régime d'historicité* in which actions, style and narrative could gain a large resonance. What characterizes the years 1967–9 is, on the one hand, an experience of *openness* in time and space and, on the other hand, a blocked, mildly repressive and stagnant society restrained by old rules. Not as convincing as before, the grand narrative of total societal Progress was threatened on many levels, starting with the educational system. From the university at Nanterre, to the Sorbonne, to the streets, despite (and partly because of) police repression, participants in the movement felt that everything was opening up, spatially and temporally.

This is why besides the 'political opportunities'[38] that are available to social movements, there are also opportunities related to the *régime d'historicité*. A movement builds its identity and generates a narrative through actions, recapitulations and expectations, but the mobilizing effects, the resonance and the outcomes of these actions, are directly connected to this *régime d'historicité*. As Elizabeth Armstrong writes, 'just as actors organize their action in response to environmental rigidity, they also respond to environmental uncertainty'.[39] Considered alongside temporality, 'environmental uncertainty' is not a stratospheric layer, or a timeless sentiment vaguely shared by some contemporaries. It can be specified, located and described.

We have come across three contextual settings that explain how opportunities related to the *régime d'historicité* were taken: a) During the 1960s, the decay of the old *régime d'historicité* brought contemporaries (mostly young people) to realize that they no longer belonged to a once consecrated field of experience and horizon of expectation. As the articulations between past and future typical of grand narratives of Progress were questioned, the values, references and codes promoted through these articulations were exposed and criticized; b) this decay created a gap in time, or a 'brèche d'historicité',[40] which encouraged people to reformulate, reconsider or critically question what was taken for granted. As the past was losing its aura of *Historia est magistra vitae* (history as life's teacher), the future lost its quality of being the predictable and rationally planned outcome of the past. The present became the only temporally habitable time, at least until a great thrust into the future was taken, or an irresistible spreading of radical gradualism instituted; c) such a reinvestment in the present informs the

---

38　Like reforms, the division of elites, the power of political allies, political threats, and the end of a regime (see for example J. Craig Jenkins, David Jacobs and Jon Agnone, 'Political Opportunities and African-American Protest, 1948–97', *American Journal of Sociology* 109 (2003), 277–303).

39　Elizabeth A. Armstrong, 'From Struggle to Settlement: The Crystallization of a Field of Lesbian/Gay Organizations in San Francisco, 1969–73', in Gerald Davis et al., eds, *Social Movements and Organization Theory* (New York: Cambridge University Press, 2005), 163–4.

40　See Hartog, *Régimes d'historicité*.

purposes and forms of a social movement's actions. As the students provoked panic and stupefaction among the authorities, a political and spatial vacuum was gradually associated with this temporal gap. By risking itself through concrete actions and organizing on the ground, outside of previous ideological grids, the movement made the possibility of the massive transformation of social relations, values, culture and knowledge 'realistic'.

These possibilities, of course, needed to be *seized* and *materialized*, which was carried out under particular conditions that we can only briefly mention here. Because they build their identities and affirm their historical consciousness as a new generation, student movements are particularly suitable for this kind of inquiry. The *mouvement du 22 mars* was able to concretely channel and alter its moment of *historicité* by rejecting the ideological labels, pre-established goals and traditional practices of most student organizations. Focusing on a highly charged *present* with an unpredictable future, the movement successfully mobilized students around issues and through practices that resonated with these new historical possibilities. Spectacular and disruptive actions, pluralistic means and objectives, sexual/ individual liberation, or the creation of small, collective, deliberative *comités d'action*, were all attempts by the *enragés* to give substance to the experimental transformations proffered by, and acted upon, their *régime d'historicité*.

Selected Bibliography

Cefaï, Daniel, *Pourquoi se mobilise-t-on? Les théories de l'action collective* (Paris: La Découverte, 2007).

Debord, Guy, *La Société du spectacle* (Paris: Buchet/Chastel, 1967).

Hartog, François, *Régimes d'historicité: présentisme et expériences du temps* (Paris: Seuil, 2003).

Koselleck, Reinhart, *Future Pasts: On the Semantics of Historical Time* (Cambridge, MA: MIT Press, 1985).

Mannheim, Karl, *Essays on the Sociology of Knowledge* (London: Routledge & Kegan Paul, 1952).

McAdam, Doug, and D.A. Snow, eds, *Readings on Social Movements: Origins, Dynamics and Outcomes* (New York: Oxford University Press, 2010).

——, John D. McCarthy and Mayer N. Zald, eds, *Comparative Perspectives on Social Movements* (Cambridge: Cambridge University Press, 1996).

Morris, A., and C. McClurg Mueller, eds, *Frontiers of Social Movement Theory* (New Haven: Yale University Press, 1992).

Sauvageot, J., et al., *La révolte étudiante: les animateurs parlent* (Paris: Seuil, 1968).

Schnapp, Alain, and Pierre Vidal-Naquet, *Journal de la commune étudiante: textes et documents. Novembre 1967–juin 1968* [1969] (Paris: Seuil, 1988).

Stoczkowski, Wiktor, *Anthropologies rédemptrices: le monde selon Lévi-Strauss* (Paris: Hermann, 2008).

Tilly, Charles, et al., *The Politics of Collective Violence* (Cambridge: Cambridge University Press, 2010).

PART 2

The Politics of Finitude

GEORGE TOMLINSON

Totalization, Temporalization and History: Marx and Sartre

> It remains the case that the totalization differs from the totality in that
> the latter *is* totalized while the former totalizes itself. In this sense, it is
> obvious that to totalize *itself* means to temporalize *itself*.[1]

This chapter picks up on what Heidegger in his 1949 'Letter on "Humanism"'
calls 'the historical in being', that dimension of being within which, for
Heidegger, a 'productive dialogue' between phenomenology and existential-
ism, on the one hand, and Marxism, on the other, 'first becomes possible'.[2]
It introduces the possibility of this dialogue through a particular, and particularly revealing, problem with *The German Ideology*: namely, Marx and
Engels offer no analysis of the relationship between time, temporality and
their materialist concept of history.[3] There are a variety of reasons why the
philosophical potential of *The German Ideology* is far from being realized,

---

1   Jean-Paul Sartre, *Critique of Dialectical Reason, Volume 1: Theory of Practical Ensembles*
    [1960] (hereafter *CDR* 1), trans. Alan Sheridan-Smith (London and New York:
    Verso, 2004), 53.
2   Martin Heidegger, 'Letter on "Humanism"' [1949], trans. Frank A. Capuzzi, in
    Martin Heidegger, *Pathmarks* [1967], ed. William McNeill (Cambridge: Cambridge
    University Press, 1998), 259. For Heidegger, since 'estrangement attains an essential
    dimension of history' in Marx, 'the Marxist view of history is superior to that of
    other historical accounts' (ibid.).
3   Giorgio Agamben emphasizes this point in his *Infancy & History: Essays on the
    Destruction of Experience* [1978], trans. Liz Heron (London and New York: Verso,
    1993), 91.

but perhaps none stands out more than the fact that this analysis is absent. As a consequence, it is unclear what a temporal reading of *The German Ideology* might yield, how complex practices and phenomena such as the creation of new needs, the dialectic of the forces and relations of production, the division of labour, class struggle, alienation and estrangement, are intelligible as *temporal* practices and *temporal* phenomena. The materialism of *The German Ideology* denotes the social activity which is labour: activity inseparable from and yet irreducible to the organic and inorganic matter which this activity creates and through which it is realized. This conception of materialism figures 'the economic' as the social production of the means of life,[4] and collapses any barrier between self-transformative action by free humans [*praxis*] and the necessary production of objects for use [*poiêsis*]. This is the basis from which history becomes a speculative and experimental concept in Marx. This is also the sense in which, for Marx, labour historicizes. But in what sense does labour temporalize? Put differently, how do we establish materiality and temporality, along with matter and time, as conceptually indissociable in Marx, such that the temporality of matter and the materiality of time can be thought within Marx's philosophy more generally?[5] To push this further, is it possible to read materiality *as* temporality in Marx?[6]

4   In addition to its colloquial meaning as victuals, *Lebensmittel* can be translated as 'means of subsistence', 'means of existence' and 'means of life'. 'Means of subsistence' is the predominant and weakest choice, as it exclusively emphasizes the reproduction of the physical existence of individuals, a dimension which Marx's concept of life [*Leben*] is necessarily grounded in but profoundly expands at the same time.

5   Étienne Balibar suggests that 'Marx's philosophy, whether or not it is in a finished form, sets itself the task of thinking the materiality of time': Étienne Balibar, *The Philosophy of Marx*, trans. Chris Turner (London and New York: Verso, 1995), 81.

6   William Haver goes so far as to claim that 'for Marx, materiality and temporality are the same thing'. William Haver, 'For a Communist Ontology', in Richard Calichman and John Namjun Kim, eds, *The Politics of Culture: Around the Work of Naoki Sakai* (London and New York: Routledge, 2010), 114. Haver does not provide it, but this reading hinges on developing a concept of materiality [*Materialität*] which simply put does not exist in Marx's corpus. This concept would emerge from – and yet would need to ontologically ground – Marx's critical reconstruction of materialism

These questions bring to centre stage the relationship between Marx and the philosophy of time. Specifically, they facilitate a confrontation between Marx's concept of labour in *The German Ideology*, a decidedly dialectical concept (internally grounded by a dialectic between the creation of the means to satisfy existing needs and the creation of new needs), and accounts of temporalization in the phenomenological and existential tradition, which are both anti-dialectical (as in the early Heidegger) and a mixture of dialectics and anti-dialectics alike (as in the later Sartre). In Heidegger and Sartre, 'temporalization' denotes the active production of a dynamic relationship between the past, the present and the future, whereas 'time' is the name for the abstract unity of these three coordinates. To put it another way, temporalization is the process of temporal differentiation: the production of the very distinction between the past, the present and the future. For Heidegger and Sartre, the concept of time does not register this process. In fact, it conceals it. For them, time is a reified category, the exteriorized product of temporalization, wherein the doubled meaning of the German *Gegenwart* as both presence and the present reveals itself.[7] Temporalization, therefore, is ontologically basic to the ordinary concept of time.[8] If this is the case, how does the temporalization of the materialist concept of history uncodify the codified tradition which is Historical Materialism? To invoke Benjamin, does the temporalization of the materialist concept of history secure its freedom from the straightjacket of historicism, from the confines of empty, homogenous time? No matter how much philosophical heterodoxy this concept implicitly entails, nor how much political agitation it explicitly

---

[*Materialismus*] in the *Theses on Feuerbach* as a dynamization of the subject–object relation in modern (post-Kantian) epistemology.

7   Heidegger invokes this doubled meaning across his corpus. In addition to Sartre, Althusser relies on Heidegger on this point. See Louis Althusser, 'The Errors of Classical Economics: An Outline for a Concept of Historical Time', in Louis Althusser and Étienne Balibar, *Reading Capital* [1968], trans. Ben Brewster (London: Verso, 1997), 95.

8   In some regards, Sartre's account of temporalization exceeds that of Heidegger's because Sartre, unlike Heidegger, situates temporalization as ontologically basic to a biological (pre-existential) time structured by the physiological needs of the human body.

provokes, perhaps existential temporalization is what this concept of history needs, in order for Marx – this is not without irony – to realize his desire for a dissident relationship with philosophy more generally.

It is possible to justify the temporalization of the materialist concept of history on the basis that it is necessary to temporalize the concept as such in Marx, a necessity borne from the standpoint in Hegel that 'time is the concept itself, that *there is*'.[9] But in what sense does temporalization destabilize the concept itself? The existential tradition is well suited to answer this question, because existential temporalization upends how we, to use a Heideggerian expression, 'initially and for the most part' understand action, activity and the act themselves. Consequently, existential temporalization intervenes into existing claims made on behalf of the originary character of *The German Ideology*. It intervenes, to give two notable examples, into Althusser's assertion that *The German Ideology* represents an 'epistemological break' and 'state of rupture' in Marx's work,[10] and Georges Labica's contention that *The German Ideology* is a groundbreaking 'construction site' for a 'scraping operation' and 'settling of accounts' with Marx's predecessors, his contemporaries and himself.[11] However, against Labica's outright reduction of all philosophy to ideology, there is a distinct possibility that philosophical discourses on temporalization might in fact *enrich* Marx's concept of history, and that this concept of history might in turn enrich these discourses, such that it forces these discourses to reckon with 'men and women, not in any fantastic isolation and fixation, but in their actual, empirically perceptible process of development under definite

9   G.W.F. Hegel, *The Phenomenology of Spirit* [1807], trans. A.V. Miller (Oxford: Oxford University Press, 1977), 487. For Hegel, this is the standpoint of absolute knowing [*absolute Wissen*], the pure movement of self-consciousness knowing itself as self-consciousness. Time as the concept itself is a standpoint which can only ever be taken in an open historical present. Hegel does not speak of absolute knowing as a closed or achieved content. There is, in other words, no such thing for Hegel as 'absolute knowledge'.

10   Louis Althusser, *For Marx* [1965], trans. Ben Brewster (London: Verso, 1996), 33 and 36.

11   Georges Labica, *Marxism and the Status of Philosophy* [1976], trans. Kate Soper and Martin Ryle (Brighton: Harvester Press, 1980), 165–72.

conditions'.[12] *The German Ideology* may convey a desire, as Althusser puts it, to 'purely and simply abolish' philosophy,[13] but this desire not only 'hardly means that there is no philosophy at work in *The German Ideology*',[14] but, we might add, hardly means that there need not be more philosophy put to work within *The German Ideology*. Marx's emancipatory project need not converge with Labica's militant (but not necessarily radical) reading of Marx's materialism as 'situating all philosophy, whether idealist or materialist, in its true place, namely in *ideology*', as rendering the notion of a Marxist philosophy 'absurd'.[15] The philosophy within Marxist philosophy need not be that philosophy (i.e. classical German idealism) in opposition to which Althusser, Labica and Marx envision a 'science of history'.[16] Herbert Marcuse's notion of 'concrete philosophy' is a clear example of this. For Marcuse, philosophy is 'the concrete distress of human existence'[17] which makes visible (and demands that we overcome) our contemporary historical situation. This philosophy, what Marcuse calls 'philosophizing' – philosophy as a concrete mode of human existence – is a far cry from the abstract thought from which Althusser, Labica and Marx seek to dissociate themselves, and with which they are arguably preoccupied, to the point where they dismiss, to name the most prominent figure, the practical and concrete dimensions of Hegel's thought. To invoke Engels, perhaps it is

12   Karl Marx and Friedrich Engels, *Die deutsche Ideologie*, in Karl Marx and Friedrich Engels, *Marx Engels Werke, Band 3* (Berlin: Dietz Verlag, 1978), 27. The translation is mine.

13   Louis Althusser, 'The Historical Task of Marxist Philosophy', in Louis Althusser, *The Humanist Controversy and Other Writings* [1966–7], ed. François Matheron, trans. G.M. Goshgarian (New York and London: Verso, 2003), 174.

14   Ibid.

15   Labica, *Marxism and the Status of Philosophy*, 280 and 365.

16   Each in his own way, Althusser, Labica and Marx fail to engage critically the place of 'non-philosophy' within Feuerbach's *Preliminary Theses on the Reform of Philosophy* [1842], a place which qualifies the decisiveness and originality of their respective formulations of a science of history.

17   Herbert Marcuse, 'On Concrete Philosophy' [1929], trans. Matthew Erlin, in Herbert Marcuse, *Heideggerian Marxism*, ed. John Abromeit and Richard Wolin (Lincoln: University of Nebraska Press, 2005), 36.

not an exit from philosophy which is warranted, but an exit from the exit from philosophy. As Balibar points out, this exit is not a simple return to the inside of philosophy unburdened by history.[18] It is an exit structured by a dialectic between philosophy and Marx's own foreign land (history), a foreign land which is itself already a dialectic between philosophy and non-philosophy.

This confrontation with existential temporalization cuts to the heart of the meaning of 'the human' in Marx, which is to say his distinctly social conception of human being. In Marx, the human is a social being because it is historically constituted as multiple individuals in relation to one another and those very relations themselves.[19] As he states across his 1844 texts: 'social being [...] is no abstract, universal power standing over and against the individual, but is the essence of every individual [...]'; 'the individual *is the social being* [...] the human's individual and generic life are not *different*'; and 'my *own* existence *is* social activity'.[20] This is the basis from which history and the human are inseparable concepts in Marx. Consider, for

18 Balibar, *The Philosophy of Marx*, 40 and 119.

19 The 'social' is not just direct communal relations. As Marx states: 'Social activity [...] exist[s] by no means *only* in the form of some *directly* communal activity [...] when I am active *scientifically* [...] when I am engaged in activity which I can seldom perform in direct community with others, then I am *social*, because I am active as a *human*. Not only is the material of my activity given to me as a social product – as is even the language in which the thinker is active – my *own* existence *is* social activity, and therefore that which I make of myself, I make of myself for society and with the consciousness of myself as a social being': Karl Marx, *Ökonomisch-philosophische Manuskripte aus dem Jahre 1844*, in Marx and Engels, *MEW, Band 40* (Berlin: Dietz Verlag, 1968), 538. The translation is mine.

20 Karl Marx, *Auszüge aus James Mills Buch 'Élémens d'économie politique'*, in Marx and Engels, *MEW, Band 40* (Berlin: Dietz Verlag, 1968), 451; Marx, *Ökonomisch-philosophische Manuskripte aus dem Jahre 1844*, 538–9; ibid. 538. 'The human, much as it may therefore be a *particular* individual (and it is precisely its particularity which makes it an individual and an actual *individual* social being), is just as much the *totality* – the ideal totality – the subjective existence of thought and experienced society for itself; just as it exists also in actuality as the intuition and the actual enjoyment of social existence, and as a totality of the human manifestation of life'. Ibid. 539. All translations are mine.

instance, his concept of nature. For Marx, the human does not make its own history alongside a self-sufficient nature, a nature in itself and as such. Rather, human history is history *as such*. The idea of a 'history of nature' in isolation from the existence of living human individuals is (for Marx) unintelligible. As he puts it: 'We know only a single science, the science of history. One can look at history from two sides and divide it into the history of nature and the history of humanity. The two sides are, however, *inseparable*; the history of nature and the history of humans are dependent on each other *so long as humankind exists*.'[21] And further: 'nature, the nature that preceded human history, is not by any means the nature in which Feuerbach lives, it is nature which today no longer exists anywhere [...] and which, therefore, does not exist for Feuerbach.'[22] Should humankind no longer exist, that would not mean that other forms of organic and inorganic matter would also not exist. Marx's claim, rather, is that these other forms of matter would be neither historical nor natural: history and nature alike come to an end with the end of human being.

Therefore, we might say that the temporalization of history is inseparable from the temporalization of the human which creates and is created by this history. But this inseparability is not grounded by nature, but rather by Marx's transhistorical concept of labour in general. As the social production of the means of life, which is a dialectical production of the means of life, labour is an ontological domain of temporalization because it constitutes the movement of negation. As in Hegel, the dialectical movement of negation is in Marx the first and most evident register of an active difference between the past, the present and the future. But is the historical status of negation thereby secured? Is negation thereby the movement of historical temporalization? *The German Ideology* offers

21 This passage in *The German Ideology* is famous, in part, because it was crossed out in a final revision of the manuscript. This translation appears in Peter Osborne, *How to Read Marx* (London: Granta Books, 2005), 38. Emphasis added. See also Alfred Sohn-Rethel, *Intellectual and Manual Labour: A Critique of Epistemology* [1970], trans. Martin Sohn-Rethel (Atlantic Highlands: Humanities Press, 1977), 18.

22 Karl Marx and Friedrich Engels, *The German Ideology* [1845], trans. S.W. Ryazanskaya (London: Lawrence & Wishart, 1965), 63.

two (deeply interwoven) dialectics as possible models of historical time: (1) the dialectic of the creation of the means to satisfy existing needs and the creation of new needs; and (2) the dialectic of the forces and relations of production. And it is negation through which the three temporal coordinates within these dialectics first becomes intelligible, such that there is futurity immanent to the present's transcendence of the past. But in what sense is the temporalization of history about more than negation? In other words, with what, or rather through what, must negation be thought in order to temporalize the materialist concept of history?

The temporalization of the materialist concept of history must situate dialectical negation in relation to historical totalization, which is to say *the totalization of the time of all human lives*. Whether it is openly acknowledged, left unstated or disavowed, this totalization is the overarching intelligibility and narrative of every post-Enlightenment conception of history from the mid-eighteenth century onwards. Within the modern philosophy of history, this is the sense in which the human is 'historical' because history is the development of the time of the human species as a *whole*. Marx does not thematize this totalization in relation to the materialist concept of history. 'World history' and the 'world-historical' figure in *The German Ideology* (primarily in relation to alienation and its speculative end in communism), but they are tautologically defined by Marx and Engels,[23] and the extent to which they function as totalizing concepts is unclear. The world market is depicted as an integral dimension of big industry and the production of world history 'for the first time',[24] but its relation to the social production of the means of life is tenuously established, and it is clearly a phenomenon specific to capitalism. As with Marx's famous eleventh thesis on Feuerbach,[25] these concepts invoke the ordinary conception of

---

23   'The proletariat can [...] only exist *world-historically*, just as communism, its activity, can only have a "world-historical" existence. World-historical existence of individuals means [...] [the] existence of individuals which is directly linked up with world history'. Ibid. 56.

24   Ibid. 78.

25   'The philosophers have only *interpreted* the world, in various ways; the point is to *change* it'. Karl Marx, *Theses on Feuerbach* [1845], in Karl Marx, *Early Writings*, trans.

'world', a conception which (at least on the surface) is much more about space than it is about time. Hence the 'ongoing totalization of the time of the human'[26] is a philosophical problem for the materialist concept of history, because the relationship between totalization and negation within this concept remains undeveloped. What is this relationship? Specifically, in what sense is totalization a kind of temporalization itself, indissociable from and yet irreducible to the movement of negation?

At this point, it is necessary to turn to the first volume of Sartre's *Critique of Dialectical Reason*. An existential reading of the relationship between two different materialisms in Marx (the new materialism of *praxis* in the *Theses on Feuerbach* and the historical materialism of needs in *The German Ideology*), *Critique of Dialectical Reason* systematically reconstructs dialectics as the very movement of totalization. For Sartre, it is individual *praxis* which ontologically grounds this reconstruction. The totalizing structure of individual *praxis* is, to use a Heideggerian expression, the 'originary ontological ground' of our existence,[27] such that totalization becomes, to use a classical Marxist expression, the 'law of dialectics'. And it is individual *praxis* from which the conceptual difference between 'totalization' and 'the totality' first reveals itself. After Sartre, totalization is a ceaselessly developing activity of synthetic unification,[28] whereas a totality is the exteriorized product of this activity, that which has been cut off from the totalizing process of its production (which it nonetheless contains sedimented within itself). However, this process of unification should not be understood as subsequent to an existing state of difference. There is no chronological succession here. Rather, following Heidegger, to whom Derrida's concept of *différance* is also indebted, totalization *is*

<hr>

Rodney Livingstone and Gregor Benton (London and New York: Penguin Books, 1992), 423.

26 Peter Osborne, 'Marx and the Philosophy of Time', *Radical Philosophy*, 147 (2008), 16.

27 Martin Heidegger, *Sein und Zeit* [1927], in Martin Heidegger, *Gesamtausgabe*, *Abteilung 1: Veröffentliche Schriften 1914–1970, Band 2* (Frankfurt am Main: Vittorio Klostermann, 1977), 311.

28 Sartre, *CDR* 1, 46.

the production of difference, a unification whose unity *is* the process of its differentiation. However, compellingly, Sartre actively dialecticizes Heidegger's anti-dialectical philosophy of difference, and consequently represents an exception to the predominant trajectory of the philosophy of difference within twentieth-century French philosophy more generally. For our purposes, this understanding of unification grounds the basic analogy between totalization and temporalization: temporalization *is*, as previously argued, the production of the very difference between the past, the present and the future.[29] But there is more than analogy at work here. There is a constitutive relationship of dependence. For Sartre, the totalizing structure of individual *praxis* totalizes precisely because it produces temporal difference. The totalizing structure of individual *praxis* is predicated on temporalization, just as the temporalizing structure of individual *praxis* is predicated on totalization. What secures this relationship of dependence? In other words, what secures the fact that individual *praxis* produces temporal difference as a differentiated unification?

The relationship between totalization and negation must now be addressed. For Sartre, totalization exteriorizes itself through totalities, worked matter in which *praxis* is embodied, but this exteriorization is always already tied to what he characterizes as the 're-interiorization' of totalities. In other words, when an exteriorized totality is re-interiorized through individual *praxis*, this interiorization is the negation of the interiority of the interior.[30] For Sartre, this is why negation constitutes the essential movement of dialectics. It is why negation is squarely at the heart of the movement of totalization, but – and this is the crux of the matter – negation does not unify the time of individual *praxis*, because negation does not provide the standpoint from which the practical dependence between temporalization and totalization is secured. At the level of the individual act, negation produces both a difference and active relation between the

29   What Sartre does not examine in sufficient detail is whether the difference between totalization and the totality is analogous to the difference between temporalization and time, such that time is the exteriorized product of temporalization, cut off from its own temporalizing process, and subject to inertia.

30   Ibid. 57.

past, the present and the future, but this difference and active relation is not thereby the difference and active relation which unifies the act as a differentiated unification. In Heideggerian terms, negation does not constitute the ontological meaning of 'care' [*Sorge*], because the temporality of negation does not constitute the meaning of the individual act as a structural whole.[31] Negation is a dynamic movement in its own right, but from the standpoint of totalization negation is only temporally intelligible as a *particular moment* of totalization. As Sartre puts it, negation only produces 'a temporary totality [...] on the basis of a provisional totalization,'[32] to which we might add, 'on the basis of a provisional temporalization'.

As a consequence, *Critique of Dialectical Reason* enables us to develop two temporal dimensions of one and the same individual act. The first – which Sartre does not thematize – is from the standpoint of dialectical negation as the internal engine of totalization. This is the sense in which a particular moment within the movement of interiorization/exteriorization can be characterized, to link up with the previous formulation in relation to Marx, as the present's transcendence of the past. This moment is a dialectical interplay between the present and the past which at the same time undeniably prioritizes the present over the past. It is the present, not the past, wherein totalization as ontologically basic to the totality, and materiality as ontologically basic to matter, becomes intelligible (for Sartre, materiality is the 'domain' of individual *praxis*, such that materiality becomes matter through individual *praxis*). We might formulate this moment as follows: the totalizing present is the dialectical negation – the

---

31   For Heidegger, care is the totalized manifold of existence, which he formally defines as follows: 'the being of Dasein means ahead-of-itself-being-already-in (the world) as being-alongside (entities encountered within-the-world)'. Martin Heidegger, *Being and Time* [1927], trans. John Macquarrie and Edward Robinson (New York: Harper Collins, 1962), 237. Heidegger establishes temporality as the ontological meaning of care in §65 of *Being and Time*. As with totalization, a 'whole' should not be conflated with a totality. As Sartre states: 'a "*whole*" is not a totality, but the unity of the totalizing act in so far as it diversifies itself and embodies itself in totalized diversities': Sartre, *CDR* 1, 48, ft. 22.

32   Ibid. 60.

simultaneous creation and negation – of the past as a totality. Or: the materiality of the present is the dialectical negation of the past as matter. To the extent that it is embodied as matter, that is, to the extent that it is totalized as a totality, the past is fated to inertia (the totality cannot undo its separation from the process of its own production). But the past is equally fated to movement, because the totalizing present cannot totalize without re-interiorizing matter (there is no *praxis* without *poiêsis*). Hence the relationship between the present and the past is a dialectical relationship between a dialectical (totalizing) present and a non-dialectical (totalized) past. As previously stated, the future is *immanent* to this relationship. The future does not lie in waiting: it is not the waiting repetition of an actual dialectic played out between the totalizing present and the totalized past. Rather, the totalizing present *is* the future of the totalized past.

But in what sense is the future different than the present? This leads us to the second temporal dimension of the individual act, one which Sartre explicitly thematizes in *Critique of Dialectical Reason*. This dimension proceeds from the standpoint of totalization *as such*, irreducible to the negation which constitutes it, wherein the production of temporal difference – which is to say the temporal unification of the act – is not secured by negation but by the *teleological structure of the act*. This is the sense in which the temporality of individual *praxis* is defined by the particular end of a particular project: every individual act makes the future present through the imagined end of the act. To be clear, this is the teleological, not the chronological, end of the act (teleology ≠ chronology, the teleological end ≠ the chronological end).[33] As with the third volume of Lukács's *Ontology of Social Being*,[34] there is, therefore, a fundamental Aristotelian dimension to *Critique of Dialectical Reason*. The future as the imagined end of the act is exactly the same future as previously described: the totalizing present which *is* the future of the totalized past. However,

33   The fact that the teleological end ≠ the chronological end simply means that the goal, the intent, the aim, etc. is an imaginary structure of the act which cannot be reduced to its actual completion, finish, etc.

34   Georg Lukács, *The Ontology of Social Being, Vol. III, Labour* [1971–3], trans. David Fernbach (London: Merlin Press, 1978).

crucially, the difference between the present and the future is not thereby flattened, because, unlike the present, the projected realization of the end of the act is not actual but imaginary. This is the sense in which the future is necessarily open: not because it does not yet exist, but because it correlates to an act of the imagination. From *this* perspective, the ontological priority is not the present but the future, as only the future guides the actual unification of the act, which is to say the actual differentiation between the past, the present and the future. Unification is, in a word, univocal: only the future of the act secures its temporal unity. And for Sartre, the end of the act, down to the basic 'restoration of the organism',[35] is grounded by *need*. It is need, specifically need as it is defined by scarcity and lack, which governs the projection of the end. Hence not only does need ontologically ground the relationships between materiality and matter, temporalization and time, and totalization and the totality, but so too does it ontologically ground the relationships of dependence between these relationships, such that temporalization is not a totalization, nor does not have materiality, in isolation from human need.

The end of the individual act is one thing, but is there such a thing as the end of history (again, in the teleological, not the chronological, sense of 'end')? Is there something which provides history (as a collective singular) with its unity? What is the meaning of the historical future? The first volume of *Critique of Dialectical Reason* provides something of a placeholder of a response to these questions with its culminating formulation of history as a 'totalization without a totalizer'.[36] For Sartre, the essence of this formulation is that totalization at the level of individual *praxis* (a totalization whose totalizer is individual *praxis*) is not – it cannot be – the same totalization which totalizes history. In other words, if history is in some sense the totalization of the time of all human lives, then after Sartre it might also be conceived of as the totalization of all individual totalizations, and, therefore, as the temporalization of all individual temporaliztions. And yet historical totalization and historical temporalization are not and cannot be

---

35   Sartre, *CDR* 1, 90.
36   Ibid. 805.

the same totalization and temporalization which is individual totalization and individual temporalization. For Sartre, we only know totalization from the standpoint of the individual, and the totalization of all individual totalizations is history, but history is not totalized by the totalization which is individual *praxis*. Historical totalization is hidden. It is, after Hegel, the 'cunning of reason', an invisible hand, to invoke Adam Smith's conception of the market, which works behind the backs of individuals.

What historical totalization compels us to examine – a question which is underdetermined in Sartre and simply unasked in Marx – is the ongoing constitution of complex relationships between individual, social and historical temporalities. Take, for instance, Marx's concept of the social individual. For Marx, this individual is already and entirely determined by society,[37] such that the social relation – not the individual – is the basic constituent of society. And yet, he also suggests that this individual is 'the great pillar of production and of wealth'.[38] At the level of the materialist concept of history, it is unclear how this concept should be read, particularly because Marx's analyses of social individuality and the social individual are completely tied to his critique of political economy (i.e. to capitalism). The point here is that it would be inadequate, if not misleading, to temporalize the social individual first and foremost from the standpoint of its individuality. But this standpoint remains the privileged point of departure within the philosophy of time. The fact is that existing discourses on temporalization are inextricably tied to the individual as the crux of that which is implicitly temporal. The individual may be a social or collective individual, as it is (to varying degrees) in Heidegger and Sartre, but the fact remains that the individual is (to date) the predominant basis of temporalization within the modern European philosophical tradition more generally. As Sartre puts it (this sentence immediately follows the quotation which frames this chapter): 'Indeed, as I have shown elsewhere, *the only*

---

37   Karl Marx, *Grundrisse: Foundations of the Critique of Political Economy* (*Rough Draft*) [1857–8], trans. Martin Nicolaus (London and New York: Penguin Books, 1993), 248.
38   Ibid. 705.

conceivable temporality is that of a totalization as an individual process.'[39] There is no prevailing philosophy of time which *begins* its account of temporalization from either the standpoint of the sociality or the historicality of the act. The philosophical tradition which we have inherited resists the possibility of theorizing temporalization from any other basis than that of the individual. The philosophy of time needs to think temporalization from an origin other than individual *praxis*, as in Sartre, and other than the 'in each case mineness' [*Jemeinigkeit*] of death, as in Heidegger. In order to be properly systematic, this philosophy must register the social and the historical as implicitly temporal in their own right, from which the complex relations between individual, social and historical temporalities can be examined in their reciprocal and asymmetric constitution.

Selected Bibliography

Althusser, Louis, *For Marx* [1965], trans. Ben Brewster (London: Verso, 1996).

——, and Balibar, Étienne, *Reading Capital* [1968], trans. Ben Brewster (London: Verso, 1997).

Balibar, Étienne, *The Philosophy of Marx*, trans. Chris Turner (London and New York: Verso, 1995).

Hegel, G.W.F., *The Phenomenology of Spirit* [1807], trans. A.V. Miller (Oxford: Oxford University Press, 1977).

Heidegger, Martin, *Being and Time* [1927], trans. John Macquarrie and Edward Robinson (New York: Harper Collins, 1962).

Labica, Georges, *Marxism and the Status of Philosophy* [1976], trans. Kate Soper and Martin Ryle (Brighton: Harvester Press, 1980).

Marx, Karl, *Theses on Feuerbach* [1845], in Marx, *Early Writings*, trans. Rodney Livingstone and Gregor Benton (London and New York: Penguin Books, 1992).

39   Jean-Paul Sartre, *CDR* 1, 53. Emphasis added. The 'as I have shown elsewhere' is a reference to Jean-Paul Sartre, *Being and Nothingness: An Essay on Phenomenological Ontology* [1943], trans. Hazel Estella Barnes (London and New York: Routledge Classics, 2003), 130–93.

——, *Grundrisse: Foundations of the Critique of Political Economy* (*Rough Draft*) [1857–8], trans. Martin Nicolaus (London and New York: Penguin Books, 1993).
——, and Engels, Friedrich, *The German Ideology* [1845], trans. S.W. Ryazanskaya (London: Lawrence & Wishart, 1965).
Sartre, Jean-Paul, *Critique of Dialectical Reason, Volume 1: Theory of Practical Ensembles* [1960], trans. Alan Sheridan-Smith (London and New York: Verso, 2004).

ADRIAN MAY

A Meteorology of the Times:
Bataille, Blanchot, *Lignes* and the Twentieth Century

The phenomenal success of French theory in the Anglo-American academy from the 1980s onwards is well known, and the influence of thinkers such as Jacques Derrida, Gilles Deleuze, Michel Foucault, and more recently Alain Badiou and Jean-Luc Nancy, is palpable across the humanities and beyond. Yet one problem with the rapid importation of these texts, often read in isolation and shorn of their original context, is that the political, cultural and intellectual stakes in France, within which they were precise interventions, are often lost. An exploration of the *revues* in which these thinkers first published is a good way to restore the historical conjuncture and the complexity of these debates, and much work has been done on the likes of *Tel Quel*, *Les Temps modernes* and *Critique* to better illuminate the post-war period.[1] Yet the contemporary era, from the mid-1980s to the present day (the very period of French theory's success in America and the United Kingdom), is less well known. The *revue Lignes* (founded in 1987), a marginal yet important milieu of contemporary thinkers, can be seen as the intellectual successor to the likes of *Tel Quel* and *Critique*, and is therefore an apt object of study to restore the material density to otherwise abstract debates.

The two key intellectual predecessors for *Lignes'* original editorial board were Georges Bataille (for Michel Surya and Francis Marmande) and

---

1   See, for example, Patrick ffrench, *The Time of Theory* (Oxford: Clarendon Press, 1995), Sylvie Patron, *Critique 1946–1996: une encyclopédie de l'esprit modern* (Paris: Éditions de l'IMEC, 2000), and Anna Boschetti, *The Intellectual Enterprise: Sartre and 'Les Temps modernes'*, trans. Richard C. McCleary (Evanston, IL: Northwestern University Press, 1988).

Maurice Blanchot (for Daniel Dobbels). Marmande has recently argued that the intellectual reaction to Georges Bataille at any given moment 'vaut toujours d'excellent indicateur d'époque', and that to trace these responses would be one way to chart a 'météorologie' of the moral, cultural and political climate in France throughout the twentieth century.[2] As a way of examining where *Lignes* is placed in the wider French milieu, this piece undertakes such a meteorology for both Bataille and Blanchot. In doing so, by returning to the 1930s and the first political texts of these two canonical figures, it will be possible to give an account of the shifting climate throughout the twentieth century, ending with *Lignes*' adoption of this philosophical genealogy to define their own project in the present. Due to space limitations, however, the early decades of their work and reception will be covered very briefly, to make room for the more complex intellectual debates which follow from the 1960s onwards.[3]

The 1930s: *Révolte, Refus, Révolution*

The political turbulence of the 1930s is easy for scholars to underestimate retrospectively, and as Jean-Michel Besnier notes, whilst today intellectual discourse is 'generally unaffected by the vertigo of militancy', in the 1930s it was accompanied by a moving fascination for action.'[4] The Great Depression hit Europe in 1932, weakening elected governments' capacity for effective action and accelerating a drift towards authoritarian extremes. The vacillation of the League of Nations in the face of rising fascist threats

---

2   Francis Marmande, *Le pur bonheur: Georges Bataille* (Fécamp: Nouvelles Éditions Lignes, 2011), 36–7.

3   For a more detailed account, see the first two chapters of my forthcoming doctoral thesis: Adrian May, '*Lignes*: Twenty-Five Years of Politics, Philosophy, Literature and Art' (University of Cambridge).

4   Jean-Michel Besnier, 'Georges Bataille in the 1930s: A Politics of the Impossible', *Yale French Studies* 38 (1990), 169–80 (170).

in Germany, Italy and Spain led many to despair: for some, only the violence of war or revolution would be able to bring a satisfactory solution. As the decade progressed and the prospects of a peaceful political solution to Europe's growing tensions seemed increasingly unlikely, Besnier adds that given 'the debilitating apathy of parliamentary democracy', the seemingly ethical choice often embraced 'revolt and risk'.[5] The discourses of Bataille, from a critical Marxist left, and Blanchot, from a Catholic conservative right, actually shared many similarities, both becoming more extreme as the decade progressed, notably producing their most violent rhetoric in 1936–7: for them it was the unopposed German re-occupation of the Rhineland in 1936 that signalled Europe's capitulation to war, not the latter Munich Agreement, and this explains their increasingly desperate tone. The key difference was Bataille's internationalism, against Blanchot's impassioned defence of the French nation.[6]

For Bataille, to counter the populist dynamics of fascism, with a charismatic leader gaining mass support, the potential forces of emancipation also needed to mobilize aesthetic and quasi-religious sentiments to whip up a frenzied, violent resistance to supplant the liberal democratic strategy of appeasement. Some have described this as a use of fascist means against fascism, whereas others, such as Walter Benjamin, told Bataille that by using this kind of logic 'You work for fascism!'.[7] With 'Contre-Attaque', 'Acéphale' and the 'Collège de Sociologie', this was an equivocal strategy, one that placed into question the ethics of aestheticized politics (an aestheticization of the political, rather than merely political art), and many would later criticize Bataille for it; Bataille himself later expressed regret for some of his actions.[8] Yet Marmande calls Bataille 'le témoin lucide,

5   Ibid.
6   For essential accounts of this period, see Michel Surya, *Georges Bataille, la mort à l'œuvre* (Paris: Gallimard, 1992), and Christophe Bident, *Maurice Blanchot, partenaire invisible* (Seyssel: Editions Champ Vallon, 1998).
7   Simonetta Falasca-Zamponi, *Rethinking the Political: The Sacred, Aesthetic Politics, and the Collège de Sociologie* (Montreal: McGill-Queen's Univeristy Press, 2011), 3.
8   See Denis Hollier, 'On Equivocation (Between Literature and Politics)', trans. Rosalind Kraus, *October* 55 (1990), 3–22, for more on this question.

compromis et peu évitable' of this period.[9] His awareness of the dangers of mass psychology in *La Structure psychologique du fascisme* proved prescient and, despite common assumptions, his writings are free of suspicious sympathies with Nazism. Whilst, after over half a century of European peace and an increasingly non-conflictual political sphere, it is easy to retrospectively criticize the violence of Bataille's rhetoric, the fact that he felt compelled to shed his habitual 'pessimisme' and collaborate within, or even initiate, such political activities shows the levels of urgency and tension palpable in the lead-up to the war.[10]

Blanchot was more clearly compromised by fascist allegiances. He started out writing acute criticisms of Hitler and his anti-Semitic policies in the moderate, nationalist press, but by 1936 and 1937, publishing in extreme-right newspapers such as *Combat* and *L'Insurgé*, he increasingly seemed to abandon analytic thought entirely, and went on to produce a repetitive, mechanically hateful rhetoric against those he saw as undermining French interests (which was pretty much everyone, from communists, fascists, anti-fascists and the Spanish to liberal democrats, Blum, and the Popular Front). The violence of these texts remains staggering to read, and especially shocking is the occasional anti-Semitism which would cast a cloud over his subsequent reception in the 1980s. Leslie Hill has since argued that 'no evidence of any real substance has ever been produced' to justify ascribing a deep-seated anti-Semitism to Blanchot,[11] and Bident characterizes him as using the 'rhétorique imitative' of an 'idéologie empruntée' from the tabloid press.[12] Nevertheless, one can only condemn these texts, and Blanchot was even partially responsible for funding the creation of *L'Insurgé*, exacerbating his culpability.

The key issue for Blanchot scholarship is whether this participation with the extreme right in the 1930s contaminates his post-war writing: in Bident's account, Blanchot began revising his ideological standpoint from

9   Francis Marmande, *Georges Bataille politique* (Lyon: Presses universitaires de Lyon, 1985), 221.
10 Ibid. 53.
11 Leslie Hill, *Blanchot: Extreme Contemporary* (London: Routledge, 1997), 37.
12 Bident, *Maurice Blanchot*, 112.

around 1938 and throughout the war, after which he produced radically different forms of writing, espousing an ethical openness to alterity more famously associated with Levinas and Derrida. Yet articles in *Aux Écoutes*, recently discussed by David Uhrig, show that in 1940 Blanchot enthusiastically greeted the installation of Pétain's Vichy regime, suggesting that his political 'conversion' was not yet underway; and whilst his shift in political position is widely recognized in the post-war period, some of the same passionate rhetoric is present in his communist texts, leading critics such as Michel Surya to question whether Blanchot's entire approach to politics is in not some way compromised.[13]

The 1940s: Engagement

Bataille and Blanchot met in 1941, and had a lifelong, close friendship. In Surya's biography, he claims that 'il est plus que vraisemblable que c'est Bataille qu'il faut créditer du revirement idéologique de Blanchot.'[14] Published ten years later, Bident's account attenuates this interpretation: Blanchot was already undergoing a process of self-scrutiny from 1938, and his post-war political engagements owe more to Dionys Mascolo (whom Bataille frequently refused to support); but Bataille certainly would have helped accelerate and confirm this change. Along with Mascolo and the heterodox Marxist grouping around Maurgerite Duras' house, in the 1960s Blanchot would take part in some of the most exemplary post-war intellectual interventions: he played a key role in the composition of the 'Manifesto of the 121' in response to the Algerian war; attempted (but ultimately failed) to publish the radical, new *Revue Internationale*; and, despite his notorious reserve, he actively participated in May '68. Whilst there is not the space

13 See the texts by Michel Surya (9–62), François Brémondy (63–121) and David Uhrig (122–39) in *Lignes* 43 (2014).
14 Surya, *Georges Bataille*, 381.

to discuss these activities in detail in the present piece, it is important to note these later interventions on Blanchot's part as signals of how far his ideological position had shifted.[15]

Whilst Blanchot's later politics attempted to form a non-dogmatic, open community of resistance and refusal which would be compatible with a liberated aesthetic practice not subservient to political ends, the immediate post-war period was marked by Sartrean engagement in which both the author and the work were required to conform to certain ideological prescriptions. Both Bataille and Blanchot agreed that literature should not be put directly into the service of politics: Bataille defended a conception of a sovereign literature that needed to explore the deepest recesses of existence free from servile moral constraints; whereas Blanchot's more radically textual approach saw writing as a space apart from daily life, politics, and the subjectivity of the author. Writing came first, above all else, and in this sense both authors seemed radically out of step with their epoch in the post-war period.

The 1950s: Decolonization, and New Critical Idioms

Yet if Bataille and Blanchot can both seem somewhat marginalized in the 1940s, they had an avenue to develop their own critical idioms via Bataille's revue *Critique*: Bataille published the articles that would become *La Littérature et le mal*, and Blanchot's contributions developed his reputation as his generation's most important critic (Jean Paulhan subsequently giving him free reign at the *Nouvelle revue française* from 1954). As Derrida notes, throughout the 1950s people began to read Bataille and Blanchot '*contre* Sartre',[16] and in this sense they became symptomatic of both a political and critical shift away from this dominant figure. With Sartre, it is never quite explicit who or what is

---

15   See Maurice Blanchot, *Écrits politiques 1958–1993* (Paris: Éditions Lignes & Manifeste, 2003), for more.

16   Jacques Derrida, quoted in Sylvie Patron, *Critique*, 195.

engaged – is it the work itself, or the author with his political convictions, or a combination of the two? Via Bataille and Blanchot, a separation occurs between text and author – much more radically in Blanchot than Bataille – which influenced the rise of structuralism and textual theories to come. Sartre's 'extraordinarily weak' presentation at the École normale superieur in April 1961 cemented the end of his intellectual influence in favour of structuralism (though his immense public standing meant that his support continued to be politically useful throughout the 1960s).[17] Meanwhile, whilst Sartre had only just rallied to the French Communist Party, from 1955–6 a huge shift in the left away from the party became palpable (especially after Khrushchev's denunciation of Stalinism in February 1956), and new intellectual groupings such as Mascolo's 'Comité d'action contre la poursuite de la guerre en Afrique du nord' put decolonization at the head of the agenda of a younger generation of thinkers, preparing the ground for Maoism and the student movements to come.[18] Bataille and Blanchot would intermittently participate in such activities, coming in from the cold somewhat with a sixties generation that would become their first serious readership.

The 1960s: The Time of Theory

Bataille died in 1962, but this decade would begin to mark his post-war notoriety, aided by the rise of what is now known as French theory. *Critique* remained a key vehicle, and issues devoted to Bataille in 1963, and Blanchot in 1966, drew together what Jean-Luc Nancy describes as a loose 'réseau' of innovative thinkers.[19] After Bataille's death, Blanchot, Derrida, Roland

---

17   Jacques Rancière, 'Only in the Form of Rupture', ed. Peter Hallward and Knox Peden, *Concept and Form: Volume 1. Key Texts from the 'Cahiers pour l'Analyse'* (London: Verso, 2012), 262.

18   See *Lignes* 33, 'Avec Dionys Mascolo' (1998).

19   Jean-Luc Nancy, *La Communauté affronté* (Paris: Éditions Galilée, 2006), 25 n. 1.

Barthes, Michel Foucault and Michel Deguy would all participate in the editorial board of *Critique*, and new approaches to literature via anthropology, sociology, psychology, psychoanalysis and philosophy, alongside the radical textual approaches now familiar to us, were developed.[20] Yet it is also crucial not to overstate Bataille and Blanchot's importance to these currents: one should question to what extent they were inspirational rather than directly influential; if they were integral to the systems of thought that developed, or merely the harbingers of a new critical mood and approach. This is a question often not investigated as thoroughly as it should be later on by those wanting to delegitimize French theory via the politics of Bataille and Blanchot, who they consider as so central to the later critical project that any delegitimation of them would bring down the entire card-house of French theory. As this chapter wishes to go on to demonstrate, reading Bataille and Blanchot through the twentieth century certainly highlights their importance as figures, but the way they are mobilized often has more to do with the current political and intellectual climate than with the actual content of their thought.

Tel Quel was of course the other key journal of what Patrick ffrench calls 'The Time of Theory',[21] and was initially quite close to *Critique*, sharing many of the same network of contributors. However, they later came to alienate Derrida, Foucault and Blanchot through their political manipulation of the now-deceased Bataille who, other than in the intense period of the 1930s, had been generally pessimistic regarding positive political action, and instead focused on a personal, sovereign revolt against bourgeois norms.[22] Dionys Mascolo had been the first to try to inscribe Bataille into post-war politics in his 1953 *Le Communisme*, inspired as much by surrealism as by Marx. Against the current Zhadnovian line of the French

---

20   See Patron, *Critique*.

21   ffrench, *The Time of Theory*.

22   See, for example, the letter sent to *La Quinzaine littéraire* by Mascolo and contemporaries in which they complain of the lack of rigour with which Bataille's thought is politically mobilized: 'Il n'est pas tolérable en revanche qu'ils en viennent à réduire ces pensées à jouer un rôle tactique dans les actions polémiques où leur volonté de croissance les entraîne': *Lignes* 33, 193–4.

Communist Party, Mascolo separated art from politics, attesting that both could be revolutionary, but that these two spheres moved at different speeds, and the two struggles were tangentially related. This position is close to the accord between Breton and Trotsky, in which all art was agreed to be emancipatory as it intrinsically liberated expression, even if the content of the work was not itself explicitly political. Even so, seeing himself drawn in to a revolutionary discourse displeased Bataille, who wrote to Mascolo reminding him of 'l'inviabilité' of using his thought in this way; subsequently, whilst he signed some anti-colonial tracts, he resisted a fuller incorporation into Mascolo's political causes, refusing to mix his personal sovereign revolt in the 'boue' of compromise.[23] Paradoxically this was the moment of Blanchot's total 'accord' with Mascolo's politics, which stretched from the anti-Gaullist *revue Le 14 juillet* in 1958 to his participation in the writers 'Comité' in May '68.[24]

Tel Quel initially shared Mascolo's view on the relative autonomy of art and politics, but following May '68 and the Maoist Cultural Revolution they began to have a greater confidence in the power of art to bring about genuinely revolutionary situations. Bataille was privileged as a thinker of transgressions that could be deployed dialectically to subvert the current order and inaugurate a cultural revolution – a position Bataille himself would have fundamentally refused. For a while, terroristically complex and experimental literary and theoretical texts were seen by Philippe Sollers and Julia Kristeva as the intellectual transgressions that could provoke a revolutionary consciousness. Foucault and Blanchot both wrote critiques of attempts to dialecticize cultural transgression into a revolutionary program: as a result, Foucault would henceforth be a silent absence from *Tel Quel*, whereas Blanchot would later be viciously attacked by Sollers as a belated return for his criticisms.[25]

---

23   Georges Bataille, *Choix de lettres, 1917–1962*, ed. Michel Surya (Paris: Gallimard, 1997), 446 and 482.

24   Maurice Blanchot, *Écrits politiques 1958–1993* (Paris: Éditions Lignes & Manifeste, 2003), 10.

25   See Michel Foucault, *Préface à la transgression* (Fécamp: Nouvelles Éditions Lignes, 2012) and, for Blanchot's critique and Soller's reaction, Christophe Halsberghe,

This critical high-point of French thought, in some ways culminating around May '68 but in theoretical preparation long before, would soon come to an end. Sollers quickly lost faith in the revolutionary program, and from the mid-1970s embraced American liberalism, becoming friends with Bernard-Henri Lévy and turning the political *Tel Quel* into the more mystical and self-congratulatory *L'Infini*. Barthes, Foucault, Blanchot and Derrida had all left the *Critique* editorial board by 1978, and the journal would never again be at the cutting edge of French thought. This was the dawn of what Félix Guattari would call 'les années d'hiver'.[26]

Some also read May 1968, alongside the Situationists and textual theory, as the definitive end of the avant-garde era, through theoretical exhaustion and the acceleration of a consumer capitalism now easily able to recuperate subversive gestures back into its economy: in fact, via the proliferation of sub-cultures and self-fashioning, resistance to the norm can itself come to seem the dominant attitude, blunting the tools of aesthetic dissent.[27] This period certainly seems to mark the exhaustion of an erotic vanguardism one can trace from Sade to Bataille, its death perhaps best represented by Pasolini's adaptation of Sade in *Salò*. Pasolini denounced his previous films' positive celebration of sexuality as merely enslaved to a liberal capitalistic idea of enjoyment; the marketization of eroticism and the 1960s sexual revolution had subsequently rendered such mobilizations of transgressive sexuality empty gestures. *Salò* instead portrayed the liberal-capitalist injunction to enjoy as a cold, fascist and repressive compulsion. French critics of the period, such as Barthes and Foucault, responded critically to Pasolini's film, ostensibly because they felt that Sade's work 'n'est pas représentable' cinematically, but perhaps also they

---

La fascination du Commandeur: Le sacré et l'écriture en France à partir du débat-Bataille (Amsterdam: Éditions Rodopi, 2006), 35–9.

26   Félix Guattari, *Les Années d'hiver: 1980–1985* (Paris: Bernard Barrault, 1986), 61.

27   For the prevalence of an attitude of resistance, see Jeffrey T. Nealon, *Foucault Beyond Foucault: Power and its Intensifications Since 1984* (Stanford: Stanford University Press, 2008), 109. On the need to boost consumption via subcultural produce, see, for example, Bernard Stiegler, *Taking Care of Youth and the Generations*, trans. Stephen Barker (Stanford: Stanford University Press, 2010), 131.

felt wounded by the intrinsic critique of their privileging of transgression as *the* most desirable function of aesthetic practice, and vaguely aware that it signalled the end of a specific cultural and intellectual era.[28]

The 1970s: Turning on Marxism and Structuralism

For some, '1977–78 constitue (sans doute plus que 1968) une rupture majeure' in French intellectual life.[29] By over-exposing Solzhenitsyn's *Gulag Archipelago*, translated into French in 1974, a hysterical anti-totalitarian rhetoric was mobilized to discredit the revolutionary, communist and progressive left and purge both the political and intellectual scene of Marxism before the 1978 elections, in which the PCF had looked likely to gain seats.[30] Subsequently, the 1980s were dominated by François Furet and a liberal-conservative group of historians. Pierre Nora formed the influential *revue Le Débat* in 1980 with the stated aim that 'il faut détruire' the current crop of French intellectuals to 'faire sa révolution démocratique'.[31] Alongside these figures, more directly attached to political and bureaucratic elites, the 'new philosophers' rose to a heavily mediatized fame: whilst the likes of André Glucksman, Alain Finkielkraut and Bernard-Henri Lévy 'offered rather simplistic and extraordinarily pessimistic political philosophies, they were enormously successful'.[32] Lastly, whilst Mitterrand did manage to bring the socialists to power in 1981 against the odds, his rapid U-turn to neoliberal policies in 1982–3 left many intellectuals at a quandary, not

---

28   Alain Naze, 'De Silling à Salo: usages pasoliniens de Sade', *Lignes* new series, 14 (2004), 107–17 (108). See also *Lignes* 18 (2005) devoted to Pasolini.
29   Jade Lindgaard and Xavier de La Porte, *Le B.A.–BA du BHL: enquête sur le plus grand intellectuel français* (Paris: Éditions La Découverte, 2004), 23.
30   See Michael Scott Christofferson, *French Intellectuals Against the Left: The Antitotalitarian Moment of the 1970s* (New York: Berghahn Books, 2004).
31   Pierre Nora, quoted in Françoise Proust, 'Débattre ou résister?' *Lignes* 35 (1998), 112.
32   Christofferson, *French Intellectuals against the Left*, 156.

wanting to give the right ammunition by criticizing the PS, but also fundamentally despairing of this new change in policy, and their ambivalence further allowed the new, more conservative intellectual hegemony to settle in. In a few short years, the intellectual heavyweights becoming increasingly famous on American and English campuses were culturally marginalized and politically disorientated in the French *années d'hiver*.

1980s: The Return of Fascism?

This initially hardly concerned the legacies of Bataille and Blanchot directly, but the shifts in the intellectual landscape, marginalizing the French theory generation, provided the terrain for those aggravated by their continued prominence to launch a more frontal assault. Now that Marxism was largely discredited, Nora and Gauchet, editors of *Le Débat*, encouraged Luc Ferry and Alain Renaut to take on Heideggarian anti-humanism, seen as the last obstacle to overturning the legacy of the 1960s generation. Their book, *La Pensée 68*, took on Foucault and Derrida as key targets, calling them obscurantist anti-democrats at prey to a reactionary '*néo*-conservatisme',[33] and when the Heidegger affair broke out in 1987, they renewed their attack. Intellectual fascism was suspected everywhere, and so the spotlight began to be cast on other thinkers in this intellectual lineage who held dubious political commitments in the 1930s, Bataille and Blanchot coming high on the list. Boris Souvarine, for example, argued that if Bataille had really had the courage of his convictions, he would have become an outright fascist.[34] In *Tel Quel* and *L'Infini*, Philippe Sollers 'surexposera, à des fins de meurtre intellectuel, le passé troublé de Blanchot', publishing texts by Jeffrey

---

33   Luc Ferry and Alain Renaut, *Heidegger et les modernes* (Paris: Bernard Grasset, 1988), 229.
34   Marmande, *Le pur bonheur*, 146.

Mehlman and Philippe Mesnard 'à vilipender cet auteur'.[35] Obviously, it is important to discuss the political excesses of Bataille and Blanchot, and serious work in this period was carried out by Leslie Hill, Christophe Bident and the review *Gramma*, amongst others. Blanchot himself, in texts written throughout the 1980s, critically though cryptically engaged with his past involvements and, in a sentence that can only refer to his own ideological conversion, stressed that: 'De l'affaire Dreyfus à Hitler et à Auschwitz, il s'est confirmé que c'est l'antisémitisme (avec le racisme et la xénophobie) qui a révélé le plus fortement l'intellectuel à lui-même'.[36] The more problematic discussions of Blanchot and Bataille were those trying to make intellectual capital out of their past actions – Daniel Lindenberg's book on the years 1937–47, *Les Années souterraines*, ends, for example, with a vague attack on the 'nihilisme' of Roland Barthes and the rest of his postwar generation, attempting to imbricate later, wholly unrelated figures in the fascist scandals of the 1930s.[37]

This coincided with an American academic obsession with French fascism, which had begun via a Benjaminian critique of the historical avant-gardes as perpetrators of aesthetic fascism (notably bringing Bataille into the debate), and was coupled with a more historical, archival investigation into the collaboration of the Vichy regime in the holocaust.[38] This again was largely scholarly and important work, but in America, too, especially after the Heidegger affair, these issues became bound up with an attempt by some in the US Academy to rid their campuses of French theory.[39] Jeffrey Mehlman, for example, starts with an important discussion of Blanchot's intellectual trajectory in the 1930s, then quickly moves on to describe a

35 Halsberghe, *La fascination du Commandeur*, 36.
36 Maurice Blanchot, *Les Intellectuels en question: Ébauche d'une réflexion* (Paris: Fourbis, 1996), 55.
37 Daniel Lindenberg, *Les Années souterraines (1937–1947)* (Paris: La Découverte, 1990), 271.
38 See Michel Lacroix, 'French Fascism: An American Obsession?', *Substance* 31.1 (2002), 56–66.
39 François Cusset, *French Theory: Foucault, Derrida, Deleuze & Cie et les mutations de la vie intellectuelle aux États-Unis* (Paris: La Découverte, 2003), 179 and 196.

'Foucault–Glucksmann "nexus"' in 1977 as also somehow complicit, in spite of the marked differences between Foucault and Glucksmann. Moreover, neither shared much with the pre-war Blanchot: superficial rhetorical similarities are mobilized to imply a hidden fascist tendency within French theory in general.[40] As suggested above, such texts tend to 'overdo' the relationship between post-structuralism and the actual writings produced by Blanchot and Bataille in the 1930s to discredit an entire genealogy:[41] yet even when thinkers such as Jean-Luc Nancy are clearly directly influenced by these texts, their intellectual engagement generally involves a critique of Bataille and Blanchot's political excesses, rather than a wholesale absorption. So whilst Richard Wolin 'sounded an alarm' on hearing that Nancy was revisiting Bataille to develop a new political approach to community,[42] what we actually find in *La Communauté désœuvrée* is 'a sober renunciation of foundationalist attitudes', as far from fascism or Bataille's violent 1930s rhetoric as can be conceived.[43]

It is important to note, then, how often these assaults on French theory have political or intellectual agendas that can distort the historical record. In America the drive against theory was part of a wider rise of neo-conservative figures in the academy attempting to impose a new political hegemony.[44] In France, as noted, it was an assault on the radical left to inaugurate a liberal-conservative normalization of French thought. So when Ferry and Renaut argue that against anti-humanism, the new humanism they proffer 'se signale par le refus d'attribuer à l'homme une essence',[45] a reader with even a minimal awareness of the work of Jean-Luc Nancy, for instance, would recognize the similarity with his explicitly anti-humanist ontology.

40   Jeffrey Mehlman, *Legacies of Anti-Semitism in France* (Minneapolis: University of Minnesota Press, 1983), 18.

41   Lacroix, 'French Fascism', 62.

42   Richard Wolin, *The Seduction of Unreason: The Intellectual Romance with Fascism, from Nietzsche to Postmodernism* (Princeton: Princeton University Press, 2004), 164.

43   Ian James, *The Fragmentary Demand: An Introduction to the Philosophy of Jean-Luc Nancy* (Stanford: Stanford University Press, 2006), 198.

44   For more on this, see Cusset, *French Theory*.

45   Ferry and Renaut, *Heidegger et les Modernes*, 15.

The difference is that Ferry and Renaut want this new humanist man to be a good liberal democrat and not question the established framework of European statehood and the consensual politics proffered by *Le Débat*, whereas Nancy constantly calls into question the very nature of democracy, community and national belonging, a project he began concurrently in the 1980s with *La Communauté désœuvrée* and the 'Centre de recherches philosophiques sur le politique'.

Lignes and Bataille

It was within this intellectual climate that *Lignes* was formed in 1987, and from Marmande's PhD thesis, *Georges Bataille politique* (1985), until the close of the 1990s, they are frequently concerned with what they see as correcting the historical record with regards to Bataille's pre-war politics. Some saw them as overstating the case somewhat. Denis Hollier, whilst largely sympathetic to Surya's *Georges Bataille, la mort à l'œuvre*, sees Surya as over-sensitive to claims that Bataille's use of fascist methods to fight fascism were 'equivocal', which, as we saw above, is an arguable position. As a result, Surya 'goes on the defensive each time he meets (or even anticipates) an accusation', trying too hard to prove that 'nothing was more foreign and even opposed to fascism than the thinking of Bataille'.[46] In conferences in the mid-90s, those associated with *Lignes* still vigorously argued with anyone who too closely associated Bataille with fascism: Christophe Bident, for example, laments that Martin Jay did not amend his comments on Bataille's equivocal past, as Jacqueline Risset had suggested to him.[47] Yet Jay's paper, largely supportive, makes just one reference to Bataille's pre-war projects being 'dangereusement approché de celui des fascistes',

46   Hollier, 'On Equivocation', 4.
47   Christophe Bident, '*Georges Bataille après tout*, sous la direction de Denis Hollier', 200. See *Georges Bataille après tout* (Paris: Belin, 1995), 35–59, for Martin Jay's text.

a defensible point.[48] A prickliness persists, then, which only dissipates at the turn of the century. Furthermore, although Surya initially wished to ensure that *Lignes* remained a relatively open, non-sectarian intellectual space, battle lines became increasingly drawn and, alongside the defence of Bataille, by the end of the 1990s the editors vigorously defend the legacy of post-structuralism, French theory and the 'Collège international de philosophie' against attacks from *Le Débat*.[49]

The Bataille debate in *Lignes* in the 1990s, however, is largely orientated against the Catholic *revue Esprit*. Whilst for *Lignes*, Bataille represents the death of God and a Nietzschean rejection of moralism, they see the attacks on Bataille, especially from *Esprit*, as symptomatic of a 1990s climate dominated by 'retours': returns to humanism, enlightenment values, classicism, but especially moralism, religion and nationalism.[50] In *Esprit*, Oliver Mongin deplores the appearance of books on S&M photography as an immoral attack on public decency; Todorov valorizes art and artists who unite good behaviour with beautiful works, denigrating George Orwell as politically suspect because of his private affairs; and almost the entirety of modern and contemporary art, but especially Duchamp, is attacked for being scatological, overly cerebral and communist, largely because objects do not look like what objects are meant to look like, as in classically mimetic art.[51] These critiques all implicitly impute Bataille, and *Lignes* as 'vieux disciples de Georges Bataille'.[52] The attack on modern art is especially reactionary and, although he is not named, one of their main targets seems to be Georges Didi-Huberman, whose re-reading of modernist aesthetics through Bataille culminated in the publication of *L'Informe*. In *Lignes*, Huberman responds with a withering critique of the

48   Jay, 'Limites de l'expérience-limite: Bataille et Foucault', ibid. 49.
49   See *Lignes* 35 (1998), 102–38.
50   See Michel Surya, 'Demains et la peur', *Lignes* 2 (1988), 203–12, and Jean-Luc Nancy, *L'oubli de la philosophie* (Paris: Éditions Galilée, 1986).
51   See Olivier Mongin, 'L'art de la pudeur', *Esprit* 150 (1989), 28–38, the dossier 'Y a-t-il encore des critères d'appréciation esthétique?', *Esprit* 173 (1991), and Michel Surya, 'Moralisation à marche forcée', *Lignes* 13 (1991), 111–35.
52   Olivier Mongin, 'Poujadisme intellectuel?', *Esprit* 164 (1990), 91–102 (92).

paucity of the *Esprit* attempts at a new art criticism, seeing it as located in 'un débat moral et *moraliste*', based on affective revulsion rather than formal, aesthetic or conceptual appreciation.[53] Elsewhere, Pierre Alferi and Olivier Cadiot also attack Bataille's influence on French poetry to demarcate their own, novel poetic practice; but again, as Surya argues, the main point of contention with Bataille seems to be his fascination with violent imagery rather than with any stylistic or formal concerns, symptomatic of 'la moralisation dominante' governing the political shift towards the right and a return of religious concerns.[54] We observe, then, a reversal from the 1960s obsession with transgression, largely inherited from the surrealist legacy, to the growing annoyance and revulsion towards such immorally subversive aesthetics and theories in the 1990s.

By the turn of the new millennium, however, the Bataille debate becomes much less polemic and, as a result, the two *Lignes* issues devoted to Bataille are more academic than conflictual.[55] This is partly perhaps due to the astonishing shift in French intellectual culture meaning that assaults on Bataille no longer seemed necessary, due to the triumph of his detractors: the cover of the *Nouvel Observateur* (15–21 February 2007) asked whether French intellectuals today intrinsically belong to the right, a stark reversal of Sartre's implied belief that engagement was inherently a left-wing activity. The social movements in 1995 'turned the air red' for a while according to Daniel Bensaïd,[56] and the onset of the financial crisis since 2007 has led to a renewed interest Marxist thought, demonstrated in *Lignes* most clearly by the publication of Alain Badiou's *L'Hypothèse communiste*: yet reading *Lignes* over the past twenty-five years, from their relatively stable position one gets the impression of watching the entire French intellectual terrain drift ever more rightwards, especially over issues of immigration and national identity – commentators such as Alain Finkielkraut, part of

---

53   Georges Didi-Huberman, 'D'un ressentiment en mal d'esthétique', *Lignes* 22 (1994), 21–62.

54   Michel Surya, 'Georges Bataille', *Lignes* 27 (1996), 190–7 (195).

55   See *Lignes* new series, 1 (2000) entitled 'Sartre–Bataille', and 17 (2005) 'Nouvelle lectures de Georges Bataille'.

56   Daniel Bensaïd, *Une Lente impatience* (Paris: Éditions Stock, 2004).

the Maoist left in the 1960s, are now more likely to complain about a perceived anti-white racism and the dissolution of French values than support
an international freedom of movement or embrace cultural difference.

Another reason is that Bataille scholarship has itself has become
more restrained. Jean-Luc Nancy states that 'many critics have hammed it
up despite what was after all Bataille's sobriety',[57] and in the *Lignes* issue
'Nouvelles lectures de Georges Bataille' Nancy is by far the most influential
figure in the responses. Rather than as subversive activity, transgression is
read here as an affirmation of exteriority, of 'being' understood as a shared
and plural site of co-appearing: the boundaries thus transgressed are those
of the self, rather than social norms. This is a wholly ontological, and no
longer moral or political conception of transgression, and the prevalence
of this approach is also symptomatic of the rise of Jean-Luc Nancy over
the last few years, being at present one of the most famous exports of the
French intellectual scene.[58]

Blanchot in *Lignes*

Blanchot occupies a much more ambivalent position in the *revue*: whilst
Bataille's extreme politics in the 1930s can still be somewhat defended for
their explicitly anti-fascist principles, the content of Blanchot's journalism,
especially between 1936 and 1937, remains indefensible for most people.
Lignes was also somewhat split, former editor Daniel Dobbels beings friends
with Blanchot's milieu, whilst Surya is sometimes obviously hostile to
some of Blanchot's work. Of key interest is an article in Surya's new collection, *La Sainteté de Bataille*, in which he laments the fact that Blanchot's

---

57   Jean-Luc Nancy, 'Exscription', trans. Katherine Lydon, *Yale French Studies* 78 (1990),
      47–65 (60).
58   For more on the ontological nature of Nancy's transgression, and its political con-
      sequences, see Martin Crowley's chapter in this volume.

La Communauté inavouable misquotes Bataille on numerous occasions to bring Bataille's 1930s texts more in line with Blanchot's later, Levinasian idiom. Familiar terms from the late Blanchot, but alien to Bataille, such as *l'etre, l'autre, autrui, le proche* and *le prochain* are inserted into citations supposedly drawn from Bataille's *œuvre*. For example, Surya notes that where Bataille wrote 's'il voit son semblable mourir', Blanchot replaces *semblable* with *autrui*, changing the register and meaning of the quotation.[59] As Surya glosses, in the Bataille of the 1930s, sacrificial death is the violent act that draws a restricted, convulsive community together, whereas Blanchot's lexical shift implies that the simple fact of our shared finitude founds a radically open community of ethical responsibility, similar to Derrida's *Politics of Friendship*. Surya polemically argues that *La Communauté inavouable* is part of Blanchot's attempts to repent for his past, and by inscribing Bataille into this more ethical register he is also trying to 'innocenter' his friends' 1930s excesses: this irritates Surya as it implies that Bataille would have something to repent for.[60]

Subsequently, Blanchot gets a much less stringent defence in *Lignes*, especially in the new series (from the year 2000 onwards) when Daniel Dobbels leaves the editorial board, meaning the journal now lacks his key defender (though the presence of Jean-Luc Nancy redresses this balance somewhat). Rather than attempt to justify his pre-war writings, however, what *Lignes* does do is reproduce documents surrounding Robert Antelme, Dionys Mascolo and Blanchot to show the political role Blanchot played in laudable post-war endeavours (including again *Le 14 juillet*, the 'Manifesto of the 121', Blanchot's attempt to found *La Revue internationale* and their public participation in May '68). These are some of the most important issues of *Lignes*' first series, and produce a serious and invaluable archive of this politicized intellectual current which would otherwise disappear.[61] Re-inscribing Blanchot back

---

59 Michel Surya, *Sainteté de Bataille* (Paris: Éditions de l'éclat, 2012), 101.
60 Ibid.
61 See *Lignes* 11 (1990), 21 (1994), and 33 (1998). The Blanchot and Antelme dossiers are published in English as Maurice Blanchot, *Political Writings, 1953–1993*, trans. Zakir Paul (New York: Fordham University Press, 2010), and Daniel Dobbels, ed., *On Robert Antelme's 'The Human Race': Essays and Commentary*, trans. Jeffrey

into public conscience as a participant of these seminal left-wing activities is both a gesture of support and fidelity, and demonstrates how far Blanchot's thought had travelled from his extreme 1930s nationalism.

Yet the *Lignes* collection of Blanchot's political writings, published in 2003, stretches only from 1958–93, leaving *Lignes* open to charges of trying to cover up Blanchot's troubled past: Steven Ungar was even able to comment that Surya was 'presumably unaware' of the existence of the 1930s texts.[62] *Lignes* had, however, tried to produce an issue on Blanchot and the 1930s, largely driven by Jean-Luc Nancy and, before his death, Philippe Lacoue-Labarthe. In 1983, these two attempted to produce an issue of *Cahiers de l'Herne*, but failed due to a lack of participation, and a later planned issue of *Lignes* also stalled as only Nancy, Lacoue-Labarthe and Badiou were willing to contribute.[63] *Les Politiques de Maurice Blanchot, 1930–93* finally appeared as *Lignes* issue 43 in March 2014, perhaps indicating that, as with Bataille, the political stakes surrounding this debate have receded enough to allow Blanchot's friends to fully appraise the stakes of his 1930s engagements in full view, without the necessity of a partisan defence. Whilst nothing in this issue radically challenges the existing portrait of Blanchot, it does highlight omissions in Bident's biography, such as Blanchot's enthusiastic early support for Maréchal Pétain's government in 1940, and subsequently the extent to which he lied to later friends such as Roger Laporte about his war-time allegiances. The articles in this issue present a welcome and uncompromising re-reading of his journalism, presenting these texts as much more explicitly 'fascist' than even before, and highlighting the need to read and think all of Blanchot's writings together.

Haight (Marlboro, VT: Marlboro Press, 2003). That the Mascolo dossier has not been republished and translated may explain the lack of attention he has received from the Anglophone academy, especially as the first series of *Lignes* is out of print. However, a digital archive of *Lignes*' first series is currently being constructed, and will hopefully make Mascolo and the *revue* more widely disseminated and discussed.

62   Steven Ungar, *Scandal and Aftereffect: Blanchot and France Since 1930* (Minneapolis: University of Minnesota Press, 1995), xviii.

63   Jean-Luc Nancy, *Maurice Blanchot, passion politique: lettre-récit de 1984 suivie d'une lettre de Dionys Mascolo* (Paris: Éditions Galilée, 2011), 20.

'Plus on accorde d'importance à la pensée de Heidegger, plus il est nécessaire de chercher à élucider le sens de l'engagement politique de 1933–34.'[64] The same can, then, be said of Blanchot. As Ian James has argued, over the last few years Jean-Luc Nancy's thought is closer to Blanchot's than ever, and it is revealing that he has as a result paid increasing attention to Blanchot's politics in recent years.[65] Yet one thing *Lignes'* dossiers on Blanchot make clear is the debt Nancy's practice of *writing* may owe to Blanchot, and this may be the largest remaining legacy of Blanchot in *Lignes*. They publish a short text called 'Le Nom de Berlin', a Blanchot text destined for his aborted *Revue Internationale* in the mid-1960s. The French original was lost, but there remained an Italian translation, which Nancy translated back into French in 1983, *Lignes* publishing it alongside the recently re-found Blanchot original in October 2000. Writing of Berlin, geographically fragmented after the erection of the Wall, Blanchot uses it as an exemplary case in which the totality of an object can only be apprehended via a fragmentary approach. This prompts further speculation on the nature of fragmentary writing, which:

> n'est pas un retrait sceptique [...] mais une méthode patiente-impatiente, mobile-immobile de recherche, et aussi l'affirmation que le sens, l'intégralité du sens ne saurait être immédiatement en nous et en ce que nous écrivons, mais qu'elle est encore à venir et que, questionnât le sens, nous ne le saisissons que comme devenir et avenir de question.[66]

As sense is a process of creation with an always deferred final signification, it is an infinite process: 'Toute parole de fragment, toute réflexion fragmentaire exigent cela: une réitération et une pluralité infinies'.[67]

Nancy first translated this text in 1983, just as he was rethinking his idea of community in *La Communauté désœuvrée*. He seems to be meditating

---

64 Blanchot, *Les Intellectuels en question*, 11.

65 James, *The Fragmentary Demand*, 227. Alongside publishing the letter from Blanchot to Laporte in *Blanchot, passion politique*, and an interview about Blanchot in *Lignes* 43 (2014), Nancy has recently published *La Communauté désavouée* (Paris: Galilée, 2014), returning once again to themes of community and politics in Blanchot.

66 Maurice Blanchot, 'Le Nom de Berlin', *Lignes* new series 3 (2000), 129–34 (132).

67 Ibid.

on these themes ten years later, roughly contemporaneous with the publication of *Le Sens du monde* (1993). In a text republished by *Lignes*, included in the *Frammenti-Interfacce-Intervalli* catalogue (1992), we can see how his meditation on the fragmentary form came to inflect his entire conception of sense creation. Although he does not reference Blanchot directly, his beginning thesis, differentiating between the fragmentary and the fractal, owes much to 'Berlin' and the dossier on the *Revue internationale*, published in *Lignes* two years previously. In preparatory texts for the *Revue*, Blanchot delineated four different types of fragments: firstly, a partial piece of a broken totality; secondly, a self-contained aphorism; thirdly, as separate steps on a voyage of research; and lastly, a completely fragmentary aesthetic in which, no longer belonging to a conception of thought where totality is possible, the realm of sense necessarily involves 'une discontinuité essentielle'.[68] In this sense, for Blanchot all literature is fragmentary. Whilst not designating these four separate categories explicitly, Nancy likewise describes a fragment as either an aphoristic, self-contained 'petite boule', or part of a dialectical schema where 'le *petit* fait couple avec le *grand*'.[69] He posits in opposition a fractal art which carries out an operation of *frayage*, contesting finalized signification to force a realization that the creation of meaning is an infinite and inter-subjective praxis. Instead of a deliberately fragmentary art, then, Nancy conceives of 'l'art comme fragmentation, et la fragmentation comme présentation de l'être (de l'existence)'.[70] For Nancy, as for Blanchot, all art is fragmentary and participates in a global effort of sense creation which presents and modifies our perception of being in the world. Likewise, although there are political stakes for Nancy's conception of art, as it relates to our global spacing and presentation within a shared world, it is not political on the level of content: art is not 'au service de quelque cause humanitaire ou politique, c'est-à-dire asservi à une signification. Au contraire, il s'agit de l'art témoignant toujours et partout de

---

68   Maurice Blanchot, 'Cours des choses', in *Écrits politiques* 63.
69   Jean-Luc Nancy, 'L'Art, fragment', *Lignes* 18 (1993), 153–73 (155–6).
70   Ibid. 158.

la nudité'.[71] Art effects *the political* in the sense that it organizes how we understand the world and our inter-related co-belonging in the world; it prepares the ground for *politics*, which happens over and above this level of sensory participation, yet within which art and literature have, in reality, little direct effectiveness. In making the direct influence of Blanchot on Nancy traceable through this restored archive, *Lignes* both preserves and furthers this intellectual trajectory, ensuring that despite the assaults against this thinker's legacy, what is important and productive in his *œuvre* survives.

Conclusion

The sketch of the previous eighty years of French intellectual culture given here is obviously partial in many respects: looking at responses to Bataille and Blancot inevitably skews the kinds of work under discussion, and orienting the debate around the position of *Lignes* evidently privileges a marginal, yet important milieu at the expense of others. Yet I hope to have at least suggested the material and theoretical contours of some key shifts in French thought: from the turbulent extremism from both left and right in the 1930s, to Sartrean engagement giving way to more heterodox Marxism in the 1960s, and the subsequent backlash from 1977 onwards, producing a seemingly inexorable drift to the right since; an obsession with transgression, derived from the surrealists and again culminating in the 1960s, shifting to a more moralistic and religious tone at the turn of the millennium; and the varied fortunes of Bataille, Blanchot and French theory which, though marginalized in France from the 1980s, still has some intellectual successors in the likes of Jean-Luc Nancy. *Lignes* maintains a critical yet generally supportive position with regards to 'French theory' in general, making it one of the last in a lineage of important French *revues* nourishing and preserving this philosophical tradition.

71   Ibid. 160.

Selected Bibliography

Bident, Christophe, *Maurice Blanchot, partenaire invisible* (Seyssel: Editions Champ Vallon, 1998).

Blanchot, Maurice, *Les Intellectuels en question: ébauche d'une réflexion* (Paris: Fourbis, 1996).

——, *Écrits politiques 1958–1993* (Paris: Éditions Lignes & Manifeste, 2003).

Christofferson, Michael Scott, *French Intellectuals Against the Left: The Antitotalitarian Moment of the 1970s* (New York: Berghahn Books, 2004).

Cusset, François, *French Theory: Foucault, Derrida, Deleuze & Cie et les mutations de la vie intellectuelle aux États-Unis* (Paris: La Découverte, 2003).

Ferry, Luc, and Alain Renaut, *Heidegger et les modernes* (Paris: Bernard Grasset, 1988).

ffrench, Patrick, *The Time of Theory* (Oxford: Clarendon Press, 1995).

Halsberghe, Christophe, *La fascination du Commandeur: le sacré et l'écriture en France à partir du débat-Bataille* (Amsterdam: Éditions Rodopi, 2006).

Hill, Leslie, *Blanchot: Extreme Contemporary* (London: Routledge, 1997).

Hollier, Dennis, 'On Equivocation (Between Literature and Politics)', trans. Rosalind Kraus, *October* 55 (1990), 3–22.

James, Ian, *The Fragmentary Demand: An Introduction to the Philosophy of Jean-Luc Nancy* (Stanford: Stanford University Press, 2006).

Lignes, first series vols 1–38 (1987–99), second series vols 1–43 (2000–14).

Marmande, Francis, *Georges Bataille politique* (Lyon: Presses universitaires de Lyon, 1985).

——, *Le pur bonheur: Georges Bataille* (Fécamp: Nouvelles Éditions Lignes, 2011).

Mehlman, Jeffrey, *Legacies of Anti-Semitism in France* (Minneapolis: University of Minnesota Press, 1983).

Nancy, Jean-Luc, 'Exscription', trans. Katherine Lydon, *Yale French Studies* 78 (1990), 47–65.

——, *Maurice Blanchot, passion politique: lettre-récit de 1984 suivie d'une lettre de Dionys Mascolo* (Paris: Éditions Galilée, 2011).

Surya, Michel, *Georges Bataille, la mort à l'œuvre* (Paris: Gallimard, 1992).

——, *Sainteté de Bataille* (Paris: Éditions de l'éclat, 2012).

Wolin, Richard, *The Seduction of Unreason: The Intellectual Romance with Fascism, from Nietzsche to Postmodernism* (Princeton: Princeton University Press, 2004).

MARTIN CROWLEY

Existence–Politics/Exposure–Sacrifice

To be human is to be finite. *Res extensa*, matter bounded corporeally in space, of course; but also, crucially, in relation to time. As Sartre observed in 1945, my existence, as a human existence, is defined by my exposure to a three-fold necessity: I am by definition – *for the time being*, perhaps – obliged to be born, to die (to find myself *within* this temporality, *nel mezzo del cammin di nostra vita*), and also to find myself existing amidst a multitude of other finite beings.[1] This may not in itself distinguish the human from other similarly finite beings, of course; for the strain of thought which derives from Heidegger's analysis of fundamental existential structures, however (and despite Heidegger's own vexed anthropocentrism), *exposure to* this finitude, and especially to this temporality, is indeed distinctively human. Even this apparently qualified form of human exceptionalism remains wholly debatable, to be sure; but this will not be my focus here. Rather, I wish to explore the ways in which this thought of human finitude may be connected to an egalitarian politics. For as Jean-Luc Nancy, in particular, has frequently insisted (*pace* Sartre), finitude is not available for appropriation – either as a resource, as the foundation of a project, or as an object for consciousness or the will. Finitude is, in this sense, radically and paradoxically shared: it is what we all, in common, are exposed to and cannot appropriate. This state of affairs presents us with a form of irreducible equality at the level of our existence as such, from which no one shaded by the name of the human is exempt (and doubtless many others besides ...), and which implies a relationship of solidarity with other similarly exposed beings, especially those whose existence is exploited and brutalized in an abusive appropriation of finitude. This, then, will be the

---

1   Jean-Paul Sartre, 'Présentation', *Les Temps modernes* 1 (1945), 3–21 (13).

argument here: that the finitude which defines our existence in common
can help us formulate the demand for an egalitarian politics.[2]

To recap. By the simple fact of my existence, I find myself exposed to
finitude. But this finitude is not mine, does not belong to me: rather, it
distances me from myself, opens a spacing as the very condition of my existence, and exposes me to the world, in the world. Finitude, here, translates
Heidegger's term *Endlichkeit*, and we should understand it not as bounded-
ness or enclosure, but rather – as Jean-Luc Nancy, in particular, has shown
– as exposure in common to an inassimilable limit.[3] The unknowable limit
of death, classically (in which this internal spacing translates primarily a
way of being in time); more broadly, however, the inappropriable fact of
my existence, of my opening onto the world. In this sense, finitude differs
crucially (as Nancy argues, and as Henri Birault notably pointed out) from
what we might call finite-ness, namely the cramped, confined, enfeebled
existence which in part of the Christian legacy, for example, defines the
human creature as inadequate before the majesty of a God by whom this
creature may or may not have been abandoned.[4] Finitude-as-exposure
certainly has its origins in this line of thought, as Birault, indeed, demonstrated. The rethinking of Heidegger by Levinas, Blanchot, Derrida and
Nancy nevertheless operates a decisive break with these origins, by shifting our understanding of the role of the limit: no longer boxed in by the

---

2   This chapter reprises and develops the arguments of my *L'Homme sans: politiques de
     la finitude* (Paris: Lignes, 2009). I would like to thank audiences at King's College
     (Halifax, Nova Scotia), Aberdeen, Nottingham and Cambridge for comments which
     have helped me draft this version, and especially the organizers of the talks in ques-
     tion – Sarah Clift, Christopher Fynsk, Neal Curtis and Christopher Watkin – for
     giving me the opportunity to expand these ideas.

3   This point may be found in various locations throughout Nancy's work. For a particu-
     larly succinct account, see 'Infinie finitude', in his *Le Sens du monde* (Paris: Galilée,
     1993), 51–6. As Frédéric Neyrat writes, drawing on Nancy: 'Il n'y a d'existence qu'avec
     – et c'est ce que signifie finitude. L'existence est finie en ce sens qu'elle est ek-sistence,
     hors d'elle-même, ex-posée': *Surexposés: Le Monde, le Capital, la Terre* (Paris: Lignes
     & Manifestes, 2004), 100.

4   See Henri Birault, 'Heidegger et la pensée de la finitude', *Revue internationale de
     philosophie* 52 (1960), 135–62.

walls of our metaphysical inferiority, we are faced instead with something like an infinitely receding horizon. Thrown, as Heidegger puts it, into an existence not of my making, I am faced by the unavoidable certainty of my death. Anticipation of this death is what makes it possible for me to grasp my existence, in advance, as the space of something like a meaning: as Sartre makes most compellingly clear, anticipated death makes possible my existential project, in what is essentially a temporality of investment. But even in this strongly dialectical version, death is not assimilated as such: it is not an encounter with, still less a crossing of the limit that allows me to leap forward into the future, but rather my understanding of my existence as defined by its exposure to this limit, which I will never experience, which – as Levinas and Blanchot particularly insist – will never form the object of my consciousness or my will.[5] To be finite, in this sense, is to have one's existence defined, happily, as exposure to a constitutive outside which will never be colonized. Exposed to an unattainable limit, then; and those who dislike the language of finitude – to whom I will return below – will find this a typically miserable formula. But what this criticism misses is the point that Nancy has regularly made, namely that this structure can equally well be described as a kind of unboundedness: the limit, as limit, never arrives. Finitude, here, is thought not as deprivation, but as opening to and of the infinite.[6]

5   See for example Emmanuel Levinas, *Le Temps et l'autre* [1948] (Paris: Presses Universitaires de France, 1991), and Maurice Blanchot, *L'Espace littéraire* (Paris: Gallimard, 1955).

6   In addition to 'Infinie finitude', already cited in note 3, above, see for example: 'toute finitude (et tout être *est* fini) est en soi excédante de sa déterminité. Elle est dans le rapport infini': Jean-Luc Nancy, *Hegel: l'inquiétude du négatif* (Paris: Hachette Littératures, 1997), 19; 'L'infini dans le fini. La finitude en tant qu'ouverture à l'infini: rien d'autre n'est en jeu. Il n'y aurait pas ce que nous nommons "finitude" – mortalité, natalité, fortuité – si, du fait même que nous le nommons, nous ne laissions pas transparaître que nous existons et que le monde existe ouvert sur l'infini, par l'infini': Jean-Luc Nancy, *L'Adoration: déconstruction du christianisme, 2* (Paris: Galilée, 2010), 11; 'Car il y a du rapport, il n'y a que ça. [...] Rapport infini que la finitude seule opère': *L'Adoration*, 126.

This understanding of finitude represents to an extent a contemporary avatar of a tradition of thought according to which the human is defined by its constitutive insufficiency (from Plato to Pico della Mirandola to Rousseau and beyond);[7] but an avatar in which the negativity of this insufficiency is replaced, as Nancy strongly insists, by an affirmative sense of exposure. The major difference presented by this understanding of finitude in relation to this tradition, however, is that – as we saw above with reference to its existential version – the openness or indetermination in question is no longer recycled as the motor for some further growth. The constitutive outside to which I am exposed as a condition of my existence remains beyond me; and rather than a lack spurring me on in my project of self-perfection, this exposure can now be affirmed as such – as, precisely, an exposure in common. It does not belong to us, and cannot be made the object of our projects, or our productive activity. But it defines our existence as existence in common. Not held in common: our existence is not our possession, collective or otherwise. But we exist in common, radically equal and in the midst of one another, whether we like it or not.

Finitude becomes political, accordingly, inasmuch as this equality of existence provides a yardstick by which to denounce any concrete inequality. This is true of any understanding of ontological equality, of course. But understanding this equality in terms of finitude allows us to go further than a merely formal, abstract denunciation. For the exposure which defines our relation to finitude is also materially manifest – in travestied form – in the suffering of the exploited, subjected to the exploitation not just of

---

7   See Bernard Stiegler, *La Technique et le temps, I: la faute d'Épiméthée* (Paris: Galilée, 1994) (in which Stiegler analyses Plato's account in the *Protagoras* of the gift of technicity (in the form of fire) to humanity as prosthetic compensation for Epimetheus's failure to endow them with any specific attribute); Pico della Mirandola, *De hominis dignitate* <http://www.brown.edu/Departments/Italian_Studies/pico/index. html> accessed 17 January 2014 (in which this lack of specific determination calls the human creature on to a kind of self-fashioning); and Jean-Jacques Rousseau, *Discours sur l'origine et les fondements de l'inégalité parmi les hommes* [1755], suivi de *La Reine fantastique* (Paris: Aubier-Montaigne, 1973) (in which this becomes the definition of the human in terms of perfectibility). And on this tradition, see Neyrat, *Surexposés*, 97–8.

their labour power, for example, but of their existence as such. (Invited, for example, to rent out their body as a site of medical experimentation.) This exploitation represents the abusive attempt to grasp, to render physically present, and to extract profit from, that existence-as-exposure which by definition is not available to this or any other form of appropriation. This is indeed what defines the injustice of exploitation as such: its attempted appropriation of the ungraspable exposure which defines our existence in common; its attempt, that is, to make the encounter with the limit happen. Within the attack on this existence that we call exploitation, this attempt to colonize our constitutive exposure and to produce it as brutalization or destitution – to *reduce* finitude to finite-ness – is already revealed as injustice.[8] And the constitutive, ungraspable exposure which defines our existence already, by virtue of this definition, aligns us with those whose existence finds itself under attack. We can reject this alignment, of course; but we cannot efface it. And its political articulation is thus in a position to challenge this rejection on its own ground.

It is, moreover, important to appreciate that this revelation of injustice is immanent to the process of exploitation: it is not dependent on any positive ability on the part of the exploited. Not that such ability is ruled out, far from it. But we have seen, and continue to see, forms of exploitation which are characterized by their determination to strip those they attack of any positive attribute, including the capacity to act. At this point, in the face of such undertakings, we have a choice to make. We can agree that the dehumanization they desire to bring about has effectively succeeded, abandon its victims to their subhuman fate, and concentrate our energies on those whose ability to act remains intact. Or we can refuse this nonsensical idea of some kind of sub-humanity – which is ruled out by the fact of our inappropriable existence in common – and confront the exploitation in question with and, where necessary, for those whose existence is under a form of attack which cannot be other than unjust.

8   As Neyrat writes: 'chaque singularité est en excès sur elle-même, et [...] le déni de finitude est ce qui ne laisse pas être cet excès en le réduisant à une quantité exploitable' (113).

This understanding of an immanent demonstration of the injustice of exploitation can be found, for example, in Sartre – for whom the existence of the exploited multitude already represents what he calls 'l'exigence radicale de l'humain dans une société inhumaine';[9] it is most thoroughly and most acutely developed, however, by the French resistant, Communist, and concentration camp survivor, Robert Antelme. In *L'Espèce humaine*, his 1947 memoir of his experiences, Antelme analyses the attempted dehumanization operated by the concentrationary system.[10] The victims of this system are stripped of all the attributes that might be thought to characterize a human being, just as their oppressors desire. Contrary to this desire, however, this subtraction from the human of all its distinctive properties does not in fact open a breach within humanity, by which the truly human might think to separate themselves from the supposedly subhuman: in a defiant reversal, Antelme insists that what is revealed by this erosion is not the sub-human, but rather the exposure to inappropriable finitude which defines the human as such. When the victim dies – and he will – he dies as a human being, not as something else. The oppressor will have failed in his wish to have his victim change species: for, with the irreducible force of the weakest residue, the human – as exposure to a limit which can never be appropriated as such – is inevitably affirmed *in and against* its attempted abolition. The oppressor's attempt to realize the encounter with the limit is bound to fail: existence is not available for appropriation in this way, and it is the denial of this that defines the injustice of the oppressor's project. What Antelme allows us to see is that the end will not come, there is no encounter with the limit; and that the solidarity implied by this unboundedness already indicates a possible force in the struggle against oppression. (Albeit also a problematic one, given the dialectical instrumentalization this may be thought to require: I will return to this below.)

9   Jean-Paul Sartre, *Situations, VII: Problèmes du marxisme, 2* (Paris: Gallimard, 1965), 346.
10   Robert Antelme, *L'Espèce humaine* [1947], édition revue et corrigée [1957] (Paris: Gallimard, Tel, 1995).

A version of this position is better known, of course, as that of Primo Levi, whose *If This Is A Man* was, like Antelme's memoir, also first published in 1947. The difference between them is political: unlike Levi, Antelme draws from his ontological thesis the conclusion that those systems – in his analysis, capitalism and colonialism – which behave as if it is indeed possible to impose divisions on the human race, must be actively resisted. For Antelme, ontological solidarity imposes Communist engagement.[11] This introduces a difficult question, which brings us in many ways to the heart of the matter, namely: the question of collective political subjectivation as this is inflected by the fact of shared finitude. Under what conditions, and by virtue of what actions, does a collective political subject take shape? And how can this process be understood when any collectivity is understood on the basis of exposure to ungraspable existence? In a case such as that described by Antelme, where oppression claims abusively to realize this inappropriable horizon, those whose exploitation is defined by the theft of all positive attributes are at risk – to put it mildly – of finding themselves exiled from any effective political subjectivation, while those who are currently spared any such treatment run the lesser but significant risk of confirming this exile by enjoying their own intact agency even as they oppose this oppression. How, then – beyond the immanent revelation of its evident injustice – is such exploitation to be resisted? To answer this, we need first to consider the signal contribution of recent times to our understanding of this process of subjectivation, namely the work of Jacques Rancière.

For Rancière, politics as such takes place only on those rare occasions (of *mésentente*, as he puts it, of 'dissensus') when a group formerly excluded from the count of effective political subjects asserts its right to be included in this count.[12] Previously, the complaints of such a group had constituted just so much noise – an unreasoning, immediate expression of displeasure,

---

11   For Antelme's formulation of this reasoning, see his 'Pauvre – prolétaire – déporté', in Robert Antelme, *Textes inédits/Sur 'L'Espèce humaine'/Essais et témoignages* (Paris: Gallimard, 1996), 25–32.

12   See Jacques Rancière, *La Mésentente* (Paris: Galilée, 1995), and *Aux bords du politique* (Paris: La Fabrique, 1998).

a background, static hum which those endowed with political agency could safely allow themselves to tune out. Now, however, demonstrating that they are indeed possessed of that reason which qualifies them as eligible for political subjecthood, the members of the group have managed to have this brute *phone* accepted as a form of meaningful *logos*. But how does this happen, and what does our account of this process imply about the possibilities and limits of political subjectivation? Beyond a purely descriptive, indeed circular answer to these questions, which simply defines politics as what happens when such an articulation succeeds – Rancière's implicit position – we need to look again at the relation between inclusion and exclusion, agency and exile.[13]

For all that he does not take this step, Rancière's analysis allows us to see that, just as an inarticulate demand will be effective only when it is taken up by someone whose voice counts, so is this meaningful voice in a position to act as a point of articulation between the political realm and those this realm excludes. In addition to understanding politics as the constitution of effective subjecthood on the basis of an indisputably reasonable voice (as in Rancière's outstanding analyses of the formation of the political names of *women* or *the proletariat*, for example), I would argue that we should also understand – and seek to realize – this process as a perpetual shuttling between inside and outside, included and excluded, reasonable and brutish. I would argue this particularly because contemporary forms of political subjectivation will have little purchase on the exploitation they face, if they are unable to proceed alongside those whose exploitation is defined by their exclusion from articulation. Who find themselves subsequently described as less than human, of course (as scum, perhaps, or a mob, a horde, *racaille*) – but this is hardly a calmly objective description, rather the act of naming is itself part of the oppression in question. In the face of these diverse practices which have as their aim the removal of any voice, the task of the currently effective political subject is perhaps that

13   For an excellent critique of Rancière along these lines, see Christopher Watkin, 'Thinking Equality Today: Badiou, Rancière, Nancy', *French Studies* 67.4 (2013), 522–34.

described best by Blanchot in his account of Antelme's *L'Espèce humaine*: namely, to pick up and to support the demand of the voiceless, to take up and to hold open the possibility of their struggle.[14]

To understand our equality as inscribed already in our existence as such gives us a basis on which to fight with and where necessary for those whose misery is defined by their exclusion from any form of effective symbolization. This exorbitant understanding allows us to refuse the fraudulent division between human and sub-human, and to refuse the repetition of this division in that between political actors and absolute victims. (Between the saved and the drowned, as Primo Levi put it, to recall the former's responsibility to the latter.) Egalitarian political subjecthood is available to all – including those unable to actualize its potential. There is no form of misery which would be somehow beneath politics, just as there is no human existence which would be somehow sub-human. The reduction of human beings to the most extreme forms of destitution reveals not some kind of shameful substance on the basis of which the human might be divided up, but rather our irreducibly common exposure to finitude, thanks to which it becomes both possible and urgent to denounce the production of this destitution as a form of domination. And when this production defines forms of impoverishment newly invented and required as the corollary to new kinds of profit, then a politics of emancipation cannot limit itself to already-existing political actors, but must open itself ever more to those subaltern groups exiled from functioning networks of articulation. Exorbitant and irredentist, impatient of its own limits, such a politics has at least the merit of insinuating itself along those contemporary capillaries in which domination becomes ever more intimate precisely by finding ways to duck under the established radar of symbolization and subjectivation.

14 Blanchot writes: 'il faut que, par l'intermédiaire d'un Sujet extérieur, lequel s'affirme alors comme représentant une structure collective (c'est, par exemple, la conscience de classe), le dépossédé soit non seulement accueilli comme "autrui" dans la justice de la parole, mais remis en situation de lutte dialectique, afin qu'il puisse se considérer à nouveau lui aussi comme une puissance, celle que détient l'homme de besoin et finalement le "prolétaire"': Maurice Blanchot, *L'Entretien infini* (Paris: Gallimard, 1969), 191–200 (197–8).

Against this merit, we need to weigh up the risks of this politics – two, in particular. First: the risk that the definition of the human in terms of finitude locks us into an account of our existence as a form of metaphysical victimhood. Secondly: the risk that any talk of politics and ontology in the same breath will lead to a fascistic political theology. Let me deal with these risks – which are real – in order.

Among those hostile to the definition of human existence in terms of exposure to finitude, whose criticism I have already evoked above, it is argued that this exposure amounts simply to a form of imprisonment.[15] This criticism rests on a – perhaps understandable – refusal to acknowledge the significance of the rethinking of the limit that I sketched above: for its proponents, there is no difference between finite-ness and finitude. For these critics (principally, Rancière and Badiou), the defining openness of this finitude reduces in particular to the miserable Christian vision – in which it does indeed, as we saw above, have its origins – of the human being as a poor, fallen creature exposed to a life of suffering from which only divine salvation offers any escape.[16] Accordingly, since our existence is in this vision by definition one of misery, all politically inflicted suffering comes to appear as a kind of metaphysical destiny, against which there is nothing to be done, and in relation to which our only forms of action are prayer and charity.

There is something to be said for this criticism: in particular, it produces an incisive and merited denunciation of the role of humanitarianism

15   As Badiou expresses it: 'Je ne crois pas enfin que l'injonction est celle de la fin, du fini et de la finitude. Ma conviction est que c'est l'infini qui fait défaut. Et je proposerais volontiers de déposer, au seuil du millénaire, tout usage des mots "fin", "fini" et "finitude". [...] Disons, proclamons: ce avec quoi il est pressant de rompre, ce avec quoi il faut en finir, c'est la finitude. Dans le motif de la finitude se concentrent le reniement de l'émancipation, le règne mortifère du pur présent, l'absence des peuples à eux-mêmes et l'éradication des vérités'. ('L'Offrande réservée', in Francis Guibal and Jean-Clet Martin, eds, *Sens en tous sens: Autour des travaux de Jean-Luc Nancy* (Paris: Galilée, 2004), 13–24 (15))

16   See for example Alain Badiou, *L'Éthique: Essai sur la conscience du mal* [1993] (Caen: Nous, 2005) and *Le Siècle* (Paris: Seuil, 2005), and Rancière, *La Mésentente, Aux bords du politique*, and 'Who Is the Subject of the Rights of Man?', *South Atlantic Quarterly* 103.2/3 (2004), 297–310.

as an alibi for the perpetuation of globalized economic exploitation – in which every disaster, from hurricane to famine to massacre, is cast as a natural disaster, the response to which can at best be palliative. But the criticism has it back to front, to my mind, when it argues that it is the definition of human existence in terms of finitude that produces this knowing depoliticization – that if we define human beings as suffering animals, then this is how they will be treated.[17] Attempted dehumanization proceeds not on the assumption of our universally miserable condition, but rather as a campaign to fabricate a supposed sub-humanity, which it can then claim to have revealed, elevating itself in return to the status of the truly, exclusively human. The refusal to define human existence in terms of exposure to finitude, on the grounds that this collapses all political agency into metaphysical victimhood, ends up accepting the terms offered by the oppressor: namely, that mute suffering makes no political claim. This is not a position we should embrace: for it locks in the distinction between fully human, effective political subjects on the one hand, and brute victims on the other. The irreducible equality declared by our existence in common as exposure to finitude rejects any such separation, and insists that in every form of exploitation, a political demand is already immanent: every victim is already a potential political subject. The task is to see whether or not any given instance of victimization can be articulated as a demand for political subjectivation: to seek to traverse the boundary between speech and silence, to relay such potential articulation. In this sense, the definition of our existence in terms of finitude functions precisely, if exorbitantly, as the kind of political speech act analysed by Rancière and embraced by Badiou: it makes an egalitarian claim which must then be tested in particular cases. The term 'human being' is indeed – as Rancière points out (*La Mésentente*, 172) – invariably used to block any such procedures of verification at source, confusing determinate forms of injustice with a generalized pit of misfortune.[18] The insistence on opening the political arena ever more to the victims of extreme destitution does of course risk this

---

17   See Badiou, *L'Éthique*, 28.
18   See *La Mésentente*, 172, and, in particular, 'Who Is the Subject of the Rights of Man?'.

kind of metaphysical slippage: the persistence of the misery of finite-ness as the shadow of finitude is of the order not of an indiscriminate destiny, however, but rather of a political possibility. Destitution is already a form of injustice not because we are all suffering creatures: in this case, it would indeed be nothing more than a destiny. On the contrary: the oppressor's pretense that destitution is merely the materialization of our miserable, all-too human lot can be challenged by the equality to which every existence lays its immanent claim. The destitute are potential political subjects not because we are all doomed to misery, but because their current condition constitutes the abusive attempt to *reduce* the finitude which is our true equality to the finite-ness in which this equality finds its ideological travesty.[19] This indicates precisely that, rather than accept the falsely neutralizing terms we are offered (in this case, for example, 'the human'), these terms need to be tested. And in this case, the definition of human existence from finitude gives us exactly the weapon we need: namely, a political articulation of this term, thanks to which the ideological function of its humanitarian phrasing – to mask the gap between existential equality and concrete equality – becomes apparent with especial clarity.

The claim may still be made, however, that such an approach operates something like a sacrifice of existence. As Nancy has argued, existence as such is unsacrificeable;[20] as Antelme demonstrates, if particular beings can be sacrificed, their existence nevertheless remains beyond the economy seeking to convert it into profit. Ironically then, the elaboration of a politics of finitude on the basis of ontological equality risks sacrificing – by instrumentalizing it as political motor – the existence it wants to affirm as beyond any economy of exploitation. This brings us, in fact, to the second criticism I mentioned above of any such politics of finitude: namely, that the link it proposes between existence and politics risks reducing to the fascistic exploitation of ontology. As Nancy shows in *La Communauté*

---

19   As Neyrat writes: '*Le sans fin du Capital masque le sans fin de l'être fini* – sa violence sature la nudité de l'être-au-monde' (107).
20   Jean-Luc Nancy, 'L'Insacrifiable', in Nancy, *Une Pensée finie* (Paris: Galilée, 1990), 65–106.

désœuvrée, the work of fascism is precisely to make death the work of the community, to consolidate the community on the basis of its assumption of death as its task.[21] (Not for nothing is the defining imagery of fascism that of the death's head, its defining slogan 'Viva la muerte!') Hence Antelme's insight that the doomed project of the Nazi oppressor is to *make present* (in space and in time) the inappropriable encounter with the limit. This fascistic appropriation of death as communal project, with its sacrifical elision of the opening – both spatial and temporal – of finitude, stands as emblematic of any attempt to develop a politics on the basis of an ontological proposition. It is not for politics to take up Being as its object. The insistence that no existence should be excluded from possible political subjectivation reads, from this perspective, like a totalitarian declaration seeking to incorporate all existence into a political project, without remainder. This has been the direction of Nancy's most recent interventions, in which he has repeatedly cautioned against the risks of over-extending the purview of politics, of over-emphasizing its ability to colonize existence, indeed of producing just such a colonization by seeking or agreeing to base political struggle on this existential ground.[22]

But we should be careful here. To argue that every existence, as such, already stakes an immanent claim to equality, is not to dictate that every existence must be politically articulated, nor that any such articulation must entail the wholesale political appropriation of existence, without remainder. Granted, it is to refuse any definitive separation between every existence, as such, and the realm of the political. But this does not have to be understood as incorporation: rather, it might be thought of as the maintenance of an open channel, through which a demand may – or, equally, may not – be heard. For there is no existence which is not already touched by the logic of sacrifice: as Blanchot's arguments in 'La Littérature et le droit à la mort' make clear (and, *mutatis mutandis*, Derrida's in 'Violence

---

21 Jean-Luc Nancy, *La Communauté désœuvrée*, nouvelle édition revue et augmentée (Paris: Christian Bourgois, Détroits, 1999).

22 See, for example, Jean-Luc Nancy, *Vérité de la démocratie* (Paris: Galilée, 2008) and, especially, Jean-Luc Nancy, *Politique et au-delà: entretien avec Philip Armstrong et Jason E. Smith* (Paris: Galilée, 2011).

et métaphysique'), as soon as I speak the words, 'any existence ...', sacrifice is minimally at work.[23] We are not at liberty to keep our hands clean of any degree of sacrificial relation to existence (unless we can manage somehow neither to act nor to enter into any form of symbolization). The fact that the encounter with the limit never arrives, that existence is never appropriated within a determinate project, does not mean that existence as such is not caught up in the business of appropriation, grasped after and minimally snagged by sacrificial gestures. That politics configured as the production or manifestation of a cause or a definitive truth is by definition maximally sacrificial, as Nancy has argued, need not imply that to posit *any* relation between politics and existence is to engage in this economy.[24] To the extent that sacrifice is always minimally at work within any form of symbolization, the structure before us is not a monochrome either/or, but rather a spectrum, from minimum to maximum. Maximally sacrificial gestures seeking to appropriate existence are, as we have seen, bound to fail; but to affirm this is already to have politicized existence, and so to have appropriated it to some extent, in the name of the refusal of appropriation. The assertion of the excess of existence over politics celebrates this excess effectively to the precise extent that it proposes its own politics of existence, a minimal politics of leaving-be. This is tangled, but inevitably so. And entanglement is not appropriation: minimal sacrifice (symbolization, figuration, configuration) understands the spatio-temporal gap of finitude as *drawn towards* the present precisely in order to refuse all attempts to *make it present*. (And if this 'in order to' engages the idiom of

---

23   See Maurice Blanchot, *La Part du feu* (Paris: Gallimard, 1949), 291–331 (esp. 312–13), and Jacques Derrida, *L'Écriture et la différence* [1967] (Paris: Seuil, Points, 1979), 117–228 (esp. 219).

24   Nancy writes: 'Il faudrait retracer l'histoire impressionnante du sacrifice politique, de la politique sacrificielle – ou de la politique *en vérité*, c'est-à-dire du "théologico-politique": depuis le sacrifice expressément religieux jusqu'aux diverses Terreurs, et à tous les sacrifices nationaux, militants, partisans. Politique de la *Cause* à laquelle le sacrifice est dû. En cela, tout le théologico-politique, jusque dans sa "sécularisation", est et ne peut être que sacrificiel. Et le sacrifice représente l'accès à la vérité, dans la négation appropriatrice de la négativité *finie* du sens' (*Le Sens du monde*, 141).

dialectical instrumentalization, it understands that we cannot do other-wise: the choice is not whether we enter this economy, but rather how we inhabit it. Abusively, grasping the gap of exposure as a means to an end; or *endlessly*, in and against this instrumentalization, in affirmation of the finitude that is our relation to this gap?)

That the transition from ontological 'is' to political 'ought' is fraught with the considerable danger of maximal sacrifice, should not distract us from the frequency with which it is in fact undertaken, including by those whose work leads us to be most nervous of this articulation. Just to be clear: I am not arguing that we can read off specific political imperatives from ontological description.[25] My claim is rather that such descriptions invite argument as to what these imperatives might be. As I have put this here, ontological description might perhaps *imply* political assertion: might be claimed to press in a particular direction (as I have argued), without this claim either issuing directly from this description, or indeed somehow escaping the arena of debate and contestation. As Sartre puts it towards the end of *L'Être et le néant*: if it is plainly impossible to derive 'ought' from 'is', it is no less plainly the case that any 'is' invites the question of whether the prescriptions we formulate will, in Sartre's phrase, take their responsibilities seriously in the face of its description.[26]

We are not, I believe, in a position to avoid moving between 'is' and 'ought': we do this all the time. The question is not whether we can avoid any kind of sacrificial relation to existence. The question is, rather, whether we can maintain this sacrifice as minimal. In order to defend existence from the exploitation to which it is subjected – that is to say, from its maximal sacrifice – we may have to engage in something like an attenuated form of that sacrificial economy with which we are in any case already bound up. If this is rightly unappealing, the alternative might not be much more

---

25   As is in fact implied by some formulations in my *L'Homme sans*, which I have accord-ingly sort to adjust here. These formulations are well criticized by Christopher Watkin, in his *Difficult Atheism: Post-Theological Thinking in Alain Badiou, Jean-Luc Nancy and Quentin Meillassoux* (Edinburgh: Edinburgh University Press, 2011), 182–3.

26   Jean-Paul Sartre, *L'Être et le néant: essai d'ontologie phénoménologique* [1943] (Paris: Gallimard, Tel, 2001), 673–4.

attractive: a strongly sacrificial – and, let us note, by definition unopposable – economic appropriation of existence on the one hand; on the other, those happy islands of respite this appropriation is prepared to grant. Some degree of articulation is necessary, if we are to refuse the major articulation that is the exploitation of existence. As Nancy writes in *Le Sens du monde*, politics must deal in figures, figuration, configuration – and some tarrying with these is essential if we wish to oppose its enthusiastically sacrificial forms.[27] By contrast, the blanket refusal of any political articulation of existence sees in this move only a crude instrumentalization, ungraspable exposure dialectically recycled as the motor of a political project. This view depends, however, upon an *a priori* separation of the existential and the political, with the former possessing a kind of originary integrity upon which the latter belatedly and illegitimately supervenes. A politics of finitude, on the other hand, refuses any such simple exteriority of politics to existence, understanding the two as entangled, at once mutually irreducible and mutually exposed. To place existence *before* politics is already to describe a relation: existence and politics are *originarily* exposed each to the other.[28] Given this, and given the inevitability (and, as I have argued, desirability) of some degree of articulation between the two, I would advocate what, in the spirit of Benjamin, we might think of as a minimal dialectical hope, or a good, minimal politicization of existence, precisely in order to oppose the maximal politicization of this existence in the form of exploitation.

The forms of domination which characterize our contemporary world are targeting our existence as such, seeking to colonize and capitalize on this existence as such, to infiltrate it with ever more intimate forms of exploitation, not least by sacrificially eliding the spacing that is our common exposure to the world. (Exposure *to* the world nowhere other than *in* the world: immanence as spaced, not as tautology or general equivalence.) This is why we cannot simply decide to emphasize the fact that existence will always exceed its attempted political appropriation: while this is certainly

27   *Le Sens du monde*, 188.
28   I argue this more fully in 'Being Beyond Politics, with Jean-Luc Nancy', *Qui Parle* 22.2 (2014), 122–45.

true, it leaves us unable to oppose this appropriation on its own ground. Against these developments, the position I have defended here asks us to accept the minimal sacrifice at work whenever we engage in the specifically political affirmation of existence, precisely in order to celebrate this existence as properly ungraspable. The desire to police and to extract profit from even the matter of this existence is by definition a form of abuse; the equality declared by our common exposure is immediately and irreducibly opposed to this attempted exploitation. This cannot be argued anywhere other than the political arena: as a consequence, we are obliged to accept both the minimal politicization of existence, and the exorbitant opening of this arena beyond its reasonable current limits. For Deleuze and Guattari, what we need is to invent forms of resistance to the present.[29] At present, it is our existence as such that is under attack. It is on this terrain, accordingly, that we have to invent part of our struggle.

Selected Bibliography

Antelme, Robert, *L'Espèce humaine* [1947], édition revue et corrigée [1957] (Paris: Gallimard, Tel, 1995).

———, *Textes inédits/Sur 'L'Espèce humaine'/Essais et témoignages* (Paris: Gallimard, 1996).

Badiou, Alain, *L'Éthique: essai sur la conscience du mal* [1993] (Caen: Nous, 2005).

———, *Le Siècle* (Paris: Seuil, 2005).

Blanchot, Maurice, *L'Espace littéraire* (Paris: Gallimard, 1955).

———, *L'Entretien infini* (Paris: Gallimard, 1969).

Crowley, Martin, *L'Homme sans: politiques de la finitude* (Paris: Lignes, 2009).

Levinas, Emmanuel, *Le Temps et l'autre* [1948] (Paris: Presses Universitaires de France, 1991).

Nancy, Jean-Luc, *Le Sens du monde* (Paris: Galilée, 1993).

---

29 Gilles Deleuze and Félix Guattari, *Qu'est-ce que la philosophie?* [1991] (Paris: Minuit, Reprises, 2008), 104.

——, *Hegel: l'inquiétude du négatif* (Paris: Hachette Littératures, 1997).

——, *La Communauté désœuvrée*, nouvelle édition revue et augmentée (Paris: Christian Bourgois, Détroits, 1999).

——, *Vérité de la démocratie* (Paris: Galilée, 2008).

——, *L'Adoration: déconstruction du christianisme, 2* (Paris: Galilée, 2010).

——, *Politique et au-delà: entretien avec Philip Armstrong et Jason E. Smith* (Paris: Galilée, 2011).

Rancière, Jacques, *La Mésentente* (Paris: Galilée, 1995).

——, *Aux bords du politique* (Paris: La Fabrique, 1998).

Sartre, Jean-Paul, *L'Être et le néant: essai d'ontologie phénoménologique* [1943] (Paris: Gallimard, Tel, 2001).

——, 'Présentation', *Les Temps modernes* 1 (1945), 3–21 (13).

——, *Situations, VII: problèmes du marxisme, 2* (Paris: Gallimard, 1965).

Stiegler, Bernard, *La Technique et le temps, I: la faute d'Épiméthée* (Paris: Galilée, 1994).

Watkin, Christopher, *Difficult Atheism: Post-Theological Thinking in Alain Badiou, Jean-Luc Nancy and Quentin Meillassoux* (Edinburgh: Edinburgh University Press, 2011).

PART 3

Abject Matter

JESSICA STACEY

Doing Time: Bastille Martyrs/Modern Saints

Although most native English speakers will be familiar with the colloquial meaning of the phrase 'doing time', when looked at critically, it presents a puzzle. A metaphor for serving a prison sentence, itself a metaphorical formulation, the phrase seems to evoke a kind of agency which, according to a basic conception of temporality as chronological – the sequence of events following on from each other – we do not have. Time might be considered as something which just happens; the most we can do is fill time, waste it, make the most of what's given to us, if we are lucky. As Penelope Corfield quips, we might talk about killing time, but 'so far no one has managed to strike a fatal blow'.[1] In prison, this lack of agency is yet more pronounced, and if we are going to use this strange formulation, 'doing time', it might seem more logical to say that, as time is something taken out of the prisoner's control, it is actually something done *to* the prisoner. In this article, I ask in what sense time can be something that the prisoner does, and how complete such an attempt to salvage agency from a situation expressly designed to disempower the subject can be. Two eighteenth-century prisoners of the Bastille provide the textual matter, their prison writings offering a non-chronological engagement with incarceration as a way to cope with, and perhaps master, the linear imposition of an indefinite sentence.

The Marquis de Sade wrote his *Les 120 journées de Sodome* circa 1785 whilst imprisoned in the Bastille, though the text was lost and did not come to light until the mid-twentieth century. Henri Masers de Latude, who was imprisoned in various Parisian fortresses from 1749 to 1784,

---

1   Penelope J. Corfield, *Time and the Shape of History* (New Haven and London: Yale University Press, 2007), xv.

published several versions of his memoirs between 1787 and 1791 (based
on earlier writings produced in situ, if we are to believe his account of his
time there), versions which increased in length and popularity, rendering
him a veritable celebrity, first of the aristocratic *salon* scene and later of
the Revolution. The two authors have enjoyed almost opposite trajectories: Latude, now practically unknown, was an exceptionally famous
figure from the first release of his memoirs right through the nineteenth
century, on the basis of his pathetic tale of unjust imprisonment and
dramatic escape from the Bastille. His memoir, dubbed 'sublime' by the
Mercure de France and suggested as required reading for all children, was
celebrated until a series of works began to attack the authenticity of his
story to the point that he is now utterly discredited, whilst Sade's works,
banned throughout the nineteenth century, were little read until the
twentieth – however, their status as a subject for literary criticism is no
longer in any doubt.[2] In spite of these differences in reception, the two
authors are united not just by their time in Bastille, but in that they are
two writers who transformed that passive time *embastillé* into the active
time of writing, and in so doing transformed themselves into Bastille
martyrs: saints of liberty and modernity. This transformation, I argue,
rests on the mythologization of three material objects: the prison, the
body, and the book.

2   For the *Mercure de France* quotation, see Claude Quétel, *Escape from the Bastille:
     The Life and Legend of Latude* (Cambridge: Polity Press, 2002), 155. The reassess-
     ment of Latude's story began with F. Funck-Brentano who, in the 1880s, accused
     the long-dead hero of having been a fraud and confidence trickster. Wikipedia now
     files him under 'con-artists by century'. Latude presented accusations of madness
     as a major factor in his persecution, which would lead him to be wrongly interred
     in a mental asylum for a time – Claude Quétel, Latude's most recent critic, posits
     that Latude was in fact suffering from insanity and that he thus wrote an exag-
     gerated account of his persecution which was not, however, entirely deliberate
     falsehood.

Figure 1:
Man Ray, Imaginary Portrait of the Marquis de Sade, 1938. Reproduced with permission from the Design and Artists Copyright Society.

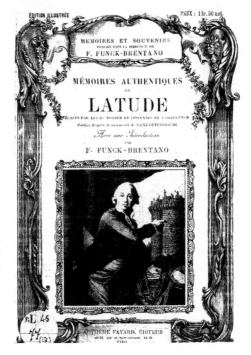

Figure 2:
This image of Latude, shown here as part of the frontispiece to a nineteenth-century edition, was created in 1791.

There exists a portrait of each author which shows an important moment on their road to their own brand of sanctity. Man Ray's 1938 portrait of Sade – imaginary, as we have only one contemporary image of the Marquis, young and in profile – has enjoyed the same success as its subject, eventually gracing the cover of Lacan's *Seminar VII*. It depicts the Bastille in flames overlooked by a triumphant bust of Sade (see Figure 1). The second image, which is no longer well-known, is the frontispiece for the 1791 version of the *Mémoirs de Henri Masers de Latude, Prisonnier pendant trente-cinq années à la Bastille et à Vincennes*, which is the version of Latude's memoirs which I shall be using for this discussion (from an identical 1793 printing). In this portrait, Latude stands in the window of a seemingly ruined building, gesturing to the Bastille in the early stages of its demolition and leaning on the rope ladder he used to escape, which he famously wove from undershirts (see Figure 2). As my purpose here is to establish what of the hagiographical might be at work in their respective trajectories, I point the reader towards a tactic shared with those medieval and early modern images of saints which depict them alongside their attributes; St Catherine of Alexandria, for example, is often shown resting a hand on her wheel in a gesture similar to that of Latude, denoting an essential component of her sainthood, but one subdued and overcome, no longer an instrument of terror.

Although both Sade and Latude were imprisoned in several locations, both were primarily associated with the Bastille, which was itself (by virtue of its fall on 14 July 1789) a symbol of the transition from despotism to liberty, the most powerful narrative of the early years of the Revolution. The reasons for Sade's imprisonment are well known – he stood accused of abusing prostitutes, poisoning one woman in what he claimed was an attempt to administer an aphrodisiac, and sodomy. The reason for Latude's incarceration is yet more ignoble; a nonentity arriving penniless to Paris from the army, he concocts a fake plot against Madame de Pompadour involving a poisoned package. He posts a parcel containing a harmless white powder, then warns the King's mistress, hoping to create a debt which might allow him to enter court. Witnesses are found, however, who saw Latude himself posting the 'poison', and he is thrown in prison (even though the authorities have tested the powder and found it to be harmless). Latude does not attempt to deny what happened, but he pleads youthful folly and focuses instead on the injustice of the length of his incarceration and the glory of his dramatic escapes.

The physical layout of the prison plays an important role in structuring both texts. There is, by this point, a tradition of describing the layout and organization of the Bastille to emphasize the way in which the monotony of prison life and the sense of being constantly watched contribute to the despair of imprisonment.[3] Annie Le Brun has noted that the extensive literature describing the plan and routine of the Bastille serves to construct a paradoxically dark, frightening, mysterious setting from what was in fact one of the most explored and formulaic spaces in eighteenth-century literature.[4] By locating the prisoner in a bureaucratic system as impenetrable as the prison itself and which limits his access to those with decision-making power, the prisoner comes to feel that the prison itself is the tyrant. Latude is unable to access any information regarding the intended length of his sentence, so time becomes a circular, unending routine, with the threat of the *cachot* (the underground cell where one is denied even the unsatisfactory temporal experience offered by normal Bastille life) lurking for bad behaviour. Sade's chateau Silling in *120 journées* follows all of these conventions; the geometry of the prison lends itself to the narrative, which is structured by the daily recitation of an Encyclopaedia of Passions, after which the libertines act out the passions described on a group of imprisoned victims, who know not the fatal end to which these gradually intensifying passions tend. That the chateau Silling should be reminiscent of the Bastille as described both in Latude's memoirs and in the detailed description given in du Perray's excursus on the prison fortress comes as no surprise, for Sade wrote the manuscript of *120 journées* whilst imprisoned there. The 'fosseé plein d'eau et très profonde', the interior courtyard with dormitories/prison cells around and, above all, the 'trois cent marches descend[ant] aux entrailles de la terre dans une espèce de cachot voûté, fermé par trois portes de fer', recall the

---

3   See as an example Brossais du Perray. *Remarques historiques et anecdotes sur le Chateau de la Bastille* (Paris, 1774).

4   Annie Le Brun, *Les châteaux de la subversion* (Paris: J.J. Pauvert, 1982), 58.

layout of the Bastille and the pre-eminent position occupied by terror of the *cachot* in the minds of prisoners such as Latude.[5]

Beyond what it lends to Sade's textual structuration, the material substance of the Bastille also plays an important role in the sanctification of the 'Bastille martyrs', which becomes a popular phrase after July 1789. The pamphlet *La Bastille au Diable* is happy to apply the term to those who have not actually expired there, including Latude, for reasons which will become clear when this discussion turns to the martyr's body. The pamphlet counsels its readers that 'Il faut lire dans le mémoire de M. de la Tude tous les détails qui concernent cette infâme prison, si l'on veut se faire une idée des souffrances que tant de généreux martyrs de la raison & de l'humanité ont dévorées dans cet épouvantable cloaque de la stupidité ministérielle'.[6] Stones from the Bastille inscribed with details of its fall and medals made from its chains are dubbed 'reliques patriotiques' by their disseminator, the self-titled Patriot Palloy, and evoked as community-binding in much the same way as in catholic devotional practices: for Lüsebrink and Reichardt, such relics are necessary to ensure 'in the long term [...] the unity of the newly born French nation regenerated from centuries of slavery and despotism'.[7] Patriot Palloy sends these relics about the country with helpers whom he called 'Apostles of Freedom', often with copies of Latude's memoirs accompanying them. Latude himself embraces this lexicon of sanctity. The rope ladder he used to escape the Bastille, and upon which he rests his hand in the frontispiece to his memoir, receives what must be considered pilgrims, and he says of a crude flute, which he fashioned during several months of confinement in a *cachot*: 'J'aurai soin, qu'après avoir servi à embellir les derniers jours de mon existence, il soit déposé à ma mort entre les mains d'un *apôtre de la liberté*, pour que, placé, à la suite, dans un de ses *temples*, il puisse avec tant d'autres *monuments du despotisme*, en retracer les attentats'.[8]

5   Marquis de Sade, *Les 120 journées de Sodome* (Paris: J.J. Pauvert, 1972), 75.

6   *La Bastille au Diable* (Paris: Chez Laurens, 1790), 36.

7   Hans-Jürgen Lüsebrink and Rolf Reichardt, *The Bastille: A History of a Symbol of Despotism and Freedom* (Durham, NC: Duke University Press, 1997), 120–1.

8   Henri Masers de Latude and citoyen Thiery, *Mémoirs de Henri Masers de Latude, ancien ingénieur, Prisonnier pendant trente-cinq années à la Bastille et à Vincennes,*

The legend of the fall of the Bastille needs this quasi-religious, myth-making brand of support; Palloy and Latude are thus involved in re-writing the past to control the future. A key component of the myth was the liberation of poor innocents, but the only prisoners liberated were a handful of counterfeiters (Sade having been moved just a few days earlier). As for any carefully executed 'assault on despotism', it is now well-known that the storming began as a disorganized march to demand gunpowder. The fate of the governor, tortured and torn to shreds by an angry mob, is judged by Lüsebrink and Reichardt as, in a time in which torture was forbidden in the Bastille and had been influentially condemned as barbaric by Voltaire, an archaism[9] – but this disturbing 'archaic' violence would prove central to the future-focused Revolution, with its many instances of mob justice. The 'real' Bastille, and the events surrounding its fall, would seem to be insufficient to the narrative of liberation which was to be built upon it, and the re-working and expansion of Latude's memoirs thus benefits both revolutionaries and Latude himself. Latude's narrative supports the mythicization of the storming of the Bastille, the transformation of its brute materiality into symbol and relic, by offering up his bodily degradation. He gains, by this collaboration, a similar transformation, which sanctifies his body and allows him to be read as a martyr.

Latude plays on the torture topos, found in many hagiographies as the suffering which the saint has to overcome to achieve union with God. The transformation of this experience relies on a particular, non-chronological temporality, of which Latude partakes. According to the temporality of martyrdom, one's empirical evidence of suffering is overridden by the prospect of salvation. Suffering takes on a religious significance, which relies on a narrative exterior to the realm of experience – in the Christian tradition, that is the narrative of Christ's birth and death as given in the Bible, with the extrapolated narrative of the creation, Fall, and the punishment

---

sous le nom de Daury; à Charenton sous celui de Danger; et à Bicêtre sous celui de Jedor, Vol. I [2 vols] (Paris: Latude, 1793), 90, my emphasis. Further references to this edition will be given in brackets in the text.

9   Lüsebrink and Reichardt, *The Bastille*, 45.

or reward meted out in an afterlife. In hagiography, salvation is bestowed after the death of the saint, but thenceforth understood to have *always been* the *telos* or final cause of the events leading to it, a teleological temporality superseding a chronological one. Lacan's metaphor for the retroactive fixing of signification, the *point de capiton* which is the last element applied to upholstery and serves to fix layers of material at a particular point, is pertinent to this kind of narrative. The crucial points here are that, firstly, pain or imprisonment signifies to the martyr the *opposite* of what is signifies to whichever tyrannical figure perpetrates it: the latter sees it as a punishment, but the former knows it to be a test leading to heavenly bliss. The tyrant, who has no access to the framing narrative, makes the mistake of seeing a particular instance of torture as an event along the chronology of his rule, whilst the saint knows that God's time supersedes the time of earthly power. Secondly, the fate of the martyr pre-figures the passage of society into a new world and a new temporality, which shows the 'old time' or the 'ancien régime' to have *always been* illusory. Emma Campbell applies Agamben's theory of threshold and community to hagiography to say that hagiography must create the 'experience of being-*within* an *outside*'.[10] Latude is aware that the best tactic to ensure his continued relevance – necessary to his very survival, for he lives on hand-outs from sympathetic well-wishers – is to position his own story of imprisonment and escape as prefiguring the storming of the Bastille and the birth of the French people into freedom. He does so in the very first sentence of his reworked memoir:

> La France, souillée pendant tant de siècles par la foiblesse de ses rois et le despotisme insolent de leurs ministres, vient enfin de secouer les chaînes sous le poids desquelles elle avoit été si long-temps accablée, et dont on croyait qu'elle avoit la bassesse de ne savoir plus rougir [...] Nous bénissons tous les jours, à jamais heureux, où nous avons vu ces indignes murailles s'écrouler au premier cri de la liberté. (vol. i, 1–2)

Returning to the fall of the Bastille at the close of the first volume, he makes clear that a new world, a new kind of time, was inaugurated on

---

10   Emma Campbell, *Medieval Saints' Lives: The Gift, Kinship and Community in Old French Hagiography* (Cambridge: Gallica, 2008), 221.

14 July 1789: 'elancés sur un autre horizon, un seul jour nous a transportés dans de nouveaux siècles' (vol. i, 201). When reproaching Malesherbes for some failure to help him, he can excuse this error by emphasizing that the crime belongs to the regime which then reigned, and thus to a totally different *siècle*, now outdated even if the calendar century remains unchanged: 'mais elle [this error] n'étoit pas de lui; ce fut l'erreur de son siècle et des circonstances: ce fut le crime du despotisme' (vol. i, 226). Latude does not need to die to become a martyr, because paradise is now to be found on earth. Witness the rhetoric of *La Bastille au Diable*: 'la Bastille [...] s'était élevée sur les débris de nos libertés [...] quand nos pères furent asservis, voilà la prison qu'éleva leur tyran.'[11] Liberty was lost, and is now reclaimed; it is at once intrinsic to the human being and an exterior quality which must be aimed at and achieved; it has both anteriority and futurity but is not fully located in the present, from which it must be regenerated after the hiatus of enslavement. The temporality of Liberty is thus startlingly similar to that of sanctity and the return to God in the Christian tradition. Just as Eden and New Jerusalem bracket the earthly time of suffering, the *ancien régime* is bracketed by man's original freedom and the new, free France.

To return to the substance of Latude's bodily degradation, a qualification is necessary – torture was not, by this time, practised in the Bastille, so our author must engage with bodily degradation more creatively. Latude is very keen to describe his bodily torments to us, unflinchingly gory in the manner of certain medieval hagiographies. These range from stigmata-like wounds on his hands and feet caused by climbing up the chimney to escape his cell in the Bastille, to the horrors of the scurvy ward in Bicêtre, where in addition to his painful illness and non-existent care he claims prisoners were given a single bowl which had to serve for both eating and defecation, and where the scabs of the water-point-monitors were to be found floating in anything prisoners were given to drink (vol. ii, 20 and 47).

Latude's torments are repeated, and repetitive. Halfway through the first volume, he is already described as near blind, toothless, falling apart

11 *La Bastille au Diable*, 5.

(105–10), and he frequently wishes to die. It is difficult for the reader to credit the healthy, masterful portrayal of the work's frontispiece, but this kind of renewal is central to the hagiographic process. Whatever state Latude is reduced to, he seems to recover enough for another escape, which then leads to a further degradation: these are the trials he must go through before his own release and the *point de capiton* of 1789. Burgwinkle and Howie have, in their study of hagiography and pornography, highlighted the way that such narratives require not only teleological unfolding, but suspension and deferral – space in which the subject's body can undergo a transformation.[12] Sarah Kay's formulation of this body is definitive: the Real of death is sublimated through a fantasy process of impossible violence and impossible renewal, and the spectacular body

> is made to occupy the position in the symbolic at which the pressure of 'das Ding' is felt: it becomes the special idea (thing/person) which transfigures the whole arbitrary structure we inhabit so as to make it seem meaningful, beautiful, or morally uplifting.[13]

Kay calls this body the 'sublime' body of the martyr, but I prefer to follow Burgwinkle and Howie in calling such a body 'spectacular', emphasizing the importance of both the spectator to its creation and the tableau in which the body is framed. Latude – or his editor – displays a developing shrewd-ness regarding this body, stating at the opening of the later version of his memoirs that, like the saint, 'la véritable histoire de ma vie n'est que celle de mes malheurs' (vol. i, 4). His seemingly never-ending torments, multiply-ing from one elaboration to the next, inspire pity, terror and wonder at his capacity to survive: emotions which are called upon to fuel revolutionary fervour. He escapes and is re-imprisoned three times, preparing for the true birth of the French people into Liberty through these repeated miscarriages. During his first escape, the wounds to his 'mains ensanglantées' (vol. i, 36) and to his feet may consciously recall stigmata. The production of his spectacular body hinges, firstly, on his descriptive ability and compulsion

12   Bill Burgwinkle and Cary Howie, *Sanctity and Pornography in Medieval Culture* (Manchester: Manchester University Press, 2010), 4.
13   Sarah Kay, *Courtly Contradictions* (Stanford: Stanford University Press, 2001), 216.

to reveal the most intimate details of his humiliation and, secondly, upon the repetition and intensification which renders his survival so extraordinary – the impossible violence and impossible renewal of Kay's formulation. The descriptions of drinking water mixed with scabs and shit, or an upper lip split in two by a constant stream of mucus (vol. i, 106), may seem irretrievably graphic, but medieval depictions of saints are marked by the same explicitness of the degradation of the body. Cary Howie, discussing the hagiography of *Marie l'Egyptienne*, relates that the holy body of the saint passes through a state of utter abjection when she retreats to the desert and exists blackened by the sun, caked in her own filth.[14]

Latude's rejuvenation recalls the oft cited spectacular renewal of female victims in Sade's works. *Les 120 journées de Sodome* shares with Latude both the language of hagiography – for, as the victims advance towards their eventual deaths, the words used are 'sacrifice', 'immoler' and 'martyriser' (e.g. 482 and 493) – and its descriptions of extreme bodily violence. The libertines make a rule which states that they cannot perform any acts on their victims which have not yet been recited (and an unspoken rule that, once something has been recited, it *must* be performed), and so with the progression of the encyclopaedia, the text, and the time of narration, the victims start to lose body parts – first digits, then limbs and breasts – before finally losing their lives. Sade completed his encyclopaedia of passions in note form, but did not produce a full version of the Silling narrative, and so only one of the deaths is fully written out. It is that of Augustine, and after being skinned, burned and blinded (all tortures found in hagiography), her death is couched in pseudo-religious language: 'on découvre ses nerfs en quatre endroits formant *la croix*, [...] Ce fut là qu'elle *rendit l'âme*; ainsi périt à quinze ans et huit mois une des plus *célestes* créatures qu'ait formée la nature.'[15]

However, the Sadean narrative comports an important difference from Latude's, for the main characters are not the victims, but the perpetrators.

14   Cary Howie, *Claustrophilia: The Erotics of Enclosure in Medieval Literature* (New York: Palgrave Macmillan, 2007), 41.
15   Sade, *Les 120 journées de Sodome*, 511, my emphasis.

Although the victim-deaths in *120 journées* resemble the deaths of martyrs, I would argue that it is the perpetrators of these tortures who become saints, for it is they and not their victims who are presented as overcoming the confines of the dominant epistemology of the day to break into a new era of freedom. Arguably, they also possess a 'spectacular saintly body' which goes beyond that of their victims, their feats of sexual endurance in obedience to the command of 'jouir' being truly extraordinary. Their assault on the values of innocence and virtue are relentless – for all the narrator's ironic rhetoric of *âmes* or *célestes créatures*, the repeated attacks of the libertines upon their victims' bodily integrity reduce such celestial beings to butchered meat, and in opening up Augustine's body, they find no soul, but only the shit which forms their chief delight: a materialist worldview triumphant.

Latude, despite his status as victim, also sometimes acts out torture as a perpetrator. In an ostensibly saintly move, he befriends the 'plus vils [...] plus rebutans' of animals: rats. Dwelling on this little society at some length, the manner in which he relates to them is hardly saintly. He considers himself 'au sein de ma famille' (vol. i, 88), but his actions towards them are those of a despot. He exercises his power over them by bestowing or limiting food, but remains sensitive to his own weakness, acknowledging that he *needs* their love and society. His enjoyment in inflicting his own torments on other beings becomes yet clearer as he relates how he cruelly catches a spider on a fly tied to a hair, and then places a bowl of water underneath. The spider, unable to escape, is constrained to the same repetitive actions as Latude himself, swinging back and forth but confined to one limited space. These games even gain the hint of an erotic charge when he elsewhere founds a new family from a pair of captured pigeons: 'Je mis tous mes soins à les consoler de leur captivité [...] Comme j'épiois leurs actions, comme je jouissois de leurs amours, je m'égarois auprès d'eux, et mon imagination rêvoit quelquefois à leurs plaisirs' (vol. i, 113). In the memoir's most tragi-comic sequence, Latude believes that a jailor is going to harm the pigeons, upon which, 'je m'élançai pour le prévenir, je les pris, et dans mon transport, je les écrasai moi-même' (115).

Both Latude and Sade seem to be acting – and writing – out a fantasy of mastery, an attempt to take control of the time being done to the two authors. However, we might ask what constitutes success in this endeavour. Ultimately, the desired object which promises the resumption of mastery over time for the disempowered prisoner is the book. The repeated act of writing facilitates a degree of control over time as it is experienced in prison, and as it will be judged by posterity. Its materiality is crucial: both manuscripts were lost, devastating their authors, then re-found, re-worked. Sade famously wrote his Bastille manuscript on a single long scroll which went missing for a century, whilst Latude wrote endless memoirs in prison which were then confiscated. He tells us that he even exchanged his own matter with one, written with Christ-like resonances in blood, on bread mashed up with saliva. An early version of the memoirs becomes an important character in the 1791 version, for it was by smuggling out a manuscript, found by a commoner named Mme Legros, his first disciple, that his release was eventually secured.

In Sade's text, the quest for a complete encyclopaedia of passions is a bid for power on the part of the libertines: a bid to master a subject, to completely categorize an aspect of the world. Although Sade never finishes the framing text and much of what we now have to work with is simply the encyclopaedia and notes on what happens (who loses an arm, who dies when), the Sadean attempt at mastery is, I believe, more complete, even though Latude enjoys such glittering, yet short-lived, social success. Striving to the status of martyr, Latude compulsively writes and re-writes his victim memoir, which expands and intensifies with each version. However, that repetition begins to subtly undermine him, for each longer memoir adds episodes such as that of the pigeons, which hint at encroaching madness. He even suggests that, after Madame Legros had secured his release, he would go into 'transports' and rage at her, perhaps going so far as to attack her (vol. ii, 176). This is important not only because Latude's claims of persecution rely heavily upon the argument that false accusations of insanity were employed not only to extend his time in prison and, even worse, to discredit the many written productions which were his only method of protesting injustice, but also because he was figured as a martyr *to reason* against the demented cruelty of *ancien régime* bureaucracy (as in *La Bastille au Diable*). Prison reports indeed gave the reason for his non-release as complete insanity, but evidence that this was a concerted tactic is not to be found, and even Malesherbes, whom Latude considered a protector and who seemed genuinely sympathetic upon hearing of the prisoner's plight, wrote after meeting him that he was 'totally insane as stated in notes given to me, and [...] showed unquestionable signs in my presence'.[16] The prisoner might be forgiven a brief loss of reason brought about by imprisonment, but the back-writing of wild accusations of improbable persecution, of a paranoid fear of assassination (for example, when he fears his tobacco has been poisoned, vol. i, 73–4), and of acting-out his persecutions on animal proxies puts the truth of his martyrdom and sainthood into question. The same repetitive structure that, in traditional hagiography, is the proof of the saint – the tyrant inflicting blow after blow and the martyr becoming ever more serene – is in Latude's repeated memoirs a site of slippage regarding the authenticity of moments differently described in different versions of the memoir, and of slippage between sanity and insanity. Accordingly, later scholars would draw from prison records the more banal conclusion that Latude was simply forgotten by his supposed persecutors, allowed to languish in his encroaching madness until he seemed beyond help, and it is as either a madman or a charlatan that he came to be judged, and then forgotten once more. The saint is a powerful figure for the Revolutionary project, but also a dangerous one, for the extraordinariness of even the successful saint can seem a pathological anathema to reason. Cary Howie calls 'claustrophilia', as opposed to claustrophobia – so, the attraction to confined spaces – the pathology of the saint, and indeed, one begins to question why Latude continually gives himself up to the authorities after his escapes, even at one point *asking* to be sent to a *cachot* (which he admits to have been somewhere between protest and délire), whilst his incessant re-writing, which continues even after he has been freed, suggests a compulsion to repeat his trauma.

Is Sade more successful? Annie le Brun has called Sade exceptional, for he takes possession of the castle which fascinates everybody, 'mais que personne n'a l'audace de reconnaître pour sien'.[17] She also argues, convincingly,

16   Quoted in Quétel, *Escape from the Bastille*, 95.
17   Le Brun, *Les châteaux de la subversion*, 177.

that he rejects the idea of the fortress as a 'mécanisme inconscient' by identifying its menace with the agency of those who dwell in it. As such, his Man Ray portrait seems particularly revelatory: whilst Latude holds his escape ladder and gestures at the Bastille in the act of being torn down, Man Ray depicts Sade as having exchanged his substance with it, the very stones of the crumbling Bastille furnishing this face and expression, securing his fame.

However, even if Sade triumphs over the Bastille by incorporating it as attribute, has he mastered hagiography? The use of an essentially religious form to metaphorize a desired assumption of modern, materialist values seems fraught with peril, for the temporality of hagiography has implications that finally exceed narratorial control. The time of the saint, as described above, violates several key tenets of Sade's work, as well as of what we might call the 'modern' project in general. Most particularly, such temporality is anti-empirical, relying on concepts beyond the realm of experience, whether that be a concept like 'God' or a concept like 'Liberty'. Latude's madness finds its mirror in the frenzy of Sade's libertines, who themselves confess that they are more machines manipulated by their new God, Nature, than free agents. They become a threat to their own narrative, to the living encyclopaedia which they are trying to create, for they are unable to control themselves and to keep to a prescribed order. Curval struggles the most, working himself into frenzies of excess, as here: 'Curval qui n'est pas maître de lui malgré les conventions, coupe un téton entier à Rosette en enculant Michette'.[18] Furthermore, the pleasure they take in blaspheming, which frequently forms part of their sexual tableaux, is suggestive of a hatred of God which actually implies a kind of recognition, which should be unnecessary to the true materialist-atheist. A remark by Blanchot seems particularly relevant here: Sade's 'pensées théoriques libèrent à tout instant les puissances irrationnelles auxquelles elles sont liées'.[19]

If both Sade's and Latude's texts can be figured as hagiographic, this points to an anachronism at the very heart of revolutionary myth. Is the ascent

18   Sade, *Les 120 journées de Sodome*, 514.
19   Quoted in Le Brun, *Les châteaux de la subversion*, 253.

to liberty, to modernity, dependent upon the teleological time of the saint? Decrying the irrationality of the Catholic cult, the drive to create a new era nevertheless depends on an anti-rational toolkit borrowed from it. Reason's martyr must not be mad – but hagiography, structurally anti-rational, cannot help but highlight what any rationalist would judge to be the pathologies of sainthood: anti-empiricism, prophecy, the compulsion to repeat, teleology, faith. The legends of the Bastille, of Latude and of Sade, mutually supportive, are all undermined by the anachronistic presence of the saint.

Selected Bibliography

Burgwinkle, Bill, and Cary Howie, *Sanctity and Pornography in Medieval Culture* (Manchester: Manchester University Press, 2010).

Campbell, Emma, *Medieval Saints' Lives: The Gift, Kinship and Community in Old French Hagiography* (Cambridge: Gallica, 2008).

Corfield, Penelope J., *Time and the Shape of History* (New Haven and London: Yale University Press, 2007).

Howie, Cary, *Claustrophilia: The Erotics of Enclosure in Medieval Literature* (New York: Palgrave Macmillan, 2007).

Kay, Sarah, *Courtly Contradictions* (Stanford: Stanford University Press, 2001).

Latude, Henri Masers de, and citoyen Thierry, *Mémoirs de Henri Masers de Latude, ancien ingénieur, Prisonnier pendant trente-cinq années à la Bastille et à Vincennes, sous le nom de Daury; à Charenton sous celui de Danger; et à Bicêtre sous celui de Jedor* (Paris: Latude, 1793).

La Bastille au Diable (Paris: Chez Laurens, 1790).

Le Brun, Annie, *Les châteaux de la subversion* (Paris: J.J. Pauvert, 1982).

Lüsebrink, Hans-Jürgen and Rolf Reichardt, *The Bastille: A History of a Symbol of Despotism and Freedom* (Durham, NC: Duke University Press, 1997).

Quétel, Claude, *Escape from the Bastille: The Life and Legend of Latude* (Cambridge: Polity Press, 2002).

Sade, Marquis de, *Les 120 journées de Sodome* (Paris: J.J. Pauvert, 1972).

DAVID GRUNDY

What's the Matter with Antonin Artaud?
Or, Why The Soul is a Pile of Shit[1]

For Aristotle, while all human beings possess a soul, its distribution differs in each individual case – or perhaps more accurately, according to class distinctions. The soul here acts as that which both subsequently reinforces and retrospectively justifies what is perceived to be the natural state enshrined in exploitative class relation. Thus, it is the possession of the soul's 'deliberative function' which distinguishes the aristocratic caste as fully human, against the animalism of women, slaves and labourers, for 'the deliberative faculty of the soul is not present at all in the slave; in a female it is present but ineffective',[2] while 'the mass of mankind are evidently quite slavish in their tastes, preferring a life suitable to beasts'.[3] The soul, then, in its complete form, is not only that which distinguishes the aristocrats from the masses, but that which distinguishes the *human as such*, that which allows men and women to be used as beasts of burden, not fully accorded human rights because they are not considered fully human, because they are considered

1   Most references to Artaud's works will be to the translations collected in *Antonin Artaud: Selected Writings*, ed. Susan Sontag, trans. Helen Weaver (Berkeley: University of California Press, 1976) [henceforth *SW*], with occasional use of *Artaud Anthology*, ed. Jack Hirschman, various translators (San Francisco: City Lights Books, 1965) [henceforth *Anthology*], unless otherwise noted.

2   Aristotle, *The Politics*, trans. T.A. Sinclair, and rev. Trevor Saunders (London: Penguin, 1992 [1981]), xiii.

3   Aristotle, *The Nicomachean Ethics*, ed. Lesley Brown, trans. David W.D. Ross (New York: Oxford University Press, 2009), 6. The combination of these two quotations from Aristotle is to be found in Cedric Robinson's Preface to the 2000 edition of *Black Marxism: The Making of the Black Radical Tradition* (Chapel Hill: University of North Carolina Press, 2000), xxxi.

to be suited for and even to actively *prefer* 'a life suitable to beasts'. To this, and to the Christian soul, Antonin Artaud says 'SHIT' – and in doing so not only proclaims 'shit *to* the spirit',[4] but that the spirit *itself* is shit:

> Caca is the matter of the soul, which I have seen so many coffins spill out in puddles before me [...] the abyss Kah-Kah, Kah the corporeal breath of shit, which is the opium of eternal survival.[5]

Here we might juxtapose Adam Cornford's re-versioning of Marx, in his essay 'Processed Shit': 'Capitalist accumulation produces order at one pole and entropy at the other, or else organized shit (capital) at one pole and disorganized shit (misery and pollution) at the other'.[6] Capital is constituted by the processed shit of the congealed and exploited labour and labourers that produce it; the soul, as shitty essence, thus acts as capital's temporal extension through the accumulation of the products of past and present exploitation – the golden future allowed by the workers whose labour it turns to gold (but which nonetheless remains only a form of processed shit) and whose persons it shits out as entropic waste, the caca[7] of capital. Such matter of time, as both money and shit, is hoarded up in caves[8] or in coffins,[9] accumulation as a hellish infinity, limbo of the shitty factory-tomb[10] – as in Sean Bonney's recent re-versioning of Baudelaire, in which 'I live in shit / my needle life a / bruteist clock',[11] or Octavio Paz's 'Sunstone', where time

4   Artaud, 'Shit to the Spirit', in *Anthology*, 106–12.
5   Artaud, 'Letter to Henri Parisot, Rodez, October 6, 1945', in *SW*, 453; original in Artaud, *Œuvres complètes, XII* (Paris: Gallimard, 1974) [henceforth *OC*].
6   Adam Cornford, 'Processed Shit: Capitalism, Racism and Entropy', *Processed World* 30 (1992–3), 30–41 (30).
7   See Artaud's numerous uses of this word in his writings of the early 1940s: in particular, the 'Letter to Pierre Loeb Artaud, Ivry, April 23, 1947', in *SW*, 518–19
8   'Stolen wealth [...] *piled up* [...] grain by grain, for thousands / of millions of years [...] stored in certain caverns with forces *prohibited by all humanity*': Artaud, 'Letter to Pierre Loeb', ibid.
9   See Artaud, 'Letter to Henri Parisot, Rodez, October 6, 1945'.
10   'The body under the skin is an overheated factory': Artaud, 'Van Gogh: The Man Suicided by Society', in *SW*, 507.
11   'Rêve Parisien', in Sean Bonney, *Baudelaire in English* (London: Veer, 2008).

turns into both money and ('abstract') shit: 'The mill that squeezes out the juice of life, / That turns eternity into empty hours, / Minutes into prisons, and time into / Copper coins and abstract shit.'[12]

Similarly, Artaud understands the soul's temporal dimension not so much as the happy eternity of heaven, but the bad infinity of limbo, caught between the past (those who inhabit limbo – pre-Christian saints and un-baptized infants – are there in part because they came *before*, came *too early*) and the fulfilled future, the entry into heaven which never comes, which is perpetually deferred. His hereditary syphilis meant that the madness and disease of his own body were at least in part the by-product of the sexual activities of his forbears, literally fucked into him, and we find traces of this horror in portrayals of the child 'bugger[ed]' by 'papa-mama', and in descriptions of 'the liver that turns the skin yellow, the brain wracked by syphilis, the intestines that expel filth', or of 'being's disease, the syphilis of its infinity'.[13] In Volume 1, Chapter 10 of *Capital*, Marx famously describes capital as re-circulating 'dead labour, which, vampire-like, lives only by sucking living labour, and lives the more, the more labour it sucks'.[14] This vampire is at once material and ghost-like, dead and alive, as in Artaud's 'spirit' which 'has ended up grabbing the place before the body that actually preceded it [...] count[ing] on what the body would lose in life in order to insure its seizure and its own subsistence / via the body that it vampirized'.[15] For our purposes, this is not only a forgetting of that abstract category the body, but of the plural *bodies* whose labour time has been converted to money, and whose bodies have been turned into a shit-and-blood soul:

12   Octavio Paz, 'Sun-Stone', in Paz, *Collected Poems 1957–1987*, ed. and trans. Elliot Weinberger (Manchester: Carcanet, 1988), 23.

13   The first reference is to Artaud, 'Here Lies', in *SW*, 538; 'the liver ... filth', is the trans-lation of Brian Massumi in Gilles Deleuze and Felix Guattari *A Thousand Plateaus* [1980] (London: Continuum, 2004), 175 (original in Artaud, *OC, VII: Hélioglabale ou l'anarchiste corounné* [1934] (Paris: Gallimard, 1982), 56); 'being's ... infinity' is the translation of Allen S. Weiss, in *The Aesthetics of Excess* (Albany: State University of New York Press, 1989), 127 (original in Artaud, *OC, XVIII: Cahiers de Rodez* (Paris: Gallimard, 1976), 115).

14   Marx, *Capital, Vol. 1*, trans. Ben Fowkes [1976] (London: Penguin Books (1990), 342.

15   Artaud, 'Shit to the Spirit', in *Anthology*, 111–12.

labour, and labourers, are 'the body that actually preceded' the 'spirit' of capital (this latter recalling the metaphor developed by Marx in the paragraph preceding his vampire characterization: 'the capitalist [...] is only capital personified. His soul is the soul of capital').[16]

Likewise, while Artaud's figuration of the 'syphilis of [...] infinity' is not so much of the past *feeding* on the present generations on whose blood it relies, it *is* a kind of haunting that the figure of the vampire-capitalist well represents, re-circulation as disease and contagion, as a bad infinity, an infinite loop that becomes the disease of being itself. Indeed, capital itself might be described as similarly diseased, infecting and catching its exploited subjects within the syphilis of this false infinity. This is why, in 'Here Lies', it is a 'stinking owner', an 'arrogant capitalist'[17] who presides over limbo, that region whose invention allows souls to be turned into profit, through prayers for their release into heaven which convert, on earth, to gilded altars, robes and church doors. As the American poet Ed Dorn puts it in his 'Theory of Truth', 'Ghiberti's doors are the doors / to the biggest bank, and bank doors / may be "the gate to paradise." The Baptistry / is clearly a bank'.[18] And behind these doors occur the exploitative actions of the priestly caste, systematized into theological doctrine, inflicted sexually and financially on their minion congregations. In the communion ritual that Artaud so loathed, this congregation is said to eat the body of Christ, through the miracle of transubstantiation; but they might better be said to be eating themselves, these wretched of the earth, these 'shit-eaters',[19] their own bodies fed back to them in the concentrated form of the wafer that their propaganda-wrung money pays for, a reverse alchemical process by which their gold is turned into the shit they are fed.

If Christian doctrine holds that one might be 're-born', through the death of the 'old' sinful body, into a new spiritual body – being 'born again',

---

16   Marx, *Capital, Vol. I*, 342.
17   Artaud, 'Here Lies', in *SW*, 547.
18   'A Theory of Truth: The North Atlantic Turbine', in Ed Dorn, *Collected Poems* (Manchester: Carcanet, 2012), 241.
19   Artaud, 'Artaud le Momo', in *SW*, 526.

both on earth (through baptism) and, after death, in heaven – Artaud holds
that this ritual is in fact cannibalism: 'For to baptize is to cook a being
against his will.'[20] The same logic applies to transubstantiation, which is
literally the cannibalistic consumption of the body of a dead man-god as
an act of symbolic renewal, the eating of the other to sustain one's own
life. If this ritual is in some way filthy, baptism implies the opposite – a
'cleansing' of filth. Yet, for Artaud, it is more like the process of cooking
found in a pun on another religious concept from 'Here Lies' – '*r° om-let
cadran*',[21] translated by Helen Weaver as 'time om-let', and also potentially
rendered as 'dial om-let' – whereby a being is destroyed and turned into
another form only in order to be consumed.

Just as Artaud elsewhere puns the Egyptian Kah – the divine breath
of life – with 'ca-ca', shit, so too here the Hindu sacred syllable 'OM' is
mocked through this punning of 'om' with 'om-let'. This sacred egg[22] is
controlled by a temporal process which can only lead to its destruction,
transformed from a living substance into a dead one in order to be eaten
and regurgitated.[23] If 'OM' is something timeless, or, more accurately, that
which contains all time, in an ultimate refusal of any notion of time's linear

---

20   Artaud, 'The Tale of Popocatepetl', in *Anthology*, 181.

21   Artaud, *OC*, 90; Weaver translation in *SW*, 546.

22   This egg might be suggestively linked to the Body without Organs, as it was, famously,
     by Deleuze and Guattari, *A Thousand Plateaus*, 169–70. See here also the hypoth-
     esis put forward in Mikhail Iampolski, *The Memory of Tiresias: Intertextuality and
     Film*, trans. Harsha Ram (Berkeley: University of California Press, 1998), 22–3, by
     which Artaud's script for The Seashell and the Clergymen draws on Ange Pechmeja's
     nineteenth-century alchemical text *L'Ouef de Knephe: Histoire Secret de Zéro*, in
     which the universal egg conjoins all the letters of the alphabet and is the source of
     all vowels.

23   Indeed, the opening of 'Here Lies' might be read as a parody of the opening of a
     famous passage in Chapter 9, Verse 17 of the *Bhagavad Gita*. 'I am the father of this
     universe, the mother, the support and the grandsire. I am the object of knowledge,
     the purifier and the syllable *om*' (translation rendered in A.C. Bhaktivedanta Swami,
     The Bhagavad Gita As It Is (Los Angeles: Bhaktivedanta Book Trust, 2006) becomes
     'I, Antonin Artaud, am my son, my father, my mother, / and myself; / leveller of the
     idiotic periplus on which procreation / is impaled, / the periplus of papa-mama /
     and child, / soot of grandma's ass' (*SW*, 540).

unfolding, Artaud transforms it into a temporally destructive force that is nonetheless trapped in a limbo of incessant violence and rebirth, caught on what he earlier describes as the 'umbilicus of limbo', 'om' contained within the original French 'ombilic', or navel. The 'dial om-lette' is the sacred syllable turned into an egg timer and into the frying egg itself, an egg which, as an 'homme-lette' – 'OM' this time as 'h-o-m-m-e' – is also man. This is what has become of the 'clockwork of the soul', the 'pain of an abortive adjustment',[24] which Artaud had earlier stated it was his task to document: OM and omelette, the abortion of the egg which is at the same time the primal birth, the destruction of life which sacrificially enables the continuation of life, through sustaining the figure who eats the omelette in order to live.

The egg in 'Om-lette', then, as birthplace and generative source, is turned into something materially and temporally measured, beaten, fried, cooked, and shat out like 'soot from grandma's ass'[25] – at once the root of the person, of the subject of these poems, Antonin Artaud, and 'the state / anti-Artaud / par excellence',[26] an egg born in order to be consumed, born in order to be eaten, born in order be destroyed, destroyed in order to be born, thus simultaneously destroyed and born in a cannibalistic-sex ritual with echoes of the Catholic rite of transubstantiation: 'the frying of je in / Chri [...] matter / which gave life / to Jeezus-cry [...] out of the dung of / my dead *self*';[27] 'a good omelette / stuffed with poison, cyanide, capers';[28] 'time [...] this mixed fry / of all the friable / of the threshold, / gone to sea again in their coffin'.[29] In the Christian myth, Jesus dies for the sins of all generations past and all generations to come: here, Artaud presents himself as Jesus Christ in what is both a statement of ultimate self-promotion, self-aggrandizement – Jesus Christ, Je Suis Christ – and ultimate abjection, crucified and pathetic baby-talk, the individual, as Jeezy Cri-Cri, a

---

24   Artaud, 'The Nerve Meter', in *SW*, 80.
25   Artaud, Here Lies, in *SW*, 540.
26   Ibid. 546.
27   Ibid. 545.
28   Ibid. 547.
29   Ibid. 551.

cry baby suffering and existing due to the unwanted procreative efforts of his predecessors, his 'papa-mama', a cry baby crucified on the family tree,[30] hung up with and through the full force and weight of the nightmare of dead generations whose suffering is in no way thus redeemed.

The reference in this last phrase is of course to Marx's 'The 18th Brumaire of Louis Bonaparte' – 'the tradition of all dead generations weighs like a nightmare on the brains of the living', in Saul K. Padover's translation[31] – but also to Walter Benjamin's notion of revolution as that present occurrence which transfers both into the past and the future, retrospectively redeeming the sufferings of all those who fought and suffered for those material effects which the revolution finally instantiates

---

30   F. Tert When's and Jack Hirschman's translation of the opening of 'Here Lies' reads 'I Antonin Artaud, am my son /, my father, my mother, / my self; / leveller of the imbecile periplum rooted / to the family tree' (*Anthology*, 238). 'Rooted' only distantly suggests crucifixion, suggesting that which is *underneath*, rather than *on* the tree. Helen Weaver's translation reverses the subject of the sentence so that it is 'the idiotic periplus on which procreation is impaled', thus exacerbating the notion of crucifixion, or impalation, but causing the abstract notion of procreation itself, rather than the person of Artaud, to be that which is crucified. Such a reversal is closer to the original, which reads '*niveleur du périple imbécile ou s'enferre l'engendrement*' (Artaud, *OC*, 77). The reflexive form of the verb used here – '*s'enferre*' – literally means to spear, or stab oneself, and is equivalent to the idiomatic English expression 'to dig a hole for oneself', i.e. to worsen one's situation through the accumulating lies one tells. The connotation is thus of engenderment as a kind of reproduction of lies, making matters worse, a self-violence with connotations of crucifixion. One might, then, translate the phrase as something like 'leveller of the imbecilic periplus on which (or where) engenderment spears / stabs / impales itself', though this does not quite capture the metaphoric mixing of the original, in which the spearing or impalation occurs in or on a periplus, a Greek log-book listing the names of ports or landmarks along a coastal route. If the exact notion of being crucified on the family tree is thus not exactly to be found in the original French, the references to Artaud as crucified Christ, the figuration of man as a tree elsewhere, and the common metaphor of 'the family tree', combined with the notion of '*s'enferre*' as a self-spearing, would seem to make this combination, this slight elaboration on Artaud's original phrasing, entirely appropriate to the gist of this particular work.

31   'The Eighteenth Brumaire of Louis Bonaparte', in *Karl Marx on Revolution*, ed. and trans. Saul K. Padover (New York: McGraw-Hill, 1971), 245.

and fulfils.[32] This is a secular-materialist eschatology whose materialism – whose matter of time – expands back to include not only *living* present matter, but the once living, now dead matter of past generations: where Marx's 'total recovery of man'[33] might, in the words of Christian Lenhardt, constitute itself as 'an ensemble of concrete historical beings, both living and dead',[34] in which, against the secular erasure of memory as a revolutionary force,[35] the past might be reclaimed, beyond religion, for revolutionary purposes.

Both Benjamin and Artaud thus appropriate religious imagery – in Benjamin's case, that of the Jewish tradition, in Artaud's, that of its Catholic elaboration – for materialist purposes. Yet while, in Benjamin's schema, the Messiah becomes something like the redemptive force of revolution (or its bearer, the proletariat), rather than the specific incarnation of Christ, the Artaud-as-Christ of 'Here Lies' is neither a revolutionary force nor an incarnate personal redeemer who will liberate past and future generations, but the present victim of precisely those past generations Benjamin's Messiah comes to save. For Benjamin, the stock of religious concepts might provide the seeds for a thinking of the temporal aspects of revolution, but, for Artaud, such

---

32 See Walter Benjamin, 'Theses on the Philosophy of History', in *Illuminations*, ed. Hannah Arendt, trans. Harry Zohn [1968] (London: Fonatana, 1973), 255–65 (256 and 262–5).

33 Marx, *Zur Kritik der Hegelschen Rechtsphilosophie. Einleitung* (my translation). For an alternative English version, see 'A Contribution to the Critique of Hegel's Philosophy of Right: Introduction', in Karl Marx, *Early Writings*, trans. Gregor Benton [1975] (London: Penguin, 1992), 256. Note that Benton translates the phrase '*völlige Wiedergewinnung des Menschen*' as 'total redemption' rather than the literal and less religiously freighted 'recovery', 'retrieval' or 'reclamation'.

34 Christian Lenhardt, 'Anamnestic Solidarity: The Proletariat and its *Manes*', *Telos* 25 (1975), 133–54 (135).

35 Susan-Buck Morss (paraphrasing Benjamin) and Lenhardt have both questioned what they see as Marx's reliance on the future as a source of revolutionary imagery: see Buck-Morss, *The Dialectics of Seeing: Walter Benjamin and the Arcades Project* (Cambridge, MA: MIT Press (991), 124 and Lenhardt, ibid. 134 ('conventional understandings of what solidarity is all about in the context of a secular theory of man and history have implied a wholesale erasure of memory').

concepts are precisely that which keeps man stuck in an infinite present hell, suffocating[36] in the nightmarish and shitty limbo of heredity, crucified by the nails of the past; and if his notion of the 'body without organs' is itself a kind of eschatology, akin to the 'heavenly body' into which, according to certain forms of Christian doctrine,[37] a sinful humanity will eventually be reborn, it is an eschatology that, unlike Benjamin's, but like Marx's, can conceive of no positive role for the past to play in the cause of present liberation.

As we have seen, for Artaud, religious dictates become a shitty opiate, a parody of the notion of 'spiritual food' which enshrines a violent feeding off one's fellow man as a supposed means of salvation, the 'insolent rabble / of all the shit-eaters / who had no other grub / in order to live / than to gobble / Artaud mômo.'[38] But this shitty opium is not only the opium of religion: Artaud's demand is ultimately, or could be made so to be, a demand to be rid of the false god of capitalism, both as capitalistic drives are rooted deep within the history of the Catholic church (allied, in France at that time, with the conservative, collaborationist establishment), and as they exist within a society in which 'nobody believes in god any more'.[39] It is an analysis of the means by which capitalist production processes keep man rooted to the organ-body as a lump of shit, worker as ape-man, as animal[40] and turd.[41]

36　See the references to suffocation in 'To Have Done', *SW*, 567–8.

37　Debates here would surround the continuity between a sinful earthly body that had nonetheless been made 'in the image of God' and a heavenly 'resurrection body' that retained, for example, gendered distinction, but did away with particular personal 'defects'. See in particular Augustine, *Concerning The City of God against the Pagans*, ed. David Knowles, trans. Henry Bettenson (London: Penguin, 1972), Book XX, 905–6, 925–7, 935, and 940–3. Early controversies surrounding the particular material form taken in resurrection are detailed in Caroline Walker Bynum, *The Resurrection of the Body in Western Christianity, 200–1336* (New York: Columbia University Press, 1995), 94–104. Key passages in such discussions were 1 Corinthians 15:40, 44 and 50–4.

38　'Artaud le Mômo', *SW*, 526.

39　Ibid. 570.

40　'I have found the way to put an end to this ape once / and for all' ('To Have Done with the Judgement of God', in *SW*, 570).

41　'You ain't shit', the American insult goes, meaning you are the lowest of the low. Eat shit and like it. Shit is processed or disposed of by inferiors who are contaminated

Reading Artaud in this way also allows us to see Konrad Bayer's dismissal, in his 1960 text 'Idiot', of all manner of ethics and creeds as 'piles of shit', as a true analysis of the state of bourgeois society and those upon whose labour it relies – the proletarians and lumpen-proletarians, the reserve-army of labour[42] – all of whom are equally lumpen, lumps of shit, turds. The etymology of 'lumpen' and 'lump' is that of a rag.[43] To be lumpen is at once to be the lump of shit that is the waste- or by- or side-product of

---

by it, who metaphorically eat it, and who metonymically (by association) become it': Cornford, 'Processed Shit: Capitalism, Racism and Entropy', 35. See also the similar observation made in Eugene Victor Wolfenstein, *Psychoanalytic-Marxism* (London: Free Association Books, 1993), 337: 'The sensuous energies of workers, women, and black people are voraciously consumed. What cannot be digested is excreted. It is something more than a metaphor when oppressed people say they are treated like shit'.

42   For Marx's development of the notion of the reserve army of labour (or 'industrial reserve army'), a concept which originally appears in Friedrich Engels' *The Condition of the Working Class in England* (London: Penguin, 2005), 118–19, see *Capital, Vol. 1*, Chapter 25, 794–802 (in particular 797). If the reserve army of labour exists on one fringe (or circle of hell) of the proletariat, the lumpen exist on the further fringe of the reserve army, twice removed: yet, as Joshua Moufawad-Paul notes, it is easy to slip over from one fringe into another circle, for these are far from stable or absolute categories (Moufawad-Paul (2012), 'The Slippery Concept of the "Lumpenproletariat"' <http://moufawad-paul.blogspot.co.uk/2012/06/slippery-concept-of-lumpenproletariat.html> accessed 16 March 2014). Thus, if Marx condemned the lumpen-proletariat as tending to align with counter-revolutionary forces (see Marx, *Karl Marx on Revolution*, 286), the Black Panther Party in the 1970s argued that the lumpen were themselves a revolutionary class: see for instance, *The Huey P. Newton Reader*, ed. David Hilliard and Donald Weise (New York: Seven Stories Press, 2002), 165–8 and 193. For more recent applications of the reserve army of labour concept to the contemporary situation, see: Andrew Glyn 'Marx's reserve army of labour is about to go global', *The Guardian* (5 April 2006) <http://www.guardian.co.uk/commentisfree/2006/apr/05/comment.businesscomment> accessed 16 March 2014; and Jacob Bard-Rosenberg, 'The New Reserve Army of Labour', *The Third Estate* <http://thethirdestate.net/2010/11/the-new-reserve-army-of-labour/> accessed 16 March 2014; and David Blanchflower, 'The Misery of Marx's Reserve Army', *New Statesman* (11 November 2010) <http://www.newstatesman.com/economy/2010/11/unemployment-unemployed> accessed 16 March 2014.

43   'lump, n.1'. (*OED Online*, Oxford University Press, March 2014.)

capitalism and to be the rag that wipes its own arse, the groups of destitutes thrown out to live in and on and off their own shit, with none or with at best grudging help from the state, which, after all, has to consider 'the current chic / of information theory [which] will tell you how / many bits of that commodity it takes to / lift one foot / lb. of shit to a starving mouth', as J.H. Prynne sarcastically puts it in his 1966 poem 'Die a Millionaire (Pronounced "Diamonds in the Air")'.[44]

So a pound of food becomes a pound of flesh becomes a pound of shit: the bourgeoisie eat shit and make their subjects eat shit, like the victims of the decadent Fascists in Pasolini's *Salò*. But if these victims eat shit only through suppressing their gag reflex,[45] the bourgeoisie eat it like the daintiest of dainty eaters, daintily nibbling nonetheless on tripe dressed up with cress, crap dressed up with cress. The capitalist system might thus be understood to be organized on two poles which are equally shitty: and here we might again recall Adam Cornford's transformation of Marx's description of capitalism as creating *wealth* at one pole of accumulation and *poverty* at the other: 'Capitalist accumulation produces order at one pole and entropy at the other, or else organized shit (capital) at one pole and disorganized shit (misery and pollution) at the other'.[46]

It is through this that we might also understand the potential accuracy of Ed Dorn's apparently excessive declaration, in the twenty-second of his *24 Love Songs* from 1969, that 'really, the world is shit / and I mean all of it';[47] and it is through this that we might understand the work of Bayer, Dorn and Artaud as *materialist* analyses by which materialism can be said to be 'a pile of shit', just as poverty can be said to be 'a pile of shit', just as God and writing and the soul can be declared to be piles of shit. But none of these are nihilistic statements of the way things are as

---

44 J.H. Prynne, *Poems* (Tarset: Bloodaxe, 2005), 15.

45 Also see, for instance, Sara Guyer's exploration of the notion of 'eating well' and 'eating badly', via Deleuze and Derrida in Guyer, 'Buccality', in Gabriele M. Schwab, ed., *Derrida, Deleuze, Psychoanalysis* (New York: Columbia University Press, 2007), 77–104.

46 Cornford, 'Processed Shit: Capitalism, Racism and Entropy', 35.

47 Dorn, *Collected Poems*, 314.

a mere means of preventing any attempts to correct that state. Rather, they are protests *against* this process, passionate condemnations of the means by which 'rational' bourgeois society enshrines *ir*rationalism, hatred, all *manner* of shit. Like Adorno and Horkheimer's analysis of the dialectic by which Enlightenment is barbarism[48] – an analysis written alongside Artaud's late texts, in the context of the devastations of the Second World War – Artaud, Bayer and Dorn call for a negative understanding of that system of negation disguised as affirmation and progress which is Western capitalism, that process in which the 'animal nature' of the human is covered over but in fact reaches its purest form, as the technologized and rational 'progress' of western capitalist civilization. They call for a negative revealing of the negative remainder of the processes of consumption and digestion by which 'Man' Eats The World and himself, in the form of his sibling, the labourer who is his fellow-human and whom this 'arrogant capitalist' sacrificially eats like Saturn consuming his children.[49]

This strange notion of eating the world perhaps needs some amplification. In his *Introduction to the Reading of Hegel*, Alexandre Kojève deploys the metaphor of eating in order to explicate the relation between 'man's' coming to self-consciousness through action and the natural world: just as 'man' transforms that world through an action which simultaneously

48 Theodor Adorno and Max Horkheimer, *Dialectic of Enlightenment*, trans. John Cumming (London: Verso: 1997 [1979]).

49 The notion of eating the world originates in the following sentences by Lisa Jeschke: 'Work could be defined as an encounter with physical objects which temporarily resist the grasp of the human ego in that ego's attempts to consume the world: mmmh, lecker → oh fuck, in my inclusive politics I have just eaten the world → and myself. In opposition, *unfolding king lear a model* is the exposition of the failure to eat': Lisa Jeschke, 'On the History of the Fool and the Theatre of Jeremy Hardingham', *Materials* 2 (2013), 85–6 (86). There is much more to be said here on the subject of incorporation, assimilation and power, particularly in relation to psychoanalysis, for which discussion space does not here permit. Note that, in the text above, the grandiloquently patriarchal use of the term 'Man' above has been retained as some sort of gesturing towards Artaud's, Canetti's and Kojève's own usage.

negates it, so eating destroys the form (and, one might argue, existence) of a thing in order to allow 'the man' who eats to conserve his own existence.

> The being that eats, for example, creates and preserves its own reality by the overcoming of a reality other than its own, by the 'transformation' of an alien reality into its own reality, by the 'assimilation', the 'internalization' of a 'foreign', 'external' reality. Generally speaking, the I of desire is an emptiness that receives a real positive content only by negating action that satisfies Desire in destroying, transforming, and 'assimilating' the desired non-I.[50]

In Kojève's Hegelian schema, this 'Man' eating the world is the *master* in the master–slave dialectic, rather than the slave (who *transforms*, rather than *annihilating* the world); it is the *master* who eats and annihilates the slave as food and as shit. Indeed, following Elias Canetti, we might consider power itself as a kind of digestion: 'underneath [power], day in, day out, is digestion and again digestion'; 'the man' who wishes to rule seeks 'to incorporate [others] into himself and to suck the substance out of them [...] when they are no more use at all, he disposes of them as he would of his excrement'.[51] Kojève's particular form of the Hegelian dialectic here acts as a negative violence by which the capitalist eats the world in order to sustain their existence, only to find that, in 'assimilating' this 'foreign' element into themselves, they have destroyed that world for *everyone*. This necessitates a new dialectic which is and must be enacted, in which the workers the capitalist has eaten and shat out are now drowning him in their own shit, digging his grave as the gravediggers he has bred, throwing and flushing him down the toilet of history in a kind of reverse procedure to Artaud's soul-as-shit, in a revolutionary process where shit can mean waste-*disposal* rather than waste-*survival*.

In any case, eating as destructive and self-destructive force might help us to explain Artaud's castigation, in a 1947 letter to Pierre Loeb, of 'the

50 Alexandre Kojève, *Introduction to the Reading of Hegel: Lectures on the Phenomenology of Spirit*, assembled by Raymond Queneau, ed. Allan Bloom, trans. James H. Nichols Jr [1947] (New York: Basic Books, 1969), 3–4.

51 Canetti, *Crowds and Power*, trans. Carol Stewart [1962] (New York: Continuum, 1973), 210.

maintainers of a digestive humanity'[52] – a humanity which we might take to
mean not that humanity which has to eat in order to survive, but that which
preys on its fellow humans in a cannibalistic process of exploited production
and consumption. Despite his fascistic tendencies – his apparent welcoming, for instance, of the plague as that which will sweep away great masses
of people in a kind of hideous cleansing[53] – Artaud's sympathies – as one
who himself suffered from a hereditary disease – invariably lie with the filthy
and starving outcast rather than with the rich man who *eats well*, for what
that man consumes is the world and its inhabitants. These are the final sentences of the last letter that he ever wrote, ten days before his death in 1948:

> I had a vision this afternoon – I saw those who are going to follow me and who are
> still not completely embodied because pigs like those at the restaurant last night eat
> too much. There are some who eat too much and others like me who can longer eat
> without *spitting*.[54]

We might consider the connection Jacob Bard-Rosenberg draws between
the recent scandal in which the frozen food company Findus packaged their
ready-made lasagne with forbidden horse-meat, instead of more palatable
varieties of animal corpse, and Lissagaray's description of the privations of
the 1870 siege of Paris, in which men and women resorted to eating dogs,
cats, and rats, and horse-flesh 'had become a delicacy':

> It is with the word 'delicacy' that we shudder most, for it poses an unusual question:
> what can we find beautiful under the duress of starvation? Today, hunger remains
> proximate to the feeling of disgust.[55]

52   Artaud, 'Letter to Pierre Loeb', in *SW*, 519.
53   'The Theatre and the Plague', in Artaud, *The Theatre and its Double*, trans. Mary
     Caroline Richards (New York: Grove Press, 1958). Artaud describes the plague as 'a
     redeeming epidemic', 'a state which is nevertheless characterized by extreme strength
     and in which all the powers of nature are freshly discovered at the moment when
     something essential is going to be accomplished', in which 'a gigantic abscess, as much
     moral as social, [will be] collectively drained' (27 and 31).
54   Artaud, 'Letter to Paule Thévenin, Tuesday, February 24, 1948', in *SW*, 585.
55   Jacob Bard-Rosenberg, 'On the Composition of Lasagne: A Caprice on Horses,
     Abstraction, and the Division of Labour', *Prolapsarian* (2013) <http://prolapsarian.

Here we might draw Artaud's disgust at the thought of eating, and particularly, of *over-eating*, into that system of social and natural exploitation which allows such extreme imbalance, which leads Artaud to recoil from even the *thought* of food. Such rejection might at first glance seem to share something of Weil's decreative martyr-ideal, in which her death through under-eating, in an act of solidarity with French resistance fighters, is suicide as a kind of passive, religiously tinged protest. However, Artaud's disgust at eating shares none of Weil's valorization of starvation as ascetic state of self-denial. Rather, it is, as hers is in part, but can never, due to its ascetic elements, fully be, an expression of *disgust* at that system which controls food's production, distribution, and consumption, at that system in which even that most natural of natural functions, that of eating in order to live, becomes unnatural, a violation of human solidarity, increased efficiency and speed of access to increased quantities of food for *some* existing at the expense of others who starve and are metaphorically eaten.[56] As Bard-Rosenberg puts it, 'what is disgusting is not just "eating horse" but rather the whole set of social mediations that make this simultaneously both possible and unknowable'.[57]

Artaud does not specify the dishes that the 'pigs' in the restaurant were eating, but, as we have suggested in this essay, they might be thought to be eating horse, to be eating shit, to be eating the world, and to be eating the

---

tumblr.com/post/43840250284/on-the-composition-of-lasagna-a-caprice-on-horses> accessed 16 March 2014.

56 For Kenneth Rexroth (in a somewhat patronizing essay, during which he frequently refers to her as a 'girl'), Weil's death-by-starvation is an 'introject[ion of] all the ills of the world into her own heart', an internalization of revolution and of 'other people' as 'mere actors in her own spiritual melodrama': 'anguish [as] an end in itself [which] takes on a holy, or unholy folly': 'Simone Weil' in Rexroth, *The World Outside the Window: The Selected Essays of Kenneth Rexroth*, ed. Bradford Morrow (New York: New Directions, 1987) 38–9. By refusing to take into her body more than others do, or can, she in fact takes their, and the world's, entire being into herself, the denial of self and the inscription of the social into the very basis of one's individual material existence paradoxically serving to reduce the social to an accessory in one's own (personal) spiritual narrative.

57 Bard-Rosenberg, 'On the Composition of Lasagne'.

congealed flesh of the living and dead labourers whose labour constitutes capital. Despite various crises and apocalyptic warnings, general quality of life within the Western world has so far not yet descended to the depths it reached during the kinds of medieval famine where, for instance, in 1033, a man might offer human flesh for sale, as meat, at market – what Cedric Robinson calls 'commercialized cannibalism'.[58] Nonetheless, we might understand, for instance through Keston Sutherland's explication of Marx's metaphor of *gallerte*, that we *do* eat processed human flesh in the form of commodities every day.[59] This is the process of coprophagic cannibalism by which workers are made into shit which they consume in the form of the commodities they make and the food they eat and by which the bourgeoisie eat the same shit. As Adam Cornford puts it, 'Shit is processed or disposed of by inferiors who are contaminated by it, who metaphorically eat it, and who metonymically (by association) become it'. Processed flesh, processed shit – in Artaud's words, 'shit, / that is, meat'.[60] What is Soylent Green, the supposedly synthetic food substance found to be made of human flesh in the classic 1973 American sci-fi movie of the same name ('Soylent Green is people!'), if not the real expression of this state of affairs? We might also consider, a couple of decades later, the fleeing East Germans turned into sausages in Christoph Schlingensief's satire on the re-unification of Germany and the promotion of free-market ideology, *Das deutsche Kettensägenmassaker*. Indeed, right now *we* – the implied 'we' of community and address to which this chapter and this book must implicitly or explicitly address itself, as students, as academics, or as those on the fringes of academia, even as workers ourselves – are, or are soon to be, eating workers, those workers as the shit that the university, through receiving sponsorship and returning tacit endorsement, participates in, the exploitation of globally outsourced labour.

58   Robinson, Preface to the 2000 edition of *Black Marxism: The Making of the Black Radical Tradition*, 13.
59   Keston Sutherland, *Stupefaction: A Radical Anatomy of Phantoms* (London: Seagull Books, 2011), 39–44.
60   Artaud, 'To Have Done', in *SW*, 560.

For Artaud, cannibalism is an example of the taboo-breaking violence which his Theatre of Cruelty presents and in which it revels, while not actually going so far as to *participate* in:

> the truthful precipitates of dreams, in which [the spectator's] taste for crime, his erotic obsessions, his savagery, his fantasies, his utopian sense of life and things, even his cannibalism, pour out on a level that is not counterfeit and illusory but internal.[61]

As taboo, cannibalism thus presents a kind of transgressive appeal for the Artaud who wishes to revolt against every aspect of bourgeois taste, in particular as it is expressed in the traditions of psychological 'realism' and 'naturalism' established by nineteenth-century theatre. Yet this is more as a kind of gesture towards extremity, a (written) flirtation with it, than an actual project for the realization of such a vision – even as a certain sadistic desire for the visceral thrill of mass suffering here assumes a latent and too often ignored fascism which suggests a problematic parallel between and extension of Artaud's theatrical vision into that of contemporaneous political developments, as Kimberly Jannarone persuasively argues in *Artaud and his Doubles*.[62] As in much of Artaud's theatre writing, the enactment of transgressive desires to be found in dreams is still contained within a dream-like spectacle: the phrase 'truthful precipitates of dreams' implies, within its metaphoric construction – a 'precipitate' is the solid formed inside a liquid substance during a chemical reaction – that the immaterial or the only nebulously material might be made solidly material, from liquid or gassy spirit to solid flesh, but the materiality of theatre is here not exactly the materiality of, say, dialectical materialism.

61 Artaud, 'Theatre of Cruelty, First Manifesto', in *SW*, 244.
62 See Kimberly Jannarone, *Artaud and his Doubles* (Ann Arbor: University of Michigan Press, 2010), particularly 189–200. See also the following quotation from a conversation with Jacques Prevel: 'Seven to eight hundred million human beings[...]should be exterminated; what is that to the three or four thousand million who inhabit the earth. Most human beings spend their life in doing nothing'. (Original in Jacques Prevel, *En Compagnie d'Antonin Artaud* (Paris: Flammarion, 1974), 191. Translation by Martin Esslin, *Antonin Artaud* (London: John Calder, 1976), 111.)

Indeed, one might argue that it is not until Artaud's later writing, when he was clinically 'mad' and had been forced to abandon the public medium of theatre work and associated manifesti for hermetic and private asylum scribblings, that his writing can finally assume a radicalism that is not a mere will to anarchy, the kind of desire for chaos, cruelty and strength through and out of suffering that led the Italian Futurists from anarchism to fascism, and that accounts for the fascistic tendencies within Artaud's own 1930s theatre writings. In figuring familial relations and, to a certain implicit extent, those of class, empire and exploitative religion, as cannibalistic, incestuous and grotesquely scatological, the material-metaphoric reality, the true grotesquerie of the capitalist-bourgeois edifice is allowed to assume an extremity true to its character: as Aimé Césaire argued of Lautréamont's *Maldoror*, such apparently wild and insane constructions might tell us as much about their society as the novels of Balzac,[63] or, in Artaud's time, Sartre and Camus, with Artaud as both harsh critic and embodiment of certain elements of material existence within the capitalist sphere.

Lautréamont and Artaud are thus part of the nightmare of history from which, to paraphrase Joyce, we are all trying to awake. The notion of nightmare is of course, as we have seen, also famously taken up by Marx – 'The tradition of all dead generations weighs like a nightmare on the brains of the living'[64] – and, in Artaud's 'Shit to the Spirit', it is connected to the negative force of spirit (or soul) as infinite void:

> Without partisans of pure spirit, of pure spirit as the origin of things, and of god as pure spirit, there never would have been any nightmares. / He [Man] doesn't know that the nightmare is the introduction of unreason by way of the void, is the anarchy in the inherent and normal logic of the brain, is the poison put into its well-being [...].[65]

Here we are brought back to the specific matter of the soul, as that which emerged from the material body as false Idea, and which now oppresses that

---

63   Aimé Césaire, *Discourse on Colonialism*, trans. Joan Pinkham [1972] (New York: Monthly Review Press, 2000), 66.
64   Marx, *Karl Marx on Revolution*.
65   Artaud, 'Shit to the Spirit', in *Anthology*, 108.

body;[66] a matter which is equally no matter, is equally 'unreason by way of the void' or is that void itself, a 'hole',[67] a nothing that is. This constraining paradox of the substance that is also a non-substance, immaterial matter or material immateriality, recalls Artaud's parodic approach to the question of God's existence: 'Is God a being? / If he is one, he is shit. / If he is not one / he does not exist'.[68] God, who is either shit or the void, is *both* shit and the void, because his shit existence presses into us the idea that he exists, an idea which constrains us, keeps us in the void of limbo as beings who do not exist, or who exist only as shit bodies, whose existence is constrained by being shit, by being the waste and excess of the industrial process, the waste disposed of by the entropic system necessitated by capitalism's drive to increased production of piles of processed shit. But the fact of God's non-existence cannot be a simple defiance, for this non-existence is the very definition of the void which does exist and keep us in constraint: 'But he does not exist, / *except* as the void that approaches with all its forms / whose most perfect image / is the advance of an incalculable group of crab lice'.[69] Similarly, the soul, like God, is nothing, but it is also shit, and, by being shit, *everything* – to appropriate Marx, it is the material soul of 'all branches of production and [...] all activities of bourgeois society'.[70] Thus, as Artaud puts it, 'There where it smells of shit / it smells of being'.[71]

---

66 'The spirit and its values and its data might never have existed if the body, which at least sweated them out, had not been there [...] Without the labour-pain of the body one day, an idea would never have been born, / and it isn't from the body that it was born, but against it, / when the idea of a gesture, / i.e., the shadow of it, / chose to live its own life. / Under the action already called: spirit': ibid. 109 and 110.

67 Artaud, 'Artaud le Mômo', in *SW*, 524.

68 Artaud, 'To Have Done', in *SW*, 561.

69 Ibid. 562. My emphasis.

70 Marx's original, heavily ironized comments concern money: 'The metallic existence of money is only the official palpable expression of the soul of money, which is present in all branches of production and in all activities of bourgeois society': Karl Marx, 'Comments on James Mill, *Éléments d'économie politique*', trans. Clemens Dutt, in Marx / Engels. *Collected Works, Volume 3: Marx and Engels 1843–1844* (New York: International Publishers, 1975), 211–28 (213).

71 Artaud, 'To Have Done', in *SW*, 559.

But if, for Artaud as for Ed Dorn and Konrad Bayer, *everything* is shit, this does not mean that it can *only ever be* or *always will be* shit, that the bad eternity of the soul Artaud figures as shit will forever spill out of coffins and onto our plates, 'set out so grudgingly / on [those] plates for the blind to eat in gratitude'.[72] The soul's natural-unnatural state might be understood as a materialism which remains metaphoric, yet which is, in Eugene Victor Wolfenstein's words, 'something more than a metaphor'.[73] Like Artaud's God, it either does not exist or exists in the form of shit, and it is that shit which must be struggled against through a materialistic-poetic analysis which is not merely Artaud's 'return to the body' – as manifested, for instance, in his emphasis on material speech as glossolalia, theatre as cry and action[74] – but a materialism that realizes the real unreality and absurdity of capital's metaphoric-actual constructs, that imitates the operation of its processed materials even as it thus cries out against it with a violent *disgust*. This is what is the matter with Antonin Artaud, in terms both of the limits of his work, as it partially reduplicates bourgeois individualism and quasi-Fascist logic, and in its great strengths in protesting against that which it partially embodies, in making us feel its visceral material disgust, so that we will no longer be able to swallow the shit we are fed without *spitting*, without calling *bullshit* on that whole pile of shit. Artaud thus realizes what is historically latent in that opening word of Jarry's 'Ubu Roi', that deformed shit, 'merdre', and it is from here perhaps, that we can get our shit started and that our shit begins.

72   Prynne, *Poems*.
73   Wolfenstein, *Psychoanalytic-Marxism*.
74   For instance: 'shouts, colors and movements'; 'This perpetual play of mirrors passing from colour to gesture and from cry to movement'; 'these howls, these rolling eyes' ('On the Balinese Theatre', in Artaud (1958), 62–4).

Selected Bibliography

Artaud, Antonin, *Antonin Artaud: Selected Writings* [*SW*], ed. Susan Sontag, trans. Helen Weaver (Berkeley: University of California Press, 1976. [Works referenced in this edition: 'The Nerve Meter' (79–90); 'Theatre of Cruelty: First Manifesto' (242–51); 'Letter to Henri Parisot, Rodez, October 6, 1945' (451–55); 'Van Gogh: The Man Suicided by Society' (483–514); 'Letter to Pierre Loeb, Ivry, April 23, 1947' (515–22); 'Artaud le Mômo' (523–36); 'Here Lies' (537–54); 'To Have Done with the Judgement of God' (555–74); 'Letter to Paule Thévenin, Tuesday, February 24, 1948' (584–8).]

——, *Artaud Anthology* [*Anthology*], ed. Jack Hirschman, various translators (San Francisco: City Lights Books, 1965). [Works referenced in this edition: 'Shit to the Spirit' (trans Jack Hirschman, 106–12); 'The Tale of Popocatepetl' (David Rattray, 181–2).]

——, *The Theatre and its* Double, trans. Mary Caroline Richards (New York: Grove Press, 1958).

——, *Œuvres complètes, VII: Hélioglabale ou l'anarchiste corounné* (Paris: Gallimard, 1982).

——, *Œuvres complètes, XII* (Paris: Gallimard, 1974).

——, *Œuvres complètes, XVIII: Cahiers de Rodez* (Paris: Gallimard, 1976).

Bard-Rosenberg, Jacob, 'On the Composition of Lasagne: A Caprice on Horses, Abstraction, and the Division of Labour', *Prolapsarian* (2013) <http://prolapsarian.tumblr.com/post/43840250284/on-the-composition-of-lasagna-a-caprice-on-horses> accessed 16 March 2014.

Cornford, Adam, 'Processed Shit: Capitalism, Racism and Entropy', *Processed World* 30 (1992–3), 30–41.

Marx, Karl, *Early Writings*, trans. Gregor Benton [1975] (London: Penguin, 1992).

——, *Capital, Vol. 1*, trans. Ben Fowkes [1976] (London: Penguin, 1990).

——, *Collected Works, Volume 3: Marx and Engels 1843–1844*, trans. Clemens Dutt (New York: International Publishers, 1975).

——, *Karl Marx on Revolution*, ed. and trans. Saul K. Padover (New York: McGraw-Hill, 1971).

RYE HOLMBOE

Merdre

Tant à merdre, qu'à phynances et à physique.[1]

—PÈRE UBU

In her invaluable if at times ungenerous account of Jarry's life and works, *Alfred Jarry: Le surmâle de lettres* (1928), Rachilde (the nom de plume of the writer and novelist Marguerite Vallette-Eymery) describes the first performance of Alfred Jarry's *Ubu Roi* (1896) in terms that have fixed the event in the artistic firmament.

Writing some thirty years after the fact, Rachilde describes an evening of riots, bawdiness and laughter. According to her account, the very first word pronounced by Père Ubu, 'merdre', a misspelling of *merde* or shit, was met with a violent uproar. The audience, which included Guillaume Apollinaire, Stéphane Mallarmé and W.B. Yeats, immediately started heckling and throwing objects at the actors on stage. In Rachilde's words, 'Un tel tumulte s'ensuivit que Gémier dut rester muet pendant un quart d'heure, et c'est long, un quart d'heure, à la scène! [...] Cela s'appelle: *un trou*' (Rachilde's emphasis).[2] What Rachilde calls *un trou* produced a mixture of hilarity and anger. 'On rit, certes; mais certains se fâchèrent aussi, et toute la représentation fut entrecoupée de manifestations en divers sens.'[3] This is unsurprising – over the course of the play *merdre* is pronounced no fewer than thirty-three times.

---

1   Alfred Jarry, *Ubu Roi* in *Œuvres complètes de Jarry*, ed. Michel Arrivé (Paris: Gallimard, 1972). IV, 3, 96.
2   Rachilde, *Alfred Jarry: le surmâle de lettres* (Paris: Arléa, 2007), 71.
3   Ibid. 82.

Rachilde's use of a metaphorics of punctures and cuts (*entrecouper* stems from the verb *couper*, to cut) to describe *merdre*'s interruptive function is suggestive. Elsewhere in her book she notes that *merdre* sounds like the infinitive *perdre*, to lose.[4] It is as if the loss of *merdre*'s referential function – the surplus letter has drained the word of content – could puncture or cut the audience's symbolic structures of interpretation. The surface paradox is that a surplus could be felt as a loss, a material excess as a moment of lack or as a cut in the signifying chain. On this view the surplus letter -R- may be understood as a foreign body that functions as both material remainder and void. Something and nothing, -R- both masks and marks the point at which the symbolic order breaks down.

In his 'Dictionnaire d'*Ubu Roi*', the semiotician and literary critic Michel Arrivé notes that the terms *merdre, phynance* and *physique* are often articulated in close proximity to one another in Jarry's play and suggests that they function as a set of equivalents. For Arrivé, Jarry's use of -*ph*- instead of -*f*- in the word *phynance* – a difference that cannot be heard but only seen in writing – indicates that the -*ph*- forms part of a private code. This is reinforced by the fact that *phynance* is used twelve times in the play, *finance* forty times, with no apparent discrimination. For example, on several occasions the farcical despot Père Ubu is called the 'Maître des Finances'. Yet when he goes into battle against the Russians, one of his hands is replaced by a 'croc à phynance', his other hand clutches a 'pistolet à phynance', while his head is protected by a 'casque à finances'.[5] Arrivé goes on to argue that in Jarry's lexical system, the terms *phynance* and *physique* undergo a process of 'neutralization'; they are equivalent and can be exchanged without altering their content.[6] Citing Jacques Lacan, elsewhere Arrivé calls this neutralizing effect 'la phonction de phonation'.[7] Given that *phynance* is a homonym and

---

4   Ibid.
5   For an exhaustive analysis of the appearance of these terms, see Michel Arrivé's invaluable book *Les Langages de Jarry: Essai de sémiotique littéraire* (Paris: Klincksieck, 1972), 166–307.
6   Ibid. 241.
7   Michel Arrivé, *Langage et psychanalyse, linguistique et inconscient: Freud, Saussure, Pichon, Lacan* (Paris: PUF, 1994), 350.

not a pun, the point is well made. Here I would add that the reciprocal relation between *merdre*, *phynance* and *physique* may also imply that the logic of *phynance* is immanent, material and substantive, a physical and physiological process akin to defecation, a process that may also be related to phantasy (to borrow Melanie Klein's homonym) and to the phantasmagorical.

The present essay constitutes an attempt to come to terms with the ways in which these various relations and procedures coagulate in the word *merdre*. My argument is that, even if it is not always directly visible, the materialization of the surplus -R- provides the exception and founds the rule that structures Jarry's system of signs. More broadly, it will be argued that the word raises important questions about the abstracting impulses of capitalism, especially as these are played out in the dynamics of the money form and in the complex interplay between the artwork and the commodity. I also want to take this opportunity to sketch out the kind of subject formation at stake in these dialectical relations. Though I will concentrate on the word *merdre* alone, it is worth remarking that, like the Christian God, Pére Ubu claims to fashion and perfect words in his own image ('Je perfectionne et embellis les mots à mon image et à ma ressemblance').[8] If this is so, then whatever can be said of *merdre* can also be said of its creator, the Maître des Finances. Père Ubu, I argue elsewhere, is the pure incarnation of capital.

To place such conceptual weight on a single letter may seem eccentric. Yet Jarry makes the importance of the surplus -R- explicit. In his posthumously published *Gestes et opinions du docteur Faustroll, pataphysicien* (1911), which tells the story of Doctor Faustroll's travels to imaginary islands with the bailiff Panmuphle and the dog-faced baboon Bosse-de-Nage, who knows no words except 'Ha Ha' (though this proves to be sufficient), the protagonist lists twenty-seven writers whose books he keeps in his library. Among them is Jarry's *Ubu Roi*. In part seven, 'Du petit nombre des élus', Faustroll extracts from each of these authors a single element. Though cryptic and random-sounding to the reader, one can assume that they are pivotal for the

---

8   Almanach Illustré du Père Ubu [XXe Siècle], Ier janvier 1901, 'Confessions d'un Enfant du Siècle. Commentaires du Père Ubu sur les événements récents', in *Tout Ubu* (Paris: Le Livre de Poche, 1962), 407.

Doctor of Pataphysics. From François Rabelais, for instance, Faustroll takes 'les sonnettes auxquelles dansèrent les diables pendant la tempête'. From Maurice Maeterlinck, 'les lumières qu'entendit la première soeur aveugle'. From Jules Verne, 'les deux lieues et demie d'écorce terrestre'. And from *Ubu Roi* (whose author he does not name) he takes 'la cinquième lettre du premier mot du premier acte'.[9] Needless to say, that letter is the letter -R-.

Surprisingly little attention has been paid to this surplus letter and to the fictions it sets in train: what might be termed its operative value. In part this is because the effects of a single letter are easily dismissed. For some, the addition of the surplus -R- constitutes little more than an attempt at euphemism. It is there 'pour masquer le gros mot', as the French literary critic Aurélie Gendrat puts it.[10] Meanwhile, at the other end of the cultural spectrum, there are those who seem to have been overwhelmed by the aura that surrounds *merdre*, such that the surplus letter's operative value has been obscured. These critics are indebted to Rachilde's not always reliable account of *Ubu Roi*'s opening night. My aim here is not to dispel this myth; that work has already been done, with some interesting results, and if it is exaggerated it is still a good story.[11] Of greater concern are the effects this

---

9   Alfred Jarry, *Gestes et opinions du docteur Faustroll, Pataphysicien* (Paris: Bibliothèque Charpentier, 1911), 13–14. For a general analysis of Jarry's library, see Ben Fischer, *The Pataphysician's Library: An Exploration of Alfred Jarry's livres pairs* (Liverpool: Liverpool University Press, 2000).

10   Aurélie Gendrat, *Ubu Roi* (Paris: Bréal, 1999), 53–4. See also: Jill Fell, 'The Manufacture of a Modern Puppet Type: The Anatomy of Alfred Jarry's Monsieur Ubu and its Significance', in Katia Pizzi, ed., *Pinocchio, Puppets and Modernity: The Mechanical Body* (New York and London: Routledge, 2012), 75; Charles Chassé, *D'Ubu-Roi au Douanier Rousseau* (Paris: Nouvelle Revue Critique, 1947); and Louis Perche, *Jarry* (Paris: Editions Universitaires, 1965). Each critic makes a similar claim.

11   See in particular Frantisek Deak, *Symbolist Theater: The Formation of an Avant-Garde* (Baltimore: Johns Hopkins University Press, 1993), 227–47. Deak deals with the production of *Ubu Roi* in the context of symbolism and the Théâtre de l'Œuvre. Much of his argument is restated by Sebastian Trainor in 'Rachilde's *Supermâle of Letters* and the Invention of the *Ubu Roi* Riot', in Graley Herren, ed., *The Comparative Drama Conference Series (no. 9): Text and Presentation, 2012* (Jefferson, NC: MacFarland, 2013), 92–109.

fiction has had in the critical imagination: what could be termed a wilful amnesia. For the most part, critics seem unwilling to recall just how strange and underwhelming Père Ubu's first word must have sounded. Of these critics, Robert Shattuck is perhaps paradigmatic. In *The Banquet Years* (1958), he claims that *Ubu Roi* marked 'the close of one era and the imminence of another', by which he means modernism and the birth of the historical avant-garde, and hangs this claim on the violent reaction *merdre* produced.[12] The kind of modernism Shattuck has in mind here is not the modernism of pure, autonomous form, the kind later advanced by Alfred H. Barr and Clement Greenberg in their writings on formal abstraction in an American context, where the emphasis falls on medium specificity and formal coherence. Shattuck's modern art is not unmediated by modern life. Rather, it is the equally mythical (if more seductive) modernism of pure negation, of revolt, of perpetual revolution against the totality of modern existence. Yet Shattuck does little to account for the effect or for the materialization of the surplus -R-. For him *merdre* is simply synonymous with an avant-gardist aesthetic of shock and its concomitant: a violent denunciation of the values and representations of the bourgeoisie.

The psychoanalyst Jacques Lacan offers what are perhaps the most suggestive words concerning *merdre*. In an intensely illuminating passage from the essay 'Remarks on Daniel Lagache's Presentation: "Psychoanalysis and the Structure of the Personality"', published in 1958 (the same year as Shattuck's *The Banquet Years*), Lacan writes that

> the condensation [*condensation*] of a simple supplementary phoneme [...] was enough to give the most vulgar French exclamation the ejaculatory value [*la jaculation jaculatoire*, which could also be translated as 'jocular value' or 'jocular jaculation'], verging on the sublime, of the place it occupies in the epic of Ubu: that of the Word from before the beginning [*le Mot d'avant le commencement*].[13]

---

12 Roger Shattuck, *The Banquet Years* (New York: Random House, 1968), 209. The idea that *Ubu Roi* was such a founding moment has been put into question, most notably by Patrick Besnier, *Alfred Jarry* (Paris: Fayard, 2005).

13 Translation modified. Jacques Lacan, 'Remarks on Daniel Lagache's Presentation: "Psychoanalysis and the Structure of the Personality"', in Jacques Lacan, *Écrits*, trans. Bruce Fink (New York and London: W.W. Norton & Company, 2006), 553.

There are several points to draw out here. The first has to do with Lacan's use of the term 'condensation' to describe the materialization of the surplus -R-. The process of condensation should be understood in relation to Sigmund Freud's notion of the dream work, first developed in *The Interpretation of Dreams* (1900).[14] The dream work involves two fundamental mechanisms: condensation and displacement. The process of displacement is related to the defence mechanisms of the ego, to a kind of censorship. The process of condensation, on the other hand, transforms the latent content of the dream into the manifest dream content. The example Freud gives to illustrate this process is the pun, in which two or more meanings can be condensed into a single word. In the work of condensation, then, various latent elements are condensed into an ostensibly unified dream image.

According to Freud, however, what is significant in dream analysis is not the recovery of the dream's latent content, the secret meaning of the dream, since this content has been altered by the retroactive effect of memory, what Freud calls secondary revision. The dream is already an interpretation. Instead, one must come to terms with the primary process through which the dream comes into being, the process through which the latent dream content is condensed into the form of a thought. As Freud put it in a footnote added to *The Interpretation of Dreams* in 1925, 'at bottom dreams are nothing other than a particular form of thinking, made possible by the conditions of the state of sleep. It is the dream work that creates that form, and it alone is the essence of dreaming – the explanation of its peculiar nature'.[15] Paradoxically, the secret of the dream work is in the work of the dream, not in its manifest content. And it would seem that for Lacan this work is analogous to the materialization of the surplus -R-.

The second point is that this process seems to have a mortifying effect. The semiotician Francis Gandon has suggested that there is a connection between Lacan's enigmatic description of *merdre* as 'the Word from before

---

14   Sigmund Freud, *The Interpretation of Dreams*, trans. A.A. Brill (New York: Macmillan, 1913), 74.

15   Sigmund Freud, cited in Slavoj Žižek, *The Sublime Object of Ideology* (London: Verso, 1989), 14.

the beginning' and a process of mortification. For him, the rejection of a signified content leads to the rejection of the subject's 'voie d'accès au symbolique'.[16] Here we are not far from Rachilde's metaphorics of punctures and cuts, and the paradoxical notion that a material surplus – 'merdre' – might be experienced as a loss – 'perdre'. Gandon then relates this rejection to the incongruous images produced by psychotic children – the two examples he uses are 'Le bâton est un poisson mort' and 'le ballon est un champignon mortel' – where the semantic disarticulation between the rhyming referents becomes the site of death.[17] On this basis, Gandon concludes, the materialization of the signifier 'est très exactement une logique du "gramme" séparé du "logos": l'unité raisonnable', a logic connected to what he terms 'la mort à l'œuvre'.[18] The aphorism Gandon uses to illustrate this point belongs to the writer Adolphe Ripotois, 'le mot, c'est la mort sans en avoir l'R', which he translates into the following diagram:

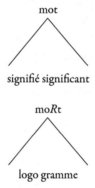

It is easy to see how *mot/merde* and *moRt/merdRe* might be interchangeable, leaving us with 'la merde, c'est la merdre sans en avoir l'R'. I will return to the play on words between -R- and air later, since it will prove decisive

16   Francis Gandon, 'X, Y, A', in *Le Signe et la Lettre: En hommage à Michel Arrivé* (Paris: L'Harmattan, 2002), 220. See also: Francis Gandon, *De Dangereux Édifices: Saussure Lecteur de Lucrèce, Les Cahiers d'Anagrammes Consacré au* De Rerum Natura (Paris: Éditions Peeters, 2001).

17   Gandon, 'X, Y, A', 220.

18   Ibid. 221.

when visualizing the processes through which something immaterial can condense itself into a material surplus, even if the pun is less successful in English. It will also bring me to the phantasmagorical logic of the commodity form and to the real effects of money. Here, though, I want to offer some preliminary remarks about how this deadening of language or mortifying effect might be related to the logic of the dream work.

Unlike other words, *merdre* does not represent something beyond itself. It is a word that does not seek to attach itself to a particular thing. In the absence of referent, it is rather like a thing or what Gandon termed a materialized signifier. The paradox is that the association between *merdre* and shit may have been heightened by virtue of this suspension of reference – *merdre* is as emphatically material and thing-like as shit; uncouth and inchoate, the word has curled up and turned in upon itself. To some extent, this internal self-sufficiency is characteristic of all swear-words, which are rarely used literally and which rarely lead beyond themselves. Swear-words might be imagined as blocks of acoustical matter whose affectivity depends upon convention, context and intonation rather than what they specifically refer to. In the expression 'fucking arsehole', for instance, the first term is used as an intensifier, the second as an adjunct, but the expression itself is nonsensical; or at least it does not lead you to imagine yourself as an arsehole that fucks.

Of course, swear-words are historical constructions, often revealing anxieties about gender and sexuation (e.g. 'bitch'), as well as social taboos and complexes (e.g. 'mother-fucker') – in Freud's terms this would be their 'latent content'. Nevertheless, their internal self-sufficiency may explain why they can be replaced with symbols such as &#%!@ – the kind often encountered in comic strips – without losing much of their intended sense. The other symbols that come to mind here are those used to represent money, as in the dollar sign -$-, which is also the symbol used by Lacan to represent the split that constitutes the Subject, a point I will return to. Here I simply want to point out that these symbols are ideogrammatic. They speak to the reader *non verbis, sed rebus*, not by words but by things. They are perhaps the closest thing modern European languages have to hieroglyphics.

With the process of condensation in mind, I want to suggest that these symbols may be analogous to those encountered in a dream: they are intelligible but they signify nothing and, when positioned in a series, they represent nothing. No image appears in the mind's eye except for the obdurate image of the symbols themselves. As such it is arguable that *merdre*'s articulation is closer to the production of an aesthetic object — a dream image perhaps, or an inanimate thing breathed momentarily into life — than it is to a communicative act. Like the symbols &#%!@, it is difficult to move beyond the word's emblematic exterior; and, like these symbols, *merdre* figures the referent it seems to refuse. *Merdre* is an afterimage of itself.

Which brings me to my third point. Lacan compares *merdre* to the Word incarnate, yet he claims that the Word only verges on the sublime. It has been argued that what Lacan means in these lines is that *merdre*'s affectivity restores the subject to a state of oneness with nature, a condition before the beginning, understood as a pre-linguistic state. On this view Père Ubu is a figure of vitality, while the articulation of *merdre* is understood as the cry of life itself: 'le cris, le cri de la passion, de l'amour, de la haine', as the French literary critic Daniel Accursi has put it, who goes so far as to say that *merdre* abolishes representation and collapses the distinction between art and life.[19] Accursi allows himself this somewhat inflated claim by viewing the figure of Père Ubu through the lens of Dadaism and its ideology of immediacy and bodily presence (what the art historian Benjamin Buchloh has derogated as 'petit-bourgeois anarchist radicality').[20] Shattuck would probably have heard a similar cry in *merdre* for the word to mark the birth of the historical avant-garde.

Yet such readings do not take into account the material specificities of what Jarry calls Père Ubu's 'accent' or 'voix spéciale', which is not characterized by spontaneity or by its liveliness of expression.[21] Nor do these readings account for Jarry's claim in *Ubu Roi*'s prologue that the actors performing on the opening night have agreed 'de se faire [...] impersonnels et de jouer enfermés dans un masque, afin d'être bien exactement l'homme intérieur et l'âme des grandes marionettes que vous allez voir'.[22] Though *Ubu Roi*

19   Daniel Accursi, *La Philosophie d'Ubu* (Paris: PUF, 1999), 55.
20   Benjamin H.D. Buchloh, 'Conceptual Art 1962–1969: From the Aesthetic of Administration to the Critique of Institutions', *October* 55 (1990), 105–43 (137).
21   Alfred Jarry, 'Lettre à Lugné-Poe' [1896], *Œuvres Complètes*, Vol. 1, 1043.
22   Jarry, *Œuvres Complètes*, Vol. 1, 399–400.

was written for marionettes, these proved too costly and time-consuming to make, so the play was performed by human actors who were asked to 'poussez au guignol le plus possible'.[23]

Rachilde, for her part, is clear in this regard. Conflating Jarry with his creation, she recalls how the former pronounced each syllable of every word, so that his speech seemed to be hammered out ['martelé'] 'comme les dents d'un engrenage rouillé': '*Ma-da-me!* disait le Père Ubu'.[24] In his suggestively titled novel *Les Faux-Monnayeurs* (1925), André Gide also uses the metaphor of a hammer to describe Jarry's speech. According to Gide, the latter would articulate words 'en martelant les syllables', while inventing bizarre words and strangely deforming others.[25] People tried to imitate him, but for Gide only Jarry could achieve 'cette voix sans timbre, sans chaleur, sans intonation, sans relief'.[26] Another contemporary compares Jarry's voice to that of a dead man. According to this account, Jarry entered the stage on *Ubu Roi*'s opening night covered in thick white make up and delivered his prologue 'd'une voix morte et de façon inintelligible'.[27] It is in this way that Père Ubu would have spoken, an effect accentuated by his cardboard mask, which would have muffled the sound of Gémier's voice.

Merdre, then, should not be cried out in a single breath. Instead, one should adopt a flat, monotonous and mechanical voice like the one that might emerge from a marionette, and emphasize each of the word's three syllables. First the r-sound rolls off the tongue; then it is interrupted with

---

23   Ibid.

24   Rachilde, *Alfred Jarry*, 29.

25   'Vêtu en traditionnel Gugusse d'hippodrome, tout, en Jarry, sentait l'apprêt: sa façon de parler surtout, qu'irritaient à l'envi plusieurs Argonautes, martelant les syllables, inventant de bizarres mots, en estropiant bizarrement certain autres, mais il n'y avait vraiment que Jarry lui-même pour obtenir cette voix sans timbre, sans chaleur, sans intonation, sans relief': André Gide, *Les Faux-Monnayeurs* (Paris: Gallimard, Folio, 1925), 287–8.

26   Ibid.

27   Georges Raymond, cited in Patrick Besnier, *Alfred Jarry* (Paris: Fayard, 2005). Also cited in Karl Pollin, *Alfred Jarry: l'expérimentation du singulier* (Amsterdam and New York: Rodopi, 2013), 11.

a d-sound that reverberates on the ridge just behind the front upper-teeth; then the r-sound rolls off the tongue again: mer-d-re. The alveolar trill [r] that frames the lingua-alveolar plosive [d] makes *merdre* particularly difficult to articulate, especially when the word is repeated, as it is in the almost palindromic 'merdre merdre merdre'.[28] To pronounce the word in this way, with a flat, almost inhuman rigour, does not make you feel more alive. It makes you feel ventriloquized. *Merdre* fills your mouth with shitre.

What must be emphasized at this point is that *merdre* underscores its own status as a construction. It draws attention to the materiality of language, to its physical fabric. The letters that comprise the word – M E R D R E – are sensuous and real in their own right. They are uprooted signs stripped down to their essential features, plastic particles of language rearranged in the space of a shape. Nauseatingly sated, *merdre* is literally brimming with letters. And if the word from before the beginning verges on the sublime, sharing what the literary critic Eric Santner has described as the 'mute "thingness" of nature', the crucial point is that it is not the language of nature that is bodied forth as real presence but the language of artifice, of artfulness.[29] Language has been denatured. The logic of incarnation has been inverted. *Merdre* is not the Word made flesh so much as the flesh made Word. *Merdre* is a lexical monstrosity, a maculate conception that shows all the flaws of incomplete metamorphosis and failed sublimation. This twisted, uncanny genesis may provide one reason behind Lacan's claim that *merdre* only verges on the sublime.

Finally, there is Lacan's near-pun 'la jaculation jaculatoire', which suggests that there is only the finest line separating the sublime from the ridiculous. Whatever claims can be made for a surplus -R-, whatever its ejaculatory value and whatever its proximity to the sublime, it is also an opaque material remainder that mocks us, not only for our inability to deal with it, but for our very attempt to deal with it. The thing might be a joke,

28 Jarry, *Ubu Roi*.
29 Eric Santner, *On Creaturely Life: Rilke, Benjamin, Sebald* (Chicago: University of Chicago Press: 2006), xv.

to which one might simply respond, like the dog-faced baboon Bosse-de-Nage, 'Ha Ha', and not lose oneself in further considerations.

***

Phallus déraciné, *ne fait pas de pareils bonds!*[30]
—ALFRED JARRY, *Le Surmâle*

So far I have tried to show how three analogous procedures coalesce in the word *merdre*: materialization, condensation and mortification. In addition, it would seem that *merdre* suffers from an internal division: the word verges on the sublime, but it is also a dumb thing, suggesting that the condensation of the surplus -R- transfigures as much as it mortifies. One might also say that -R- splits the identity of things in two. *Merdre* is both animated and drained, sacred and profane, seductive and superfluous, sublime and excremental. These states of things might be termed, respectively, 'thingitude' and 'thingness', terms which could also describe the puppet or the marionette, objects that are strange, animate and dreamlike – fetish objects perhaps – but also inert, crudely material and thinglike. As the literary critic Kenneth Gross put it in his essay on the uncanny life of puppets, 'what you feel is the presence of a composite or double body, animate and inanimate at once [...], it may be a body within a body, or a soul within a soul'.[31]

In this section I want to argue that the division between thingness and thingitude is an effect of what has been termed the real abstraction of capital. It will be argued that the materialization of the surplus -R- has a function analogous to that of money, and that the dream work arguably operating in *merdre* is homologous to the logic whereby the commodity form attains its imaginary unity. Jarry once called his theatre 'un théâtre ABSTRAIT', placing

30   Jarry, *Œuvres Complètes*, 339.
31   Kenneth Gross, *Puppet: An Essay on Uncanny Life* (Chicago: University of Chicago Press, 2011), 55.

the term in capital letters as if to emphasize its materiality.[32] Accordingly, it will be argued that the mode of abstraction staged in *Ubu Roi* cuts against the grain of convention and common sense. Symbolic forms conventionally suggest something immaterial, spiritual or pure. Through a mechanism of what the semiotician and literary critic Michael Riffaterre has termed 'semantic indirection', akin perhaps to the process of displacement in the dream work, they intimate a higher, ideational, 'abstract' reality detached from concrete life.[33] In Jarry's object-world, however – the figural and insistently material world of the puppet theatre – symbolic forms are animated but gravity-bound, unable to become airborne. To return once more to Rachilde's metaphorics, one might say that they are punctured or cut, always on the brink of imploding, of collapsing in on themselves. It will be argued that it is this desublimation of symbolic forms that makes Jarry's theatre really ABSTRAIT.

In *The Sublime Object of Ideology*, Slavoj Žižek draws a parallel between Freud's analysis of dreams and Karl Marx's analysis of commodities. In both cases, Žižek writes, 'the "secret" to be unveiled through analysis is not the content hidden by the form [...] but, on the contrary, the "*secret*" of this form itself'. If classical political economy understood the labour theory of value – the notion that the value of a commodity is equal to the quantity of socially necessary labour time for its production – what remained unexplained in its analyses were the various processes through which this latent content had assumed that particular form. What remained undetermined was the definitive source of a commodity's value. Thus the commodity-form remained an enigmatic, mysterious thing. In Marx's words from his well-known passage on the commodity fetish:

> A commodity appears, at first sight, a very trivial thing, and easily understood. Its analysis shows that it is, in reality, a very queer thing, abounding in metaphysical

---

32 'Nous croyons être sûrs d'assister à une naissance du théâtre, car pour la première fois, il y a en France (ou en Belgique, à Cand, nous ne voyons pas la France dans un territoire inanimé maie dans une langue, et Maeterlinck est aussi justement à nous que nous répudions Mistral) un théâtre ABSTRAIT': Alfred Jarry, 'Douze arguments sur le théâtre', in *Tout Ubu* (Paris: Livre de Poche, 1962), 146–7.

33 Michael Riffaterre, *Semiotics of Poetry* (London: Methuen, 1980), 2.

subtleties and theological niceties. So far as it is a value in use, there is nothing mysterious about it [...]. It is as clear as noon-day that man, by his industry, changes the forms of the materials furnished by Nature, in such a way as to make them useful to him. The form of wood, for instance, is altered, by making a table out of it. Yet, for all that, the table continues to be that common, every-day thing, wood. But, so soon as it steps forth as a commodity, it is changed into something transcendent. It not only stands with its feet on the ground, but, in relation to all other commodities, it stands on its head, and evolves out of its wooden brain grotesque ideas, far more wonderful than 'table-turning' ever was.[34]

It will have been noted that the phantasmagorical table functions in a way comparable to *merdre*: it too is a radically desublimated symbol, and it too has been animated by money, which transforms it into an exchange-value. In order to account for this uncanny vitality, Žižek turns to the Marxian economist Alfred Sohn-Rethel's notion of 'real abstraction'.[35] Sohn-Rethel developed this notion in *Intellectual and Manual Labour*, in which he argues that 'the formal analysis of the commodity holds the key [...] to the historical explanation of the abstract conceptual mode of thinking'.[36] Paraphrasing this passage, Žižek claims that the transcendental preconditions of thought – the various categories which found the *a priori* frame of 'objective' knowledge – are identical to those that structure the act of commodity exchange. 'Before thought could arrive at pure *abstraction*', Žižek writes, 'the abstraction was already at work in the social effectivity of the market'. As Marx's description of the phantasmagorical table suggests, abstraction was already at work in the exchange of commodities, which allows Žižek to argue that 'the real abstraction [read: the commodity fetish] is the unconscious of the transcendental subject'.[37] The subject is an afterimage of the commodity form.

---

34   Karl Marx, *Capital: A Critique of Political Economy, Vol. 1*, trans. Ben Fowkes (New York: Vintage, 1977), 163.
35   See Alfred Sohn-Rethel, *Intellectual and Manual Labour: A Critique of Epistemology* (London: Macmillan, 1978).
36   Sohn-Rethel, cited in Žižek, *The Sublime Object of Ideology*, 16.
37   Ibid. 19.

The example Žižek uses to illustrate this point is the money-commodity (though what he says can equally apply to the dancing table, or indeed to *merdre*). For Žižek the money-commodity suffers from an internal division. It is as if it had two bodies, a 'body within the body', as he puts it.[38] The one is material and contingent – simple things like coins or notes that are subject to degradation – the other is immaterial and unchanging, almost sublime. The caveat is that the money-commodity's two bodies, though never completely separate from one another, don't add up. Why? Because the money-commodity does not contain value as such, at least not in the same way that a commodity's material qualities determine its use-value. Like a commodity's value-form, the money-commodity is a form distinct from the actual, contingent, material body of money itself. It is a purely ideal form. It is for this reason that Žižek claims that the nature of real abstraction is that of a 'postulate implied by the effective act of exchange'.[39] In other words, that of a certain 'as if' [*als ob*] (the expression is Sohn-Rethel's). As Žižek writes, italicizing the expression, 'during the act of exchange, individuals process *as if* the commodity is not submitted to physical, material exchanges; *as if* it is excluded from the natural cycle of generation and corruption'.[40]

For Žižek this process is premised on a moment of fetishistic disavowal. People are perfectly conscious of the fact that money is neutral, that it is simply the expression of a social relation, but they behave as if it consisted of an immutable substance, 'a substance over which time had no power'.[41] The point to draw here, however, is not that the reality of money is a fiction. Rather, it is the fictive dimension of money that makes exchange-value real. That the value-form of money is immaterial and incorporeal does not prevent it from having a real existence, a 'sublime materiality',[42] as Žižek puts it. Yet the money-commodity only verges on the sublime since, like the dream image, it is a material composite, a maculate conception.

38 Ibid. 18.
39 Ibid.
40 Ibid.
41 Ibid.
42 Ibid.

Its unity is imaginary. It is for this reason that Žižek compares its second body to the Sadean victim who can endure whatever physical torments and survive with its beauty untouched. The dream of unity is preserved through a kind of symbolic mortification.

I want to suggest that it is here that the logic of *phynance, physique* and *merdre* coincide. The point is that value does not inhere in shit (read: money or commodities). Value is as immaterial as air. Yet we behave *as if* value inhered in shit, *as if* this value came from nowhere. That is why *phynance* is also a physical and physiological process akin to defecation, one that is intimately tied to the space of phantasy. In other words, the logic of the 'as if' is such that something as immaterial as air can condense itself into a surplus -R-. The loss of *merdre*'s referential function makes the word both ABSTRAIT – in the sense of an aesthetic object that has lost its mimetic function – and more real, in that it therefore becomes more thing-like or shit-like or 'reified'. And this process is experienced as both a loss of meaning – *perdre* – and as a material excess – *merdre*. To repeat an earlier point, the materialization of the surplus -R- both masks and marks the point at which the symbolic order breaks down.

Marcel Duchamp seems to have touched upon this notion in a *calembour* where (to return to the title of Gide's novel) the artwork or aesthetic object emerges as counterfeit money: 'Arrhe est à art ce que merdre est à merde', where arrhe means a deposit of money.[43] Duchamp translated this analogy into the following fractional equation:

$$\frac{arrhe}{art} = \frac{merdre}{merde}$$

With the process of mortification in mind, one could now add a third element:

$$\frac{arrhe}{art} = \frac{merdre}{merde} = \frac{mort}{mot}$$

43   Marcel Duchamp, cited in Thierry de Duve, *Sewn in the Sweatshop of Marx: Beuys, Warhol, Klein, Duchamp* (Chicago: University of Chicago Press, 2012), 66.

What the above analysis suggests is that these equations are more than static correspondences. Real abstraction is a process as indifferent as the laws of physics. It is a process that could be defined as a process of concretion or the becoming concrete of the ABSTRAIT. One might also say that real abstraction is the process through which something as immaterial as air can condense itself or materialize itself into a surplus -R-, a surplus that splits the identity of things in two. The analogy between the dream work and real abstraction may therefore be summed up by the simple equation:

$$R = \$$$

And $\$$ is the symbol used by Lacan to represent the split that constitutes the Subject.

Selected Bibliography

Accursi, Daniel, *La Philosophie d'Ubu* (Paris: PUF, 1999).

Arrivé, Michel, *Les Langages de Jarry: essai de sémiotique littéraire* (Paris: Klincksieck, 1972).

Duve, Thierry de, *Sewn in the Sweatshop of Marx: Beuys, Warhol, Klein, Duchamp* (Chicago: University of Chicago Press, 2012).

Jarry, Alfred, *Œuvres Complètes de Jarry*, ed. Michel Arrivé (Paris: Gallimard, 1972).

——, *Gestes et opinions du docteur Faustroll, Pataphysicien*: (Paris: Bibliothèque Charpentier, 1911).

Marx, Karl, *Capital: A Critique of Political Economy*, Vol. *1*, trans. Ben Fowkes (New York: Vintage, 1977).

Shattuck, Roger, *The Banquet Years* (New York: Random House, 1968).

Sohn-Rethel, Alfred, *Intellectual and Manual Labour: A Critique of Epistemology* (London: Macmillan, 1978).

Žižek, Slavoj, *The Sublime Object of Ideology* (London: Verso, 1989).

PART 4

Transformations of Temporality and Materiality

JENNIFER JOHNSON

Surface Matters: Georges Rouault's Materiality

This paper will offer a short exploration of the work of the French painter Georges Rouault (1871–1958), and the questions of materiality and meaning raised by his painting in the first years of the twentieth century. In 1890, Rouault entered the Ecole des Beaux-Arts to study painting, and, from 1891, was a student of the Symbolist Gustave Moreau, alongside Matisse and Marquet. The death of Moreau in 1898, by then a much-revered mentor to Rouault, prompted a period of crisis for the painter during which time he moved away from the literary symbolism of his much-lauded early works to an increasingly thick, roughly applied facture that the critics found impenetrable; a materiality that appeared to obscure and to block meaning. Rouault has a difficult relationship to narratives of modernism. At times, his attention to surface facture has much in common with Fauvist mark-making, but at the same time Rouault's painterly marks resist Fauvism's tendency towards abstraction by remaining yoked to representation. Rouault combines an apparently highly modernist pictorial vocabulary with a subject matter seemingly dredged-up, or lingering-on, from the previous century – prostitutes, clowns, circus scenes – as well as religious themes such as the head of Christ. From the start, this subject matter was seen as distancing Rouault from 'mainstream' modernism. There is not space here to consider these works at length, or to take in fully the theological and philosophical complexities of Rouault's work.[1] Therefore, the following discussion will examine in detail

---

1   See my forthcoming thesis, 'Georges Rouault's Modernism and the Question of Materiality' (University of Oxford). Excellent studies of Rouault include: Stephen Schloesser, ed., *Mystic Masque: Semblance and Reality in Georges Rouault 1871–1958* (Boston: McMullen Museum of Art, 2008); Soo Yun Kang, *Rouault in Perspective: Contextual and Theoretical Study of his Art* (Boston and Oxford: International

just one of these works, *Tête de clown tragique*, and argue that Rouault's project presents a subtle and nuanced resistance to modernism's celebration of the materiality of the surface, or rather, an insistence that meaning resides therein, twinned with a simultaneous questioning of whether paint – paint understood as *matter* – *can* contain meaning in this way.

Georges Rouault, *Tête de clown tragique* (1904–5), 37cm × 26.5cm,
Kunsthaus, Zurich / gift of Dr Max Bangerter, Montreux.

When the critic Louis Vauxcelles saw Rouault's entries to the 1904 Salon d'Automne in Paris (eight oils and thirty-six watercolours and pastels,

Scholars Publication, 2000); and Pierre Courthion, *Georges Rouault* (Paris: Flammarion, 1962).

probably including *Tête de clown tragique*),[2] he wrote that one could distinguish nothing: 'nothing save a paste made up of caviar, blacking, and pitch', and went on to wonder what sort of light there must be in Monsieur Rouault's studio: what over-smoked glass concealed nature and light to this 'misogynous dreamer who plunges into the depths of Erebus?'[3] He was not alone; Rouault's works were also described as 'coal-daubed nightmares', as 'dark mistakes', as barbarous images without any rapport whatsoever with 'true art', as a 'babbling collection of horrors', and as a slapping of paint onto canvas that ended simply in incomprehensible, chaotic forms. The critics' terms emphasize a perceived 'lowness' to Rouault's pictorial vocabulary. Nothing can be distinguished except the paint, which is reduced to 'paste', to 'caviar', and then, lower still, to 'blacking and pitch'. In evoking other materials to describe the paint, the paint matter is denied (and apparently refuses) the status of signifier. It does not seem to carry meaning, but to block interpretative efforts – it is physically in the way. The image of the darkened, smoky glass that conceals opposes Leon Battista Alberti's well-known metaphor of the painting as a window, to be seen through, in which the paint matter becomes transparent and, usually, points to something beyond itself.

Vauxcelles is describing an encounter in which his expectations of Rouault's painting are thwarted. One way of understanding Vauxcelles' difficulty would be to re-articulate the encounter in the terms offered by the recent theoretical work collectively described as New Materialisms,[4] which

---

2   As Rouault only sporadically and intermittently signed and dated his works – often returning to and reworking them as he rarely considered his paintings to be 'finished' – as well as repeating general titles such as 'filles' or 'clown' for dozens of works, it is difficult to date these works exactly, and to match them to the details of the works hung at the Salons d'Automne and Indépendants during 1904–9. This is exacerbated by Rouault's tendency to change or add to titles retrospectively. The 1904 catalogue includes listings for '1621: *Clown*, pastel', '1623: *Monsieur Clown*', and five listings, 1093–97, as 'Croquis de cirque', which might all refer to *Tête de clown tragique*, as might the listing for work '1490: *Clown*' in the 1906 Salon d'Automne catalogue.

3   Louis Vauxcelles, *Gil Blas*, 14 October 1904, quoted and translated in Irina Fortunesca, ed., *Rouault*, trans. Richard Hilliard (Bucharest and London: Abbey Library, 1975), 12.

4   See, amongst others: Bruno Latour, *We Have Never Been Modern* (Cambridge, MA: Harvard University Press, 1991); Graham Harman, 'Realism without Materialism',

– although not necessarily particularly new, nor strictly materialist – turn
towards matter, challenging the reduction of the non-human world to mere
inanimate matter, and re-envisaging the notion of things and objects as trou-
blesome to sign-narratives. In the article that inaugurated 'Thing Theory',
one aspect of New Materialisms, published in *Critical Inquiry* in 2001, Bill
Brown describes a moment in A.S. Byatt's novel *The Biographer's Tale* where
the main protagonist – a doctoral student – 'Fed up with Lacan as with
deconstructions of the Wolf-man', looks up at a grimy, dirty window and
'epiphanically thinks, "I must have *things*"'.[5] It is, writes Brown, a moment of
relinquishing theory to relish the world at hand: 'A real, very dirty window,
shutting out the sun. A *thing*'.[6] Whilst there is momentary relief for Byatt's
protagonist, it is based upon a false assumption about the stability of 'things';
the stability of the material over the immaterial. In fact, as Brown explains,
we only encounter things in their thingness through chance interruptions;
moments of contingency that 'disclose a physicality of things'.[7] These interruptions and confrontations occur when an object stops working for us –
in Byatt's novel it is the interruption of the usual habit of looking *through*
windows that provides the rare instance of looking *at* a window as an opaque
thing. Vauxcelles is describing a similar experience: Rouault's painting does
not respond to the usual ways of looking at paintings, which forces Vauxcelles
to confront the works as things. Vauxcelles sees 'nothing' but at the same
time acknowledges the presence of an almost excessive materiality. It is this
opaque, impenetrable – viscous even – thingness that the paste, the caviar,
the blacking and pitch attempt to describe. Vauxcelles' experience faced with
this paint-matter is not the quest for certainty represented by things over
theory, but a realization that to encounter something in a thing-like state
is to encounter a threshold 'between the nameable and unnameable, the

---

SubStance 40.2 (2011), 55–72; Jane Bennett, *Vibrant Matter: A Political Ecology of
Things* (Durham, NC: Duke University Press, 2010); Diana Coole and Samantha
Frost, *New Materialisms: Ontology, Agency, and Politics* (Durham, NC: Duke
University Press, 2010).

5   Bill Brown, 'Thing Theory', *Critical Inquiry* 28.1 (2001), 1.

6   A.S. Byatt, *The Biographer's Tale* (New York: Alfred A. Knopf, 2001), 2.

7   Brown, 'Thing Theory', 4.

figurable and unfigurable, the identifiable and unidentifiable'.[8] On the one hand it is the thing faced honestly and directly: on the other it is something not fully – perhaps not even partially – apprehended.

The opaque window can also be seen as emblematic of the modernist concern with the status of the surface. Another such window appears in James Joyce's short story 'The Sisters' from *The Dubliners*, where the narrator's gaze through a window is obstructed by a 'darkened blind'.[9] The window becomes a surface, and its materiality is attended to. It is 'read' by the viewer as a sign of the death that has occurred inside the house. As in Vauxcelles' account of Rouault's 'black canvases', there is an absence, there is 'nothing' to see (echoed by the death inside the house), but at the same time there is the dark materiality of the window that has become a shape, or a thing. This apparent threat to signification made it hard for Rouault's first viewers to make sense of his work, but in their baffled responses there are also hints that they sensed meaningful possibilities in his paintings, even if they were unable to articulate those meanings with any clarity.

Tête de clown tragique, painted circa 1904–5, is one of the eighty-three works devoted to circus themes painted by Rouault between 1902 and 1910. Typical of Rouault's experiments with mixed media during this period, it is a combination of watercolour, pastel, and gouache on paper. It is also one of Rouault's literally darkest works: a face, the features roughly demarcated by thick gestural black marks, emerges from a mass of dark streaks and patches in which the accoutrements of a clown – a hat, circular collar, and oversized buttons on the chest – are laid out in equally rough patches of blue outlined in black with a flash of white denoting the direction of the pleats of the collar. The patches of colour are applied in a scumbled or scribbled manner, through which the colour and texture of the paper is visible. The thick black lines have a heaviness combined with a gestural dynamism that appears to hew the face out of its ground in a manner that recalls the surface of a block used in wood-cutting, or a crudely executed wood-engraving. Although the face – or, specifically, certain facial features; cheek bones, eye

8   Ibid. 5.
9   James Joyce, *Dubliners* (London: Grant Richards, 1914), 9.

sockets, nose and jaw – emerges from the paper, it never escapes entirely from the work as a whole. The torso of the clown fills the entirety of the canvas – exceeds it, even, as the hat and shoulders are cut off by the edges of the paper. It has something of the theatrical portrait to it – up-front and confrontational, but at the same time caught up and kept at a distance by the tangled web of painterly marks. The dark active lines operate across the paper giving the surface a sense of unity, drawing attention to it in a manner that effectively collapses the figure-ground distinction. At the same time, this unity is tenuous, giving way everywhere to disorder, to daubs and dashes. Demonstrative of this is the monkey which, with prolonged attention (and especially if one is familiar with the recurrence of the same loosely indicated animal across Rouault's circus works), can be divined on the shoulder of the clown, filling the top left of the painting. A jumble of marks, the monkey serves to utterly dissolve any sense of depth between foreground and background by pictorially belonging to the mark-making of the ground, but simultaneously 'belonging' to (sitting on) the subject.

Darkness is the absence of light, and light is conventionally one of the organizing principles of painting: Paul de Man writes that 'Light implies space which, in turn, implies the possibility of spatial differentiation, the play of distance and proximity that organizes perception as the foreground-background juxtaposition that links it to the aesthetics of painting'.[10] If the Impressionist and Neo-Impressionist interest in light was to do with its phenomenal power in revealing the world as it is seen, Rouault's use of black opposes space and proposes a matter that hides or closes off the representation of a recognizable world. To some extent this sounds like a Greenbergian reading – representation ceding to abstract mark-making is, after all, precisely what he looked for in modernism. But Clement Greenberg was unimpressed, describing Rouault as a pornographic, sadomasochistic embarrassment to modern art.[11] The critic's response is hyperbolic but

10   Paul de Man, 'Anthropomorphism and Trope in the Lyric', *The Rhetoric of Romanticism* (New York: Columbia University Press, 1984), 258.
11   Clement Greenberg 'Georges Rouault' [1945], in Greenberg, *Art and Culture: Critical Essays* [1961] (Boston: Beacon Press, 1989), 86.

revealing; Rouault's works disrupt Greenberg's account of the purity of painterliness, retaining what Greenberg saw as a literariness that had no place in painting. What specifically distinguishes Rouault from this story here is that the image remains uncertainly suspended between representation and abstraction, teetering on the verge of both but committing to neither. This is also played out in the visual space within which the clown is located. If the monkey is a disequilibrious presence, there is an answering stabilizing or steadying presence in the painting. In the top right-hand corner of the work there is a broad vertical brush mark that appears to denote a structure – an 'edge' of something – conventionally 'behind' the clown's hat. Whether this 'edge' belongs to a door, a wall, or a poster (several of Rouault's paintings of clowns have the rectangular shapes of advertisements around and behind the figures) is not important; what is important is that it is not clear, it is *not* the specifically located spaces of Toulouse-Lautrec's or Seurat's circus scenes. What this particular structuring but unspecific mark in *Tête de clown tragique* puts under strain is the attempt to privilege either form or content. It is a painting of a clown, but at the same time it is a painting haunted by the image of a clown (haunted by its subject matter in a manner akin (albeit via a very different aesthetic) to the way that Picasso's 1911 cubist work *Man with a Pipe* offers up what T.J. Clark describes as 'the generalized ghost of a man')[12] – what is nameable and what is unnameable, identifiable and unidentifiable, is ambiguous or deeply uncertain: clown or paint?

What is 'clown' in the work, then, has its own unverifiable status built into it because, although as we have noted, the marks hew out the face of a clown amongst themselves, they posit nothing more than this. The mixed media draws attention to the differing textures of the materials used, but no direct claim upon the 'outside' world is made by these marks; they contain no instrumental relation to the textures of the clown, to fabric or flesh, or even three-dimensionality. However, that – apparently paradoxically – we speak of the 'clown' in Rouault's work immediately creates an excess of meaning to the marks as 'mere' or 'pure' paint.

12   T.J. Clark, 'Cubism and Collectivity', *Farewell to an Idea: Episodes in a History of Modernism* (New Haven and London: Yale University Press: 1999), 216.

It is a claim of the New Materialisms that they abandon the terminology of matter as an inert substance,[13] that matter is always more than 'mere' matter, but arguably paint-matter has always had a peculiarly dual status as part-matter part-actor in the event that is painting. Materially, Rouault's marks are not 'pure' matter – they are corrupted or muddied by the activity of painting, their application is, at least to some extent, bound up with the appearance of the head of the clown in their midst. On the other hand, these marks declare themselves, first and foremost, as material things – they do not, as we have said, give way to representing the clown's coat or collar. We can tell what kind of brush was used, and we can divine more about the substance of the paint matter than we do about the subject, but, nevertheless, they remain tied up with the subject. The marks 'show their own workings', but this does not allow us to work back through the operation, as it were, to pull apart the paint and the clown. Judith Butler has pointed out that in both Latin and Greek, 'matter (*materia* and *hyle*) is neither a simple, brute positivity or referent nor a blank surface or slate awaiting an external signification, but is always in some sense temporalized',[14] and this is also the case for Marx's account of materialism, when 'matter' is understood as a principle of *transformation*, 'presuming and inducing a future'. Matter – and this seems particularly relevant to trying to grasp the role of a paint-matter that declares itself whilst simultaneously going about its conventional work – contains potentiality (its Aristotelian definition). In this sense, Butler writes: 'to know the significance of something is to know how and why it matters, where to matter means at once "to materialize" and "to mean"'.[15] Rouault's picture posits both the marks and the clown as the 'something' to know the significance of, which leaves both wrapped up in each other's process of materialization (what Butler calls the 'indissolubility

---

13   Diana Coole and Samantha Frost, 'Introducing the New Materialisms', in Coole and Frost, eds, *New Materialisms: Ontology, Agency, and Politics* (Durham, NC: Duke University Press, 2010), 9.

14   Judith Butler, *Bodies that Matter: On the Discursive Limits of 'Sex'* (London: Routledge, 1993), 7.

15   Ibid. 7.

of materiality and signification'),[16] re-orienting the uncertainty between paint and clown towards a question about what it is to *make* meaning.

The conception of matter as a principle of transformation loses the exteriority that notions of 'pure' matter or inert matter are supposed to secure.[17] However, Butler's question here is markedly different from that of the New Materialists, and it provides a useful distinction. In Butler's terms we have to ask whether language, in this case painterly mark-making, can simply refer to materiality, or if language or painting are also the 'very condition under which materiality may be said to appear?' Although New Materialists such as Jane Bennett also draw upon a history of thought in which materiality is figured 'not as inert or even particularly passively resistant but as active and energetic,'[18] for Bennett matter is an *active principle* and 'though it inhabits us and our inventions, also acts as an outside or alien power.'[19] This assumes an a priori meaningfulness to matter, and suggests the possibility of separating a meaningful matter from the processes to which it is subjected, or a materiality that is not in fact indissolubly bound up with another discourse. As Diana Coole puts it, 'Is it not possible to imagine matter quite differently: as perhaps a lively materiality that is self-transformative and already saturated with the agent capabilities and existential significance that are typically located in a separate, ideal, and subjectivist realm?'[20] This is tricky for painting, which is inherently *both* a material object and a temporalized process. It is true that the material qualities of the medium have always had a role in aesthetics and the notion of a 'truth to materials', which arose in the nineteenth century – most notably in the writings of John Ruskin who made it both an aesthetic and an ethic[21] – drew particular attention to an empathetic relationship between the work of the artist and his or her

16 Ibid. 6.
17 Ibid. 6 and 31.
18 Jane Bennett, 'A Vitalist Stopover on the Way to a New Materialism', in *New Materialisms: Ontology, Agency, and Politics*, 47.
19 Ibid.
20 Diana Coole, 'The Inertia of Matter and the Generativity of Flesh', *New Materialisms: Ontology, Agency, and Politics*, 92.
21 John Ruskin, *The Seven Lamps of Architecture* (London: Smith, Elder, & Co., 1849).

materials. Furthermore, as modernist painting increasingly reflected upon its own condition, it more explicitly proposed a conversation or mutability between paint-matter and subject that transgresses the conventional object/subject divide. However, at the same time, if paint-matter is meaningful in and of itself, it is because it has acquired a history of its own use, application, associations, reception, and 'meaningfulness'. The problem that this 'history' challenges is the attribution of these qualities to the matter itself: on the one hand, the qualities of wood are always those of wood, but the way they were brought to bear upon the representation at work in a work of art was rarely ever (in the late nineteenth and early twentieth century) because they were just 'there', speaking for themselves. The associations that paint-matter has acquired have, to a large extent, been put there through the activities of centuries of painters. Certainly as regards Rouault's materiality, it is the wielding of paint-matter as a thing of expression that draws our attention to that matter, and by 1904 painting had reached a point where that attention already *meant something to* painting.

For Butler, the risk of instating an idea of matter as prior or external to discourse as a means to look to such matter to ground or verify the falsity, injury or violation of the discursive, is that we may well discover that matter itself is saturated with discourses.[22] In Butler's terms, the indissolubility of materiality and signification is intended to unsettle, to trigger a loss of epistemological certainty that does not result in the annihilation of either element but may initiate new ways of understanding the mattering of matter. Where painting is concerned, then, Butler's deconstructive approach also allows for the possibility that not all materiality is conceptualized materially – what of the excess we have mentioned, the possibility that Rouault's marks tantalizingly pose, that they do, might, or try to, mean more than they physically are? One way of rephrasing the point we have reached with Rouault's marks is to cannibalize Butler's terms, and say that whilst painting is the condition under which materiality may be said to appear, *materiality* is the condition under which painting may be said to *mean*.

22   Although this can be read as contentious in her argument for gendered bodies, it
       posits an important aspect of painting.

So, if Rouault's materiality seems to block meaning, to deny the possibility of seeing through to the 'picture', this materiality in itself contains the potential to be meaningful. The critics' use of vocabulary such as 'coal', 'blacking, and pitch' to describe Rouault's paint-matter aligns his work with industrial labour and its materials, an associative texture that establishes the modernity and contemporary social engagement of Rouault's work, and evokes comparisons with the imagery of Zola's 1885 naturalist novel *Germinal* or Daumier's darkly satirical drawings of urban life in the nineteenth century.[23] At the same time, Rouault's marks also press into service the associations and values invested in this crude application of paint by his predecessors – particularly Gustave Courbet's materialism and the anarchism of Neo-Impressionists such as Paul Signac or Maximilian Luce. Over half a century earlier, Courbet's thick impasto had rejected the metaphysical, stating firmly – via his palette knife – that art was not mentally conceived but physically constructed. His brute materiality replicated, on an analogous level, the material qualities of the physical things represented. As we have said, Rouault's work makes no such instrumental claim, but he, like Courbet, was accused of reducing everything to matter, and Rouault uses the echoes of Courbet's materialism to his own ends. For one thing it represented honesty and realism, and an empathy with the lower classes of Parisian society, with which Rouault was increasingly keen to associate himself. Sympathetic critics of Rouault have turned to a narrative of pity and transcendence in the face of these works, in which art 'rescues' these themes and the society in which they exist, and where the 'lower' the terms to which the artist descends the 'higher' the message can be deemed to be. But arguably, what the original critics reacted to was the *lack* of transcendence, the pure, vulgar physicality of the works. Rouault's thick materiality also recalls the efforts of Signac and Luce to align their painterly work with that of the artisan or labourer. Rouault depoliticizes this work – he is no anarchist – and uses these associations partly to distance himself from what was conventionally seen as 'modernity' by aligning himself with the idea

23   See my forthcoming thesis, 'Georges Rouault's Modernism and the Question of Materiality' (University of Oxford).

of Christ the artisan, therefore also positioning himself within theological modernism. 'I am not of these streets, but of the Age of the Cathedrals', he wrote. Contradictorily, however, he also increasingly recounted the circumstances of his birth, in a cellar in Belleville in the last bloody days of the 1871 Commune; seeking, it seems, to redefine himself as a specifically Parisian painter born out of that painful darkness.[24] These histories and associations are not literally or immediately 'in' the matter of the mark, but are *contained in the materiality of the mark*, where materiality is understood as matter and signification intimately, and irrevocably, linked.

This is what is most epistemologically challenging about Rouault's work; for what the irreducible materiality of his marks posit is *not* the *separation* between the materiality of the signifier and the signified, which lends itself to a transcendent-like manoeuvre, but the *closeness*, the 'indissolubility'. Matter, Rouault's work proposes, always binds itself to representation – and representation is always bound to matter. The concept of artifice is important for Rouault's *œuvre*: derived from the Anglo-Norman and Middle French *artifice* or *artefice*, it is the action of making (workmanship or craftsmanship), and the product of that action (an object or piece of work). It has since acquired the negative associations of the modern use of 'artificial', and is therefore also artfulness, cunning, trickery – a manoeuvre or device intending to deceive or trick. All of these resonances are entwined in the materiality of Rouault's marks because, as we have seen, just as the marks seem to reveal themselves in an 'honest' declaration of themselves as something made (as opposed to the 'deception' of mimetic illusion), which has the immediate appearance of a 'truth claim' or act of demystification, this is the same point at which this 'revelation' is found to be wrapped up in a dense nexus of potentially signifying schemas. That is to say that the laying bare of its materiality is found to be another dissimulating strategy within the mark. If there is a truth claim, it is in the rejection of such truth claims and the ironic reflection this offers upon the ideology of demystification. This is a vital part of the disorientation and ambivalence in the relation between the physical mark and what it lays claim to or signifies – the result

---

24   Georges Rouault, *Sur l'art et sur la vie: le métier de peindre* (Paris: Bibliothèque Médiations, 1971), 16 and 175.

is an apparent impasse, or, more accurately, a state of aporia. This aporia is enhanced by the conjunction of these marks with subject matter that often depicts subjects or images designed to 'stand-in' for other realities, or which stand in relation to another reality or idea: the clown is exemplary of this, as a masked figure used to critique, parody and philosophize on so-called reality. Rouault's works deny the immediacy often associated with modernist painting. Instead they are bound up with representation on several levels, each of which gives way to the next – a kind of burrowing below the surface seemingly antithetical to the obdurate physicality of the mark.

Selected Bibliography

Bennett, Jane, 'A Vitalist Stopover on the Way to a New Materialism', in Diana Coole and Samantha Frost, eds, *New Materialisms: Ontology, Agency, and Politics* (Durham, NC: Duke University Press, 2010), 47–69.

——, *Vibrant Matter: A Political Ecology of Things* (Durham, NC: Duke University Press, 2010).

Brown, Bill, 'Thing Theory', *Critical Inquiry* 28.1 (2001), 1–22.

Butler, Judith, *Bodies that Matter: On the Discursive Limits of 'Sex'* (London: Routledge, 1993).

Byatt, A.S., *The Biographer's Tale* (New York: Alfred A. Knopf, 2001).

Clark, T.J., *Farewell to an Idea: Episodes in a History of Modernism* (New Haven and London: Yale University Press: 1999).

Coole, Diana, 'The Inertia of Matter and the Generativity of Flesh', in Diana Coole and Samantha Frost, eds, *New Materialisms: Ontology, Agency, and Politics* (Durham, NC: Duke University Press, 2010), 92–115.

——, and Samantha Frost, 'Introducing the New Materialisms', in Diana Coole and Samantha Frost, eds, *New Materialisms: Ontology, Agency, and Politics* (Durham, NC: Duke University Press, 2010), 1–44.

Courthion, Pierre, *Georges Rouault* (Paris: Flammarion, 1962).

Fortunesca, Irina, ed., *Rouault*, trans. Richard Hilliard (Bucharest and London: Abbey Library, 1975).

Greenberg, Clement, *Art and Culture: Critical Essays* [1961] (Boston: Beacon Press, 1989).

Harman, Graham, 'Realism without Materialism', *SubStance* 40.2 (2011), 55–72.

Joyce, James, *Dubliners* (London: Grant Richards, 1914).

Kang, Soo Yun, *Rouault in Perspective: Contextual and Theoretical Study of his Art* (Boston and Oxford: International Scholars Publication, 2000).

Latour, Bruno, *We Have Never Been Modern*, trans. Catherine Porter (Cambridge, MA: Harvard University Press, 1991).

Man, Paul de, *The Rhetoric of Romanticism* (New York: Columbia University Press, 1984).

Rouault, Georges, *Sur l'art et sur la vie: le métier de peindre* (Paris: Bibliothèque Médiations, 1971).

Ruskin, John, *The Seven Lamps of Architecture* (London: Smith, Elder, & Co., 1849).

Schloesser, Stephen, ed., *Mystic Masque: Semblance and Reality in Georges Rouault 1871–1958* (Boston: McMullen Museum of Art, 2008).

LOUIS DAUBRESSE

Quand l'endroit du temps rencontre son envers au cinéma: Une dialectique des opposés

Parmi les grandes questions qui se posent lorsque l'on parle du temps, l'une revient de manière récurrente: dans quel sens se dirige-t-il? 'Une de ces ténèbres, parmi les plus belles sinon les plus obscures, est celle qui nous empêche de préciser la direction du temps'[1] disait Borgès. Sommes-nous certains que le Temps ne possède qu'une seule flèche? Se pourrait-il que le Temps possède d'autres priorités et ne soit pas univoque?

A la fin du 19ème siècle, une nouvelle technologie a permis de libérer le Temps de son caractère unilatéral pour lui offrir une autre direction. Cette technologie, c'est l'appareil cinématographique. Ses inventeurs, les célèbres frères Lumière, ont très vite réalisé toute l'étendue de son potentiel. En effet, dès 1896, soit un an à peine après la toute première projection publique dans l'histoire du cinéma, un film allait révolutionner de l'intérieur la perception que l'homme avait du Temps. *Démolition d'un mur* était une prise de vue toute simple, dans laquelle des ouvriers s'affairent pour faire renverser un muret à coups de pioche. Celui-ci s'écroule au sol. Quelques secondes plus tard, nous revoyons la même prise de vue, mais en marche arrière. La manivelle de l'appareil de projection est manipulée en sens inverse. Se produit à l'écran un événement inédit aux yeux des spectateurs de l'époque: le mur se soulève comme par miracle et se redresse, replacé sur ses fondations. Ainsi, par la simple magie de la réversion pelliculaire, le mur entièrement détruit a été restauré dans son état d'origine. Dans cette simple projection, les frères Lumière ont rendu possible un phénomène totalement inimaginable auparavant: l'engendrement d'un envers directionnel du Temps.

---

1   Jorge Luis Borges, 'Histoire de l'éternité (1936)', in Borges, *Œuvres complètes* (Paris: Editions Gallimard, Collection Bibliothèque de la Pléiade, 1993), 367.

Par un simple changement de défilement pelliculaire, l'envers temporel se dissocie de son endroit. Le projecteur cinématographique peut nous offrir la vision d'un monde aux valeurs physiques contraires où les personnages évoluent à reculons et rajeunissent au lieu de vieillir.[2]

Dès lors, le cinéma s'est d'une certaine façon mis à prendre conscience de ses propres aptitudes à déformer le temps, par condensation, dilatation, suspension ou inversion. Tous ces mouvements impossibles dans notre système entropique sont réalisables dans la machine à remonter le temps, celle du cinéma:

> Les diverses possibilités de manipulation que (l'image-mouvement) laisse cependant ouvertes (à savoir restitution donnée à une vitesse plus ou moins grande ou dans un ordre peut-être l'inverse de celui enregistré), suggère que tout l'esprit du cinéma porte non plus sur la faculté de restituer un mouvement, mais de jouer sur celui-ci. Non que ce dernier doive disparaître comme tel, mais il n'est plus saisi que dans sa relation à l'ensemble qui doit demeurer à travers lui, ou qui se met à s'animer d'une vie qui lui est propre. Il n'y a plus à feindre l'illusion de mouvement, quand c'est l'image et le tout de l'image qui sont d'emblée mouvement, mouvement de mouvements.[3]

Après les frères Lumière, le procédé technique du défilement inversé allait connaître un destin plus ou moins mouvementé au cinéma. Il sera régulièrement utilisé dans des comédies burlesques ou dans des œuvres poétiques de Jean Cocteau avant de se transformer en micro-figure visuelle dans le classicisme hollywoodien puis de rejaillir dans le domaine expérimental ou dans le clip vidéo.

---

2   'La représentation d'un événement "tourné" à rebours et projeté à l'endroit, nous révèle un espace-temps où l'effet remplace la cause; où tout ce qui devrait s'attirer, se repousse; où l'accélération de la pesanteur est un ralentissement de la légèreté, centrifuge et non centripète; où tous les vecteurs sont inversés. Et pourtant cet univers n'est pas incompréhensible, et la parole même, avec de l'habitude, peut y être devinée. Alors on songe au redressement mystérieux des images rétiniennes, à ce dormeur construisant un rêve qui paraît se conclure sur la sonnerie d'un réveil, alors qu'il est parti d'elle. Et l'on se demande qui connaît le véritable sens de l'écoulement du temps?': Jean Epstein, 'Photogénie de l'impondérable (1935)', in *Ecrits sur le cinéma 1* (Paris: Editions Seghers, 1973), 250–1.

3   Alain Menil, *L'écran du temps* (Lyon: Editions PUL, 1991), 17.

Toutefois notre réflexion ne portera pas sur l'histoire de l'inversion pelliculaire au cinéma ni sur les philosophies de l'envers du temps. Nous voulons nous focaliser sur l'expérimentation de cet effet de vitesse dans un cadre précis: celui d'une combinaison entre progression et régression. Il s'avère que le cinéma est le seul domaine possible où l'envers temporel peut rivaliser avec l'endroit. Toute la difficulté théorique tient au fait que l'envers est vu comme le contraire absolu de l'endroit et *vice-versa*. Notre cheminement intellectuel aura pour objectif de dépasser cet antagonisme conceptuel et d'imaginer une hybridation de ces deux entités que tout oppose, mais seulement en apparence. En effet, il serait faux de croire que l'endroit et l'envers du temps sont totalement dissociables l'un de l'autre. Plusieurs cinéastes ont tenté de confronter ces contraires temporels, par le biais de différents dispositifs imagiers. Trois exemples retiendront notre attention: *Sugar/Water*, un clip musical tourné par Michel Gondry en 1996, et deux films expérimentaux, *Pièce touchée* (réalisé par Martin Arnold) et *Scaling* (de Mike Hoolboom).

Nous étudierons tour à tour chacune de ces trois œuvres en en analysant d'abord l'élaboration technique, puis les combinaisons entre inversion et extension et enfin les incidences sur la matière temporelle. Nous verrons en quoi l'expérience de ces films s'avère singulière.

Pièce touchée ou la contiguïté des contraires

Ce film de Martin Arnold illustre la question des interpénétrations entre progression et régression, avers et envers, élaborant au travers de la pellicule un espace où la coexistence des antagonismes est rendue envisageable et cohérente.

Le projet du réalisateur est de se consacrer uniquement au support pelliculaire, à la manière des détournements opérés par Ken Jacobs ou Bruce Conner, mais avec des visées distinctes:

> [Martin Arnold] décolle le signifié du signifiant, en suspendant le sens et le mouvement des images de films de série B; [il] s'attaque au cliché du bonheur tel que

l'Amérique des années 1950 le fabrique et le reproduit: un mari rentre chez lui (un intérieur au confort moderne) et trouve sa femme belle et disponible (lisant un magazine dont on imagine qu'il contient les mêmes valeurs), et l'embrasse. Cette scène, qui dure 18 secondes, est extraite d'un film de Joseph M. Newman, *The Human Jungle* (1954).[4]

Dans le court-métrage de *found footage* de Martin Arnold, 'l'action va se dérouler sur un quart d'heure dans une forme qui insiste, en y revenant sans cesse et en progressant très lentement, sur les gestes effectués par les deux personnages'.[5] *Pièce touchée* débute par un temps de latence, durant lequel on note une absence de mouvement apparent. C'est la dialectique entre progression et régression qui va permettre ensuite l'apparition et l'évolution du mouvement. La porte s'ouvre puis se ferme, se rouvre, se referme, mais l'entrebâillement est de plus en plus important. La bande sonore est occupée par un son mécanique. Est-il de nature intradiégétique? Nous aurions tendance à dire que non, puisqu'il ne saurait être assimilé à aucun corps, aucun objet visible ou hors-champ dans le profilmique. Il s'agit du son provenant du matériel pelliculaire lui-même. La lumière s'éteint, puis est rallumée: on est très proche de l'essence même du *flicker* (procédé que Térésa Faucon désigne comme 'montage de photogrammes, produisant un effet de papillonnement, de clignotement renvoyant le montage au principe mécanique de l'intermittence cinématographique').[6] Les images photogrammiques se mettent en porte-à-faux les unes par rapport aux autres, du fait d'un renversement des repères droite-gauche des unes par rapport aux autres, mais qui finissent par produire une impression de continuité narrative: le mari se débat du mieux qu'il peut pour pénétrer dans le salon; la porte qu'il franchit semble être un portillon duquel il n'arrive pas s'extirper; indécis, il éteint et rallume la lumière inlassablement; une force invisible l'empêche d'avancer vers sa dulcinée malgré toutes ses tentatives infructueuses pour se déplacer dans l'espace.

4   Françoise Parfait, *Vidéo, un art contemporain* (Paris: Editions du regard, 2004), 302–4.
5   Ibid. 304.
6   Térésa Faucon, *Penser et expérimenter le montage* (Paris: Presses Sorbonne Nouvelle, 2010), 148.

Les coupes sont de plus en plus fréquentes. Il y a variation du rythme des coupes franches. Quant au personnage, il reste dans une indécision permanente: avance-t-il? Recule-t-il? L'histoire connaît néanmoins une certaine progression, les régressions finissent par être considérées comme de faux envers (interprétées comme des coulées temporelles qui participent à l'avancement de la situation). Du fait de cette dialectique inédite, l'anecdote initiale inscrite dans le réel diégétique se déploie sur un laps de temps dilaté. Elle est écartelée entre des marches avant et des marches arrière. Le ralenti est parfois utilisé pour amplifier le mouvement. L'inversion spatiale gauche-droite crée, à force, un rapport de forces entre deux espaces-temps. Lequel va avoir l'ascendant sur l'autre? Lequel s'inclinera? Le personnage masculin se penche pour offrir un baiser tant attendu à son épouse. C'est le climax de tout ce court métrage. Les yeux des personnages clignotent, renvoyant au scintillement du montage et au battement visuel éprouvé par le spectateur. Lorsque le baiser dans la pure tradition hollywoodienne survient, le spectateur réalise toute la difficulté de l'épreuve spatio-temporelle que viennent de vivre les deux personnages. Arnold ironise sur la magnificence de cette embrassade, sur laquelle il refuse de s'éterniser. De nouvelles alternances gauche-droite surgissent à l'image. La saccade produit un effet de surimpression des deux images, du fait de la persistance rétinienne spectatorielle. Autour d'une même posture oscillent les mouvements des personnages et de la caméra. Cette posture sert d'axe temporel à partir duquel les progressions et les régressions se jouent. La femme se lève de son fauteuil, puis se baisse, se lève, se baisse ... Comme si son corps était condamné à l'indécision entre deux gestes.

Un nouveau changement spatial intervient: le haut et le bas ont basculé. S'entrecroisent des plans dont les repères cartésiens sont en porte-à-faux, de sorte à ce qu'on ne sache plus où est l'endroit spatial et où est le reflet. Il règne une impression de contiguïté entre les plans: au-delà de l'égarement des sensations, tous les mouvements profilmiques ou pelliculaires semblent tendre vers une même direction. Ils s'établissent en une suite logique et translationnelle vers un advenir. L'endroit et l'envers ne sont plus qu'une seule et unique coulée de temps et d'espace. Le film s'achève sur une stase pelliculaire et un arrêt définitif de cet incroyable emboîtement des contraires aspirant à une unilatéralité. De cet affrontement entre deux mouvements spatio-temporels (l'un étant l'opposé exact de l'autre), où les personnages agissent dans un déploiement et un repliement corporels, ressort l'idée d'un balancement équilibré. Leurs actions sont suivies de leurs contre-actions. La progression du mouvement se fait par à-coups, par le biais de petites marges de durée qui créent peu à peu un décalage du mouvement pour l'amener vers l'après.

Alors que les gestes semblent progresser malgré toutes les apparentes résistances du matériau pelliculaire, alors que le mouvement semble parvenir à sa finalité, une impétueuse régression temporelle nous ramène à l'instant précédent, le mouvement retournant alors vers son point d'origine. La régression fait obstruction à sa complète et définitive réalisation. Les soubresauts liés à cette dialectique induisent une ténacité physique non seulement du mouvement lui-même dans sa mise en acte, mais aussi de l'instant. L'instant refuse d'être évacué pour un instant postérieur. L'instant veut persister dans le présent du photogramme. A l'articulation entre les deux directions temporelles s'ajoute cette articulation spatiale. L'image est mise en raccordement avec son reflet horizontal ou son inclinaison verticale. Les enchaînements de plans convoquant les deux antipodes peuvent s'accélérer jusqu'au *flicker*, et sont donc proches du subliminal. Le spectateur peut presque lire une surimpression entre les deux espaces inversés l'un par rapport à l'autre. Les temps contraires s'articulent toujours l'un par rapport à l'autre, au point d'être indissociables. Le film finit par ressembler à un manège infernal semblable à une bulle de temps, une prison hors du temps chronologique.

Une structure de l'équivalence dans *Sugar Water*

Peut-être faut-il d'emblée souligner le caractère presque inconcevable de cette idée de réversibilité dynamique. [...] Nous savons [...] l'importance, dans l'Antiquité, de l'idée d'un temps circulaire, revenant périodiquement à ses origines. Mais l'éternel retour lui-même est marqué par la flèche du temps, comme le rythme des saisons ou celui des générations humaines. Aucune spéculation, aucun savoir n'a jamais affirmé l'équivalence entre ce qui se fait et ce qui se défait, entre une plante qui pousse, fleurit et meurt, et une plante qui ressuscite, rajeunit et retourne vers sa graine primitive, entre un homme qui mûrit et apprend et un homme qui devient progressivement enfant, puis embryon, puis cellule.[7]

Bien qu'impossible dans l'univers linéaire et à sens unique comme il semble que ce soit le cas pour le nôtre, cette réversibilité dynamique peut être administrée phénoménologiquement par le biais du cinématographe. C'est se faire l'avocat du diable, mais pourtant tout est concevable à partir de la machine-cinéma, y compris les théories scientifiques les plus invraisemblables sur le temps. C'est de ce fait qu'Epstein affirmait l'intelligence supérieure d'un tel appareil d'enregistrement et de métamorphose du temps.[8]

Mettons ainsi en perspective ces pensées théoriques avec le clip de Cibo Matto, réalisé par Michel Gondry: *Sugar Water*. Il s'agit d'un palindrome cinématographique.[9] Le clip *Sugar Water* se construit également sur un *split-screen* par juxtaposition de deux écrans. Leur cloisonnement

7   Ilya Prigogine and Isabelle Stengers, *Entre le temps et l'éternité* (Paris: Editions Flammarion, 2009), 38–9.

8   'La vraie machine à comprendre le temps doit donc être un instrument capable de faire voir les variations, les différences du temps, à grossir celles qui existent et, au besoin, à en créer de nouvelles, de même que le microscope et le télescope introduisent d'immenses variations de longueur, de largeur, de hauteur, au moyen desquelles nous explorons l'espace. De plus, cette vraie machine à connaître le temps ne doit pas transposer les variations temporelles en proportions spatiales, comme font les graphiques des statisticiens, mais elle doit représenter les changements de temps dans le temps même, en valeur de durée'. Jean Epstein, 'L'intelligence d'une machine (1946)' in *Ecrits sur le cinéma I*, 369.

9   Pour rappel, en littérature, le palindrome est une figure rhétorique, impliquant des mots ou des textes dont l'ordre des lettres reste le même que l'on les lise de gauche en droit ou de droite en gauche. La signification ne change donc pas. Cependant, pour que le palindrome fonctionne, il faut supprimer les connexions syllabiques, les espaces entre chaque mot, les marques diacritiques (accents ou trémas par exemple) sur chacun des lettres. Il existe des palindromes très célèbres comme 'Elu par cette crapule' ou 'Esope reste ici et se repose'. Dans la langue anglaise, on peut se rappeler au bon souvenir des 'Eva, can I stab bats in a cave?' ou encore 'God! A red nugget! A fat egg under a dog!'. Au cinéma, le palindrome se construit sur un plan ou sur succession de plans que l'on fait défiler dans un sens puis dans l'autre, de sorte que le dernier plan du film soit l'inversion temporelle du premier.

à l'image s'effectue par le biais d'une coupure écranique verticale. Dans l'image de gauche, Yuka Honda est couchée sur un lit, dans l'image de droite, Miho Hatori l'est également. On serait tentés de croire à la mise en scène de leurs quotidiens respectifs, mis en parallèle l'un par rapport à l'autre. Mais il s'avère que la structure narrative est beaucoup plus sophistiquée que ça. D'une part, le personnage interprété par Yuka Honda évolue dans un espace-temps diégétique semblable au nôtre, tandis que celui joué par Miho Hatori est pris dans un envers spatio-temporel. Yuka Honda est dans une phase d'extension tandis que Miho Hatori est dans une phase de régression. L'image écranique est à considérer à l'endroit pour Yuka Honda, mais en reflet chez Miho Hatori (la gauche et la droite ont été perverties).

D'autre part, le scénario du clip crée des interactions entre le parcours des deux personnages, bien que l'un soit à reculons par rapport à l'autre. Les actions décrites prennent en compte l'inversion causale:

- Honda ferme sa fenêtre au tout début du clip et fait accidentellement tomber un pot de fleurs, alors que Hatori ferme la sienne tout en assistant à l'envolée d'un pot de fleurs, provenant du trottoir d'en face, qui vient se poser sur le rebord du balcon ...
- Honda efface au chiffon des inscriptions GAR et TER sur la vitre, effectuées au rouge à lèvres; Hatori efface au rouge à lèvres les inscriptions SU et WA sur sa propre vitre.
- Honda prend une douche; Hatori, elle, ouvre une boite de sucre, la suspend au dessus d'elle (il s'agit là d'une autre recomposition du titre du clip, 'SUGAR/WATER'); des grains de sucre s'exfiltrent du sol, de ses cheveux, de ses épaules, tous aspirés vers la boite en sucre dans laquelle ils convergent.
- Honda s'essuie respectivement avec une serviette puis un sèche-cheveux; Hatori semble faire de même.
- Honda et Hatori enfilent toutes deux un survêtement et sortent de leurs appartements respectifs, la première pas à pas, l'autre en marche arrière.
- L'une ouvre sa boite aux lettres pour y récupérer un courrier (un papier carton sur lequel est marqué 'You K' 'Illed' 'E' et 'M'), l'autre place dans sa propre boite aux lettres un courrier;

- Un chat entre à reculons dans une chatière au sein de l'univers diégétique de Hatori, alors qu'un autre chat (serait-ce le même?) sort d'une chatière dans l'espace-temps de Honda ...
- Honda et Hatori descendent un grand escalier raide et quittent leur immeuble résidentiel.
- Lorsqu'elle sort dans une ruelle, Honda met le courrier qu'elle vient de lire dans une boite postale; Hatori récupère quant à elle un courrier dans une boite postale commune aux couleurs et aux dimensions identiques (encore une fois, il y a lieu de se demander s'il s'agit de la même boite postale).

Tout d'un coup, alors qu'Honda a pris le volant de sa voiture, et qu'Hatori se dirige vers un lieu où un accident semble s'être produit, nous nous rendons compte qu'une collision entre la première et la seconde va (ou vient) (d')avoir lieu ... Lorsque Honda percute Hatori, nous arrivons à un point de contact entre les deux univers spatio-temporels, le premier fait d'endroit et le second d'envers ... C'est le plan de symétrie de ce palindrome complexe. Honda accourt vers Hatori, couchée au sol. Sur le corps vraisemblablement inerte de cette dernière se trouve ce papier en carton sur lequel nous distinguons les inscriptions 'You K Illed E M', certaines lettres étant marquées à l'envers à la manière d'un reflet de miroir; néanmoins, le message devient immédiatement visible pour le spectateur, un 'Tu M'As Tué' désormais compréhensible et logique au vu des événements. C'est là que la réversion s'effectue. Chaque personnage bascule dans l'autre image, en passant au travers de cette séparation écranique imaginaire. L'espace-temps d'Honda est désormais à rebours, tandis que celui d'Hatori apparaît maintenant comme un univers de l'endroit.

Toutes les actions que nous aurons vu dans la première partie du clip se reproduisent mais dans une causalité retournée: Hatori et Honda retournent dans leur appartement, la première en marchant en avant, l'autre à reculons. Hatori et Honda se déshabillent. La première se verse ensuite du sucre sur le corps (d'où le titre du clip, à traduire par 'Eau sucrée'). La seconde, mouillée, prend une douche pour s'essuyer ... Le clip s'achève là où il a commencé, alors que les deux jeunes femmes se remettent au lit. Le devenir inverse se sera déplacé de Hatori à Honda, dont les trajectoires se

croisent. Cependant, il faut noter que l'on ne connaîtra pas l'étape anté-
rieure à l'accident dans le parcours d'Hatori, ni l'étape postérieure dans celui
de Honda. L'antériorité du trajet de la première n'existe que dans l'envers,
l'avenir de la seconde ne se construit que par inversion du processus. La
figure du palindrome cinématographe est perfectionnée jusqu'aux limites
du possible dans *Sugar Water*. Michel Gondry propose une vraie boucle en
split-screen qui se déplie et se replie sur les mêmes images. Le palindrome
classique se constitue d'une vision linéaire de la chose doublée de sa réarti-
culation en sens inversé. Ici, la marche avant et la marche arrière se simulta-
néisent. L'écran fractionné montre deux espaces-temps symétriques et non
dénués de connexions: bipolarité et simultanéité d'anecdotes visuelles et
d'événements semblables.

Dans cet espace composite, le plan de gauche sera le plan de l'endroit jusqu'au bout, tandis que le plan de droite sera celui de l'envers. Le
clip lui-même se veut comme méta-espace de l'endroit et de l'envers, une
sorte d'hyper-temps fait de croisements entre l'inversion et la linéarité.
Toujours dans cet esprit de réversibilité qui transforme une temporali-
té en son contraire. Au commencement de *Sugar Water* l'endroit a déjà
vomi son envers. Sans qu'elle ne soit au préalable formulée par le trajet de
l'endroit, la matière de l'envers existe en toute autonomie. L'envers n'aura
pas attendu l'apparition et l'accomplissement de l'endroit pour s'accom-
plir à l'écran par une inversion à la fois spatiale et temporelle. L'endroit ne
peut prétendre utiliser l'envers comme son faire-valoir. D'aucun des deux
ne saurait se considérer comme l'ascendant de l'autre. Ils sont traités sur
un pied d'égalité. L'effet *split-screen* se charge quant à lui de les mettre en
contradiction tout en manifestant, par quelques accessoires (le pot de
fleurs, la lettre en papier-carton, le chat noir), leur interaction nécessaire
et durable. Car l'envers comme l'endroit ne sauraient survivre ici sans leurs
antagonistes respectifs.

L'état temporel que Michel Gondry institue tend vers une situation
d'équilibre des forces régressives et extensives. Cet équilibre induit la réversibilité de l'endroit mais aussi celle de l'envers. Chacun des deux espaces-
temps est passible de réversion, pour se muter en envers de l'endroit ou en
envers de l'envers, c'est-à-dire un retour en l'endroit. Ressurgit la logique
de migration des corps, que ce soit à l'échelle macroscopique ou au niveau

microscopique. Il y a toujours des fluctuations même dans un état apparent d'équilibre ou dit stationnaire:

> A l'état stationnaire, par définition, la production d'entropie est compensée en permanence par l'apport d'entropie lié aux échanges avec le milieu: le système est le siège d'une activité permanente, production d'entropie, qui est maintenue au prix d'échanges continuels avec le milieu. L'état d'équilibre correspond au cas particulier où les échanges avec le milieu ne font pas varier l'entropie [...].[10]

Dans *Sugar Water*, il y a une équivalence parfaite entre les phénomènes de dissolution et ceux de condensation, entre les événements de désintégration et ceux de formation. Le clip est en lui-même dans une circularité parfaite et infaillible. Le travail d'équivalence entre ce qui se dissipe et ce qui se concentre, entre ce qui se dégrade et ce qui se solidifie prend, corps par un montage cinématographique empreint de dualité et de perspectives dichotomiques. Le temps peut également se mouvoir en une circularité parfaite, s'épanouir depuis un point d'origine pour y revenir encore et encore: de la source, il s'en retourne à la source. Le fonctionnement cyclique du temps implique une réversibilité continuelle et inusable. La circularité temporelle et la réversibilité dynamique vont ainsi de paire.

Scaling: Un alliage multidimensionnel

Scaling est, dans la logique de notre cheminement, un film qui tombe à point nommé. La coexistence de deux temporalités contraires y connaît son point culminant. Ce film en noir-et-blanc de Mike Hoolboom, tourné en 1986, est à nos yeux la tentative la plus explicite pour la conciliation entre l'envers et l'endroit, pas seulement du temps mais aussi de l'espace.

Résumons la situation, qui semble à première vue très sommaire: un homme nu tourne le dos à la caméra et fait face à un mur. Nous nous rendons

10   Prigone and Stengers, *Entre le temps et l'éternité*, 71.

compte qu'il est en train de peindre cette façade murale avec une couleur entièrement noire. Un noir absorbant et ostensible. Très vite apparaît à l'écran un autre individu, lui aussi nu, lui aussi en train de peindre ce même mur ... Mais il s'avère que les deux individus ne font pas partie du même espace-temps et qu'ils ne sont qu'un seul et même personnage, dédoublé en deux plans différents et superposés l'un sur l'autre. Il y a donc deux couches d'images, tout comme il y a deux façades murales qui semblent, du point de vue diégétique, se synthétiser en une seule. Ci-dessous, un tableau permet de résumer l'organisation interne du film.

	Début du film	Milieu du film	Fin du film
Premier plan	X	X+1	X+2
Second plan	X+2	X+1	X

Voici donc ce que l'on est amenés à voir: un des deux corps peint la surface murale avec un noir opaque, l'autre semble peindre par-dessus la surface noire avec du blanc. Mais il s'avère que le geste effectué par le deuxième personnage avec le pinceau n'est pas du tout conforme. Au lien de faire des mouvements appliqués de haut en bas, il les accentue de bas en haut, comme s'il raclait la peinture noire pour l'éliminer progressivement! Ce second plan qui est en surimpression sur le premier est à la fois son envers temporel et son verso spatial: plan qui est projeté en sens inverse et qui est retourné horizontalement. Le résultat en est une étrange combinaison de deux unités où des actions disjointes y sont réalisées. Le personnage peint à l'endroit et dépeint à l'envers. Dans le premier cas, il recouvre le blanc avec une couche noire, dans le second cas, il élimine le noir en faisant ressortir le blanc.

On assiste donc à un face-à-face chromatique où le noir et le blanc cherchent chacun à s'approprier l'espace de cette surface. Mais le jeu se complique avec le surgissement d'une troisième couche monochrome: la superposition du noir et du blanc produit une troisième couleur d'apparence grisâtre. De l'antagonisme physique de ces deux plans résulte la révélation d'un troisième plan. Ce plan-là est celui que l'on peut voir à l'écran comme le Tout, incluant en son réel diégétique le constituant du premier plan et du deuxième plan. La surface murale est teintée d'un gris composite, dont l'étendue va se déplacer progressivement dans l'espace, effacée par les coups de pinceau des deux protagonistes pour réapparaître en une autre zone murale. Si l'on cherche à interpréter cette présence envahissante du gris au sein de l'espace filmique, au-delà de la logique chromatique, nous pourrions dire qu'il incarne le dépassement de cette dialectique envers/endroit. Il excède cette opposition primaire, vainc en quelque sorte la dualité qui faisait jusqu'à présent de l'endroit et de l'envers deux rivaux que tout sépare. Ce gris-là est la fécondation de ces deux entités spatio-temporelles. L'envers et l'endroit ne se détruisent plus mutuellement, ne se dénigrent plus réciproquement. Ils cherchent, d'une certaine manière, un accouplement, malgré les résistances matérielles. *Scaling* est le lieu de réunion des inverses. Leur fusion permet l'enfantement de cette matière grise, qui s'est attribuée non seulement les deux couches chromatiques que sont le noir et le blanc, mais aussi, symboliquement parlant, toutes les dimensions spatiales et les deux dimensions temporelles. L'envers et l'endroit ont bien malgré eux donné naissance à cette substance hybride et amalgamatrice.

Dans cette structure décidément des plus déroutantes, il faut relever le fait que la narration de *Scaling* se base sur un effet de symétrie spatio-temporelle, à l'instar du système très particulier que Michel Gondry a mis en place pour son palindrome *Sugar Water*. La seconde moitié du court-métrage est l'inversion de la première, avec une interversion des deux corps au sein de l'espace. Le premier corps, celui de l'endroit, a habité la partie latérale gauche face au mur, tandis que le second corps, celui de l'envers, était resté disposé dans la partie latérale droite. Lorsque les deux plans superposés arrivent à mi-longueur de leur durée totale, un croisement spatial s'opère dans cette macrostructure symétrique. *Scaling* détourne l'idée même du palindrome : la réversion se produit au même moment où débute la version. Il n'y a pas dissociation temporelle entre le plan d'endroit et son équivalent en sens inverse. Régression et progression sont projetées simultanément par le biais d'un effet de superposition photogrammique. L'envers et l'endroit sont désormais presque indistinguables l'un de l'autre, comme le dirait Françoise Proust :

[...] Envers et endroit sont indécidables : les créatures sont à la fois en mouvement et en repos, elles semblent et tomber sans s'arrêter et suspendues, immobiles, sans fil, en l'air : désormais, il n'y a plus personne derrière le miroir. [...] Le miroir est lui-même devenu automate. Il n'y a rien à voir derrière le miroir: le miroir, le double, est premier. Le monde est un jeu de miroirs ou de réflexions et il n'y a plus de monde à l'envers ou de monde à l'endroit, il n'y a que des doubles faces, des recto verso.[11]

La confusion entre l'endroit et l'envers frôle la perfection même si elle ne l'atteint pas entièrement. Le double mouvement qui se profile dans *Scaling* semble être un et indivisible plus que dédoublé. La régression affecte le mouvement à l'endroit (l'acte de peindre), tandis que la progression affecte le mouvement à l'envers (l'acte de dépeindre). Les deux corps du même personnage semblent cohabiter, travaillant d'une même dynamique. On aurait même envie de dire qu'ils sont dans une logique de complémentarité: l'envers et l'endroit s'appuient l'un sur l'autre pour maintenir leur équilibre respectif. L'endroit est subsidiaire de l'envers et l'envers est subsidiaire de l'endroit. L'inversion complote étrangement avec l'extension pour produire une surface qui est l'expression imagière de leur adéquation physique, substantielle, spirituelle ... *Scaling* propose donc un objet cinématographique sans commune mesure, une forme d'alliage multidimensionnel dont les sous-parties hétérogènes se sont assimilées au bénéfice d'une coalition imagière qui a imprégné tout l'écran.

Pour conclure notre réflexion, nous pouvons constater que ces trois œuvres se construisent autour d'une spatialisation du temps et d'une temporalisation de l'espace. Mais, au-delà de cette première appréciation, nous pouvons noter autre chose: par procédé d'articulation, par équivalence systémique, ou même par fusion totale, ces trois films neutralisent les valeurs de l'endroit et de l'envers, en les plaçant non plus dans une forme contradictoire mais dans un dispositif de co-influence. On pourrait même aller plus loin: toutes fonctionnent toutes sur la base d'un système a-causal (dans lequel la traditionnelle chaîne causes-effets n'existe pas). Dans *Pièce touchée*, *Sugar Water* ou *Scaling*, il n'est finalement plus question de réversion ou de temps chronologique. En effet, la frontière entre endroit et envers est devenue poreuse. Mieux que cela, endroit et envers s'interpénètrent. La logique de binarisme entre les deux est alors éliminée. Nous sommes bien

11   Françoise Proust, *L'Histoire à contretemps. Le temps historique chez Walter Benjamin* (Paris: Editions du Cerf, 1994), 124–5.

dans un amalgame des opposés. Grâce à leur alliance, le temps progressif et le temps inversé fécondent un espace-temps sans flèche ni linéarité. Dans chacun de ces trois courts-métrages, l'emboitage des envers antagonistes donne naissance à une sorte de méta-espace fusionnel. Le temps y abandonne son unilatéralité et sa flèche directionnelle. Il apparaît comme antilinéaire, désordonné, tiraillé entre ses mouvements contraires. Il s'agit d'un temps né de cette synthèse des deux temps précédemment cités: un temps que l'on pourrait affirmer comme étant hors des temps, un temps qui n'est plus anisotrope. Nous assistons donc à l'émergence d'un temps isotropique.

Bibliographie

Arnold, Martin, *Pièce touchée* [videorecording] <https://www.youtube.com/watch?v=AnDagpv4kUk> accessed 3 May 2014.

Borges, Jorge Luis, *Œuvres complètes* (Paris: Editions Gallimard: Collection Bibliothèque de la Pléiade, 1993).

Epstein, Jean, *Ecrits sur le cinéma 1* (Paris: Editions Seghers, 1973).

Faucon, Térésa, *Penser et expérimenter le montage* (Paris: Presses Sorbonne Nouvelle, 2010).

Gondry, Michel, 'Sugar Water' in *The Work of Director Michel Gondry* [videorecording] (New York: The Criterion Collection, 2003).

Hoolboom, Mike, 'Scaling' in *Imitations of Life* [videorecording] (Chicago: Video Data Bank, 2003).

Menil, Alain, *L'écran du temps* (Lyon: Editions PUL, 1991).

Parfait, Françoise, *Vidéo, un art contemporain* (Paris: Editions du regard, 2004).

Prigogine, Ilya, and Isabelle Stengers, *Entre le temps et l'éternité* (Paris: Editions Flammarion, 2009).

Proust, Françoise, *L'Histoire à contretemps. Le temps historique chez Walter Benjamin* (Paris: Editions du Cerf, 1994).

CHRISTINA CHALMERS

Frank O'Hara's Anti-Cocteau Movement

> Quand les hommes sont morts, ils entrent dans l'histoire. Quand les
> statues sont mortes, elles entrent dans l'art. Cette botanique de la mort,
> c'est ce que nous appelons la culture.
> —ALAIN RESNAIS AND CHRIS MARKER,
> *Les Statues Meurent Aussi*

I hazard to bring together two works which meditate in contracted and expanded forms on questions of culture as related to botany and death. The late and under-appreciated Frank O'Hara's poem 'Biotherm' (1966) immediately announces its own relation to acculturation, botany and decay in its very title. According to Bill Berkson, who provides a glossary to the poem in his essay 'Air and Such', 'Biotherm' refers to a sunburn preparation which 'stands for life energy, skin, food or other sustenance, and is imagined as a preservative (of the "pretty rose").'[1] For Berkson *bio therm* is 'life (or body) heat'; a symbol for the liveliness and intimacy which he sees as the central themes of the poem.[2] It can be usefully compared, via an oblique reference to Jean Cocteau within the poem itself, to Cocteau's short amateur film 'La Villa Santo-Sospir', which uses temporal reversals to differently reflect on the relation between florality and death. I will offer some preliminary thoughts on how 'cette botanique de la mort' proceeds through O'Hara and Cocteau's formal strategies, including strategies of reversal and negation.

In this chapter, then, I will situate Frank O'Hara and Jean Cocteau in relation to one another, arguing that O'Hara performs a reading of certain

---

1   Bill Berkson, *Companion to Biotherm* (San Francisco: Arion Press, 1990), 16.
2   Ibid.

effects predominant in Cocteau's films which approximate his paradigmatic style. In beginning from Frank O'Hara's considerations of Cocteau,
though, I won't consider the influence of Cocteau's poetry or theatre on
O'Hara, but attempt to think through a particular relation between their
different cinematic and literary effects. Keston Sutherland argues for studying O'Hara's 'difference from' earlier 'moments in modernism' through
looking at the way he ingests French influence; this might be extended to
the influence of French cinema on O'Hara, particularly these instances of
Cocteau's work.[3] One of O'Hara's few references to Cocteau is elliptically
critical and densely charged with considerations on Cocteau's aesthetic.

I want to concentrate on a characteristically pregnant O'Hara line,
which extends multiply into Cocteau's work. This line occurs in 'Biotherm',
a long poem written for his friend Bill Berkson, the year before O'Hara's
death. This is how it begins:

> The best thing in the world   but I better be quick about it
> better be gone tomorrow
>   better be gone last night and
>   next Thursday better be gone
> better be
>   always   or what's the use the sky
>   the endless clouds trailing we leading them by the bandanna, red.[4]

The effect of the emphasis on 'quickness' and the fast cutting here is to
impress immediately on the reader the significance of temporal movement
in the poem. To proceed in thinking about how 'Biotherm' presents concepts
of preservation and death, it is important to note the ways that its temporal
economy is organized. 'Biotherm' criticism has been centrally concentrated
on how the poem creates an impression of the forward movement of time;
this is related to concepts of literary economy and expression which are often

3   Keston Sutherland, 'Close Writing', in Robert Hampson and Will Montgomery,
      eds, *Frank O'Hara Now* (Liverpool: Liverpool University Press, 2010), 123–4.
4   Frank O'Hara, *The Collected Poems of Frank O'Hara*, ed. Donald Allen (London:
      University of California Press, 1995), 436. Future page references will follow quota-
      tions in brackets.

borrowed from the context of abstract expressionism. Critics set O'Hara within the context of his own analyses of abstract expressionist art. This argument might be bolstered by a knowledge of O'Hara's comments on 'Biotherm' in a letter to Donald Allen, in which he says about the poem that 'I am enjoying trying to keep going'.[5] Some, like Mutlu Konuk Blasing, argue that there is pure bodily expression and unimpeded mobility in 'Biotherm', relating the poem to Harold Rosenberg's action painting aesthetics.[6] Berkson has it that the poem 'pushes off, shuttling and sometimes seemingly untethered'.[7] O'Hara undercuts the possibilities for static monumentality that a Poundian kind of epic poem allows, developing a structure which is centrally concerned with manipulating duration, quickly cutting between different passages and never quite ossifying into something so perceptible as a unified style.

Berkson also mentions that the poem has 'ever-expanding scope and possibility as the lines accumulate', yet there is 'no lapse of intensity withal, no sprawl: each new passage invents yet another mode of compression'.[8] This represents a conception of movement as intensification which is different to Blasing's idea of action painting. Blasing's thesis about O'Hara's writing might have been supported by readers such as Ginsberg, but it also represses some of the 'push' and 'pull' of the poem.[9] Both conceptions, however, converge on a concept of duration as coinciding with innovation rather than mere reiteration, reconstruction or otherwise reversal. Significant movements in the poem are those between expansion and

5   Quoted in Marjorie Perloff, *Frank O'Hara: Poet Among Painters* (New York: G. Braziller, 1977), 173.

6   Mutlu Konuk Blasing, 'Frank O'Hara's Poetics of Speech: The Example of "Biotherm"', *Contemporary Literature* 23:1 (1982), 52–64.

7   Berkson, *Companion to Biotherm*, 9.

8   Ibid. 8.

9   Allen Ginsberg describes *Second Avenue* as a new literary abstract art, opening up new spheres of 'meaningless' free composition (Allen Ginsberg, 'Abstraction in Poetry', quoted in Marjorie Perloff, 'Frank O'Hara and the Aesthetics of Attention', *boundary 2* 4:3 (1976), 798). Elsewhere O'Hara asks Larry Rivers to analyse draft poems according to whether: 'the surface isn't kept "up" [...] if they show nostalgia for the avant-garde, or if they don't have "push" and "'pull"': Frank O'Hara, 'Letter to Larry Rivers', quoted in Perloff, 'Frank O'Hara and the Aesthetics of Attention', 795.

compression; there is extension and diffusion of words across the page, but also concentration into small lyric poems embedded in the larger structure. Movement in time, then, seems to force different pressures on words; in drawing fragments of language and literary detritus in its drift, the poem's architectonic structure is formed. There is movement between wildly divergent registers, narratives, spaces and references. This telescoping between different scales at such awkward speed significantly represents a departure from the high modernist heaviness of a Poundian or Olsonian version of epic fragmentation.[10] Evocations of sky and clouds transform instantaneously into intimate conversation or passages about eating food; then we flip channel to the B-movie *Practically Yours* or to Mae West or Greta Garbo.

As noted above, Berkson's argument about the constant innovation of 'modes of compression' suggests that the poem intensifies as well as advances indiscriminately. The poem repeats phrases and words in uneven patterns; 'better be gone', 'red', 'bandannas', 'roses', 'cinzano-soda', 'vodka', 'clouds', 'waves' and many others appear and reappear in new contexts. They sink and resurface on the poem's 'ego-ridden sea' (448). Repetition across sections is a binding structural dynamic. The 'dulcet waves' of a mock imagist passage, for example, recur at the poem's close, where 'I wave toward you freely' and the 'infinite waves of skin smelly and crushed' (448) absorb the poem. Different pressures are applied to the word 'wave', oscillating between senses of physical communication and the sea's symbolism. This is only an insincere fusion of self and nature; O'Hara constructs these parallels only to distance them. 'Wave''s recurrence mimics the poem's structural surging between lyric intensity and the stature of its closing frame. It is also plurivocal and humorous, mocking swellings of epic grandiosity, especially the kind which relies on the static quality of naturalized images such as 'waves' as an anchor for the monumental. Intensification is an intensification into a more fully realized, more fully humorous insincerity and performativity.

'Biotherm''s structure and kinds of movement are very significant for O'Hara's consideration of Cocteau. His reference to Cocteau and allusion

10   For more on the differences between O'Hara and Pound, see Lytle Shaw, *Frank O'Hara: The Poetics of Coterie* (Iowa City: University of Iowa Press, 2006).

to Cocteau's films is contained within an evocation of the back-and-forth of imagined dialogue:

> Lo! the Caracas transport lunch with George Al Leslie 5:30 I'll
> be over at 5
> I hope you will I'm dying of loneliness
> here with my red blue green and natch pencils and the erasers
> the mirror behind me and the desk in front of me
> like an anti-Cocteau movement (441)

Geoff Ward glosses the passage in the following way:

> In Cocteau's *Orphée*, Orpheus dives through mirrors of mercury to reach the realm of Heurtebise, death, and cryptic poetry coming through the radio, like a proto-Jack Spicer movement. The desk, by contrast, has erasers and pencils on it, but no metaphysics about or in it. Once again the bumped-into, the constraining work-tool, life's hard furniture, are the agents of freedom more than deep spaces without resistance, which may only lead to forms of death.[11]

He formulates O'Hara's phrase as an affirmation of life against death; the desk functioning as a frustrating but nevertheless redemptive mediator with freedom. This is part of his argument that the poem exemplifies and affirms that which emerges from frustration and spleen, rather than artistic transcendence: the poem is 'a qualified triumph of the disjunctive'.[12] Cocteau represents an artistic metaphysics of the mirror world which for Ward is synonymous with 'forms of death'. Curiously, Ward does not substantiate this supposed escape from 'forms of death' in the context of the passage, and does not consider that O'Hara's 'death by loneliness' might be connected to the very separation that O'Hara here describes; that it might also be his own 'anti-Cocteau movement' which atomizes him and maintains the loneliness of the desk worker. O'Hara is, then, positioning himself as a desk-worker 'dying of loneliness' because of his isolation from the artistic mirror world; he cannot inhabit Cocteau's Orphic-artistic identity while at work. His attitude towards this artistic 'metaphysics', in the phrase 'anti-Cocteau

---

11 Geoff Ward, "'Housing the Deliberations": New York, War, and Frank O'Hara', in *Frank O'Hara Now*, 26.
12 Ibid. 25.

movement', is ambivalent. This partly returns us to O'Hara's performativity and insincerity, which holds such phrases suspended in ambiguity.

Further ambiguities abound. In Berkson's glossary to the poem, he argues that this line is a reference to *Le Sang d'un Poète*, taking the exemplary mirror as metonymic of this film rather than *Orphée*. His argument is that the passage 'describes Frank O'Hara's typical position in his office at the Museum of Modern Art, which here he distinguishes from the "movement" into the mirror in Jean Cocteau's film *The Blood of a Poet*'.[13] It is revealing that each critic manages to make this into a reference to different films; there are others, too, that could be adduced. This might imply that the reference also encapsulates something that is specific to Cocteau's style rather than the particular constellation of elements in individual films. The image of the mirror world, which in *Orphée* is 'The Zone' where the Death Princess metes out justice, and in *Le Sang d'un Poète* is an imagined otherworldly hotel, is itself merely a symbol of these imagined other realms, which exist in many of Cocteau's films. The mirror functions to signify that which is reflected backwards, both identical and non-identical; that which is both an entirely separate realm, and an uncanny, deathly reversal of the world's very functioning. It is worth building on this analysis of Cocteau's *style* to bring out some of O'Hara's commentary on Cocteau and its contradictions.

Something characteristic of Cocteau's work is contained in this phrase 'anti-Cocteau movement', but O'Hara reformulates it as his own relation to Cocteau, circling it back into self-referentiality. As both Ward and Berkson suggest, O'Hara's position in relation to Cocteau is linked to a nexus of associations to work and leisure which 'Biotherm' as a whole meditates on, constantly mentioning lunch dates, parties, the cinema and other typical fillers of leisure-time. More importantly, both critics also suggest that the kinds of artifice that Cocteau glorifies represent a 'metaphysics'. This, I argue, coincides with a consciousness of Cocteau's own orphic myth of art's power to reverse necessity and death, which I will come to shortly.

The phrase is involved with the rest of the poem's considerations about temporal movement and direction. In the phrase 'anti-Cocteau', I cannot

13   Berkson, *Companion to Biotherm*, 19.

help but hear 'clockwise', a kind of sub-articulation which links it to temporal direction, both linear time and circular time as notated on the clock. Even without this parallel, O'Hara's oppositional movement, away from Cocteau, means that he moves in a different direction from Cocteau; if Cocteau is moving forwards into the future, O'Hara is moving backwards. But the phrase further exemplifies a movement that is particular to Cocteau's films themselves. In both *Orphée* and *Le Sang d'un Poète*, characters seem to be animated by a specific kind of oppositional force. There is gravity-defying, or anti-gravitational movement; direction becomes confused, and the world's poles fumble around in an alternative magnetism. Further, if we were to project and examine the movements implied in O'Hara and Cocteau's works, it is Cocteau who seems to be more concerned with moving backwards, both in his filmic technique – his use of reverse motion – and in his ubiquitous concern with mythology and genesis; the relations of monumentality and fluidity which are examined and estranged in his use of backwards movement. Cocteau's is a looping of the present into the past via mythic symbols which unite images of orphic authorial power, inscribed as both internal and external to the art-work itself. Cocteau's own authorial process is dramatized in symbolic exhibitions of the power of filmic technique to resurrect, mythologizing the process. This is most conspicuous in his use of reverse motion, which is often taken to be a central characteristic of his style. O'Hara, by contrast, is taken to be more interested in constant mobility; repetitions, reiterations, reversals of phrases are estranged by their performative articulation. In Cocteau there is a mythic but rarely simply humorous potential in the use of repetition, reversals and strained movements.

In the short film *La Villa Santo-Sospir*, we are shown images of the villa of Cocteau's patron Francine Weiswiller, which Picasso and Cocteau have decorated with frescoes. Their paintings and line drawings of mythical characters on the walls, including depictions of Orpheus, Dionysus and Narcissus, are one of the main features of the villa displayed in the film. The amateur camerawork reveals different parts of the villa in an undulating movement through its corridors and across these decorated walls. After travelling through the villa by camera, we later see frames which are filled by conspicuously blank, white walls. Entering into these frames, a hand wipes line drawings of mythical figures back onto the walls. This effect is created using reverse motion. Parallel to these processes of re-revelation, where images that have been wiped out are re-created, Cocteau uses reverse motion to seemingly bring flowers back into bloom. Near the end of the film, we move to the villa's garden, where we view further examples of this reversal trope. A hand opens, in which a crumpled flower appears to be patching itself back into bloom. A series of similar sequences follow in turn. After a few moments, we realize that the film is being played backwards; but as James Williams notes, 'there are moments when it is not clear whether we are watching forward or reverse motion'.[14]

What is it that essentially links this backwards-movement of de-crumpling flowers with the exhibition of depictions of classical heroes and gods? A direct link is created between the rendering of classical mythology in the wall design and the idea of backwards or counter-movements in the film. We might posit, then, that Cocteau sees these processes – of reversal and of the re-revelation of myth – as contiguous processes. The reversal of the frame and of time is a return to myth, rather than an attempt to move away from mythic, linear time as identified with fate, the necessity of death and decay.[15] The reversal of death, the re-blooming of flowers, is no less a mythic recognition of temporal inevitability. For Williams there is 'no obvious meaning to be read into this playful perversion of cinematic form', but the very juxtaposition of this technique, given dynamic form as an image of a re-blooming flower and the shots of painted drawings of mythical figures, is significant for the valence with which Cocteau wishes to imbue the frames.[16] In this backwards movement through frames, there is an evocation of re-naissance, of coming back to life; this backwards movement is a metaphorical node in Cocteau's work which functions in conversation with his attachment to myth. The image of re-completion in the blooming flower represents a re-naturalization, a return to unity;

14   James Williams, *Jean Cocteau* (London: Reakton, 2008), 208.
15   For more on fate as identified with mythic time, see Walter Benjamin's descriptions of mythic and divine violence in his 'Critique of Violence': Walter Benjamin, *One-Way Street and Other Writings*, trans. Edmund Jephcott and Kingsley Shorter (London: New Left Books, 1979).
16   Williams, *Jean Cocteau*, 208.

going backwards establishes the return of a symbolic natural state rather than a de-naturalized state which represents the estranging of necessity in art or technical artifice. In the image of the flower, there is a resurgence of the past in the present, as well as a realization of past unity as a trope of the future and a collapsing of the present into the past. This is identified with the classicism of Cocteau's evocation of his own myth-making power, in which technical artifice is veiled rather than performed.

The way that the film-maker achieves these reverse effects is by one of three means; either printing the film backwards, going from the final frame to the first frame; or spooling the film in reverse order. What actually manages to make this reverse-motion functional, though, is the disjunction between soundtrack and image. In *Orphée*, for example, reverse motion is used when the Princess reanimates her victims within the realm of death; part of the sense of amazement this is supposed to elicit is created because her voice plays forwards whereas the images, the frames, loop into reverse motion and then return to forwards temporal development. Likewise, in *La Villa Santo-Sospir*, the continuity on the level of the soundtrack, which does not play backwards, contradicts a discontinuity on the level of the image, which does. Why should the technology – and this strategy of disjunction – which allows the film-maker to reverse film be reified so that it becomes a symbol of his own power? Cocteau uses a strategy of disjunction but loops it back into unity, rather than allowing for a fuller revelation of this disjunction as montage.

Analogously, in *Le Sang d'un Poète*, a man in a sombrero is repeatedly shot and resurrected through reverse-motion. This is even more clearly an attempt to show Cocteau's own control over life and death as represented by figures within the film; the agency which effects this reversal is not represented within the film but is ascribed to Cocteau himself. Cocteau does not occupy the position of the avenger, bringing characters back to life from his position as controller of the frame as a kind of divine, external figure, blasting apart linear temporality as identified with fate.[17] Instead, I

---

17 For further comments on a difference between the mythic and the divine which might illuminate this difference between the divine avenger and the mythic gods, see Benjamin's 'Critique of Violence'.

will argue, his bringing back to life of characters – or flowers – or in short, his temporal reversals, remain within the temporality of fate; the device of reverse-motion does not, like montage might, fundamentally question linear temporality as identified with death and fate, but remains within its own controlling power. The fragmentariness of montage, its discontinuity, is re-written as a trope of unity. This is a kind of suturing.

Bringing the discontinuous fragments and frames together against a soundtrack which remains continuous and 'linear', suturing the wound, Cocteau presents reverse motion as a spectacle to provoke awe. In the re-blooming of flowers, this suturing is literalized, as the broken petals are patched together again. This imagery can be brought into confrontation with some of Lacan's considerations on 'suturing' as related to 'logical time'. For Lacan, suturing signifies a return to logical time:

> L'instant de voir ne peut intervenir ici que comme suture, junction de l'imaginaire et du symbolique, et il est repris dans une dialectique, cette sorte de progrès temporel qui s'appelle la hâte, l'élan, le mouvement en avant, qui se conclut sur le *fascinum*.[18]

I will not fully consider the implications of presenting Cocteau alongside Lacan here. However, it is provoking to consider the potentiality of thinking the 'conjunctions' of external authorial power and the representations of reversal within Cocteau's films – one might argue, the imaginary and the symbolic – that Cocteau uses in his image of the flower, the mirror realm and in his use of reverse motion. These reversals return his films to temporal progress. Cocteau's 'botanique de la mort', the attempt to reverse death, makes the film-maker analogous to a force for resurrection only within a filmic economy which remains wedded to this 'thrust' of 'forward movement' and logical time.

While the power of the camera to control and delimit movement is taken as synecdochic of the poet's and artist's mythologizing role and ability to counteract death's dominion, what it actually represents is a return to logical temporality as fate in the form of this suturing. Though

---

18   Jacques Lacan, *Le Séminaire de Jacques Lacan, Book 11*, ed. Jacques-Alain Miller (Paris: Seuil, 1964), 107.

superficially disruptive of forwards motion, linear, logical temporality maintains its pull in that it insists on the reproduction of the past rather than its disruption; Cocteau holds up a mirror, creates a backwards time which parallels forwards time, but he does not go so far as to shatter the mirror. Critics such as Williams have argued that the use of reverse-motion techniques in Cocteau's work is so pervasive as to be 'embarrassing'.[19] The anti-gravitational filmic style is an expression of artistic resistance to temporality as fate through the alternate pull of mythopoeia; but this strategy maintains those forms, sliding blithely through them, only in reverse, and never quite intensifying into fragmentariness. This contrasts sharply with O'Hara, who uses his evocation of the 'anti-' and the 'backwards' as part of his intensified, fragmentary poem.

To return to 'Biotherm', we note how the poem is taken to eschew mythology through a deflationary use of allusion, attempting to blast monumental poetry into linguistic shards; his is a monumentality denuded of discrete regulation, as Lytle Shaw argues. Shaw writes that he turns

> Pound's desire for discrete, bounded terms, proper names with carefully controlled piths and gists, and an epic third-person audience model into a referential field characterized by fluidity, appropriation, and 'indiscrete' nods toward second-person audience figures inside the poems.[20]

The poem 'threatened Poundian discretion'.[21] O'Hara's frustrated spleen not only responds to Pound, but replaces and overcomes the merely violent reversals of Orphism. There are no mythic transcendences, linked to the potentialities of mythic-artistic violence; instead there are gritted teeth, quotidian annoyance, cynicism, a raw energy which Cocteau's almost comforting aesthetic overrides. But there is something counter to logic – at least a formal logic – in O'Hara's idea that he represents an 'anti-Cocteau movement'. His 'anti-movement' is in fact a reversal of a reversal; a movement against a style in which mythic backwards movement predominates.

---

19   James Williams, *Jean Cocteau* (Manchester: Manchester University Press, 2006), 93.
20   Shaw, *Frank O'Hara*, 65.
21   Ibid. 75.

If we return to the clock analogy, this would mean that while Cocteau is moving forwards, and O'Hara is moving backwards, Cocteau's progression is backwards, where O'Hara's supposed retrogression is a double negative, returning to forwards movement.

Returning to the passage in 'Biotherm', we can see that these reflections are very relevant to the question of the position of 'anti-movement' in relation to 'loneliness', and O'Hara's implied relation to the 'deep spaces without resistance' which Ward identified in Cocteau. This relation was taken to be ambivalent; O'Hara's relation to Cocteau estranged by the performative articulation and imagined discourse within which he was evoked. The tone of the phrase is left suspended; but this ambivalence is also within the phrase 'anti-Cocteau movement' itself and its relation to one of Cocteau's most extensively used filmic techniques.

The double negative returns O'Hara to unity, progressive, 'logical' forwards time, but it also makes the phrase double, polyvocal.[22] It becomes, looping through Cocteau, a linguistic doubling game, something characteristic of O'Hara; double awarenesses are held in suspension, reflecting an ambivalence in the phrase. O'Hara's relation to 'logical time' is always suspended within the performative space of his own articulation, which is fragmented, double, never operating without a sense of the necessity to perform an authorial role, style and persona; Cocteau wants to collapse his authorial mythology into being.

We can also view this difference from Cocteau in the performativity with which O'Hara evokes his own capacity to bring back the dead. The ability to turn the clock back, reversing death, recalls a phrase of O'Hara's in the poem 'Ode to Joy'. If technique, reified as a symbol of Art itself, has the capacity to counteract Death, there will indeed be 'no more dying', a state imagined in 'Ode to Joy'. There is, however, a double-sidedness in O'Hara's self-aware utopian evocations in this poem:

> We shall have everything we want and there'll be no more dying
> On the pretty plains or in the supper clubs (281)

22   See Drew Milne, 'Performance over Being: Frank O'Hara's Artifice', *Textual Practice* 25.2 (2011), 297–313.

Michael Clune reads 'Ode to Joy' as a transmutation of the personal into the collective via the market in a kind of indefinitely extended bourgeois paradise.[23] Such inability to grasp O'Hara's performativity or humour leads some critics towards misjudgements, such as Clune's argument that poems such as 'Personal Poem' and 'Ode to Joy' exemplify a Hayekian-Friedmanian thesis that 'Free choice is the route to a total relation to America'.[24] Its tone, however, involves a kind of artifice and performativity which makes it irreducible to actual gleeful investment in the free market, which Clune reads into the idea of having 'everything we want'. Something similar might be said for 'Biotherm', in which a disruptive performativity both distances and estranges the reader through the artifice that it evokes, refusing the kinds of comforting suture that Cocteau's recourse to mythologizing and re-animation provide.

Stable meaning is, then, upset by insincere modulations of tone. This ambivalence is related to O'Hara's performativity, his irony, which is operative in the comment on Cocteau in 'Biotherm'. This is partly why the 'death by loneliness' that he experiences in the poem can be interpreted by critics in such divergent ways. Any kind of mythology which gives the artist power over temporality, such as Cocteau's, is repeated so often as to become cliché; O'Hara's phrase 'anti-Cocteau movement' is aware of the cliché of reverse motion in Cocteau and comments indirectly on this. He recognizes that Cocteau's style is hackneyed device and tricksmanship. The phrase transliterates and echoes Cocteau's key in an ironization of the romanticization of backwards movement. O'Hara's insincerity here is a kind of doubling and estrangement which connects to the content of the phrase 'anti-Cocteau movement', which doubles senses of reversal. This strategy of doubling is a more effective form of disruption and fragmentation, forcing a reflection on different kinds of reversal through the mediating interlocutor of Cocteau, distancing the reader, than Cocteau's own pacifying, saccharine tropes of reversal. A fierce vibration of opposites is at work in this piece of criticism.

23   Michael Clune, '"Everything We Want": Frank O'Hara and the Aesthetics of Free Choice', *PMLA* 120.1 (2005), 188.
24   Ibid. 187.

Selected Bibliography

Benjamin, Walter, *One-Way Street and Other Writings*, trans. Edmund Jephcott and Kingsley Shorter (London: New Left Books, 1979).

Berkson, Bill, *Companion to Biotherm* (San Francisco: Arion Press, 1990).

Blasing, Mutlu Konuk, 'Frank O'Hara's Poetics of Speech: The Example of "Biotherm"', *Contemporary Literature* 23.1 (Winter 1982), 52–64.

Clune, Michael, '"Everything We Want": Frank O'Hara and the Aesthetics of Free Choice', *PMLA* 120.1 (2005), 181–96.

Lacan, Jacques, *Le Séminaire de Jacques Lacan*, Book 11, ed. Jacques-Alain Miller (Paris: Seuil, 1964).

Milne, Drew, 'Performance over Being: Frank O'Hara's Artifice', *Textual Practice* 25.2 (2011), 97–313.

O'Hara, Frank, *The Collected Poems of Frank O'Hara*, ed. Donald Allen (London: University of California Press, 1995).

Perloff, Marjorie, 'Frank O'Hara and the Aesthetics of Attention' *boundary 2* 4.3 (1976), 779–806.

——, *Frank O'Hara: Poet Among Painters* (New York: G. Braziller, 1977).

Shaw, Lytle, *Frank O'Hara: The Poetics of Coterie* (Iowa City: University of Iowa Press, 2006).

Sutherland, Keston, 'Close Writing', in Robert Hampson and Will Montgomery, eds, *Frank O'Hara Now* (Liverpool: Liverpool University Press, 2010), 120–30.

Ward, Geoff, '"Housing the Deliberations": New York, War, and Frank O'Hara', in Robert Hampson and Will Montgomery, eds, *Frank O'Hara Now* (Liverpool: Liverpool University Press, 2010), 13–28.

Williams, James, *Jean Cocteau* (Manchester: Manchester University Press, 2006).

——, *Jean Cocteau* (London: Reaktion, 2008).

PART 5

Topological Writing

ANDREW OTWAY

Rhythmanalysis and Bertin's *Les Heures Marseillaises*

The heterodox Marxist and sociologist Henri Lefebvre's collection of essays *Élements de rythmanalyse* was published posthumously in 1991, a year after his death. This text can be read as a final volume in a series of works on a critical philosophy of everyday life. It not only presents the culmination of his thought on the interconnectedness of time and space but also analyses rhythms of everyday life from several different perspectives, with the ultimate aspiration of contributing to a radical socio-political change in society. In *Rhythmanalysis* Lefebvre discusses the conflict between (but also the inevitable conjunction of) the organic *rhythms* of the body and the natural world associated with a conception of cyclical time, on the one hand, and social, 'artificial' and mechanistic *repetitions* as part of an opposing conception of linear time on the other hand. Kofman and Lebas say: 'Rhythmanalysis is the means by which we understand the struggle against time within time itself'.[1] Ten years before he wrote *Rhythmanalysis*, Lefebvre had suggested that the 'important thing [...] is the progressive crushing of rhythms and cycles by linear repetition. It must be emphasized that only the linear is fully amenable to being fully quantified and homogenized'.[2] Capitalism and its state support need society to exist in a quantifiable and homogenized time to be able to thrive; in Marxist terms, Lefebvre draws up the following opposition: 'Like all products, like space, [quantified] time divides and splits into use and use-value on the one hand, and exchange

---

1   Henri Lefebvre, *Writings on Cities*, ed. and trans. Eleonor Kofman and Elizabeth Lebas (Oxford: Blackwell, 1996), 31.

2   Henri Lefebvre, *The Critique of Everyday Life, Vol. 3*, trans. Gregory Elliott (London: Verso, 2005), 130.

and exchange value on the other. On the one hand it is sold and on the other it is lived'.[3]

There is a socially and politically repressive side to everyday life, for Lefebvre's critical philosophy, and a liberatory side. This opposition applies to his notion of rhythmanalysis, too. On the repressive side he examined, for example, the phenomenon of *dressage* and the part rhythm plays in this all-pervasive form of social conditioning or 'training'. *Dressage* for Lefebvre is not only a technique of animal training; it is also a technique whereby the combined powers of capitalism and the state train sections of society by employing a combination of natural and artificial rhythms which compel people, for example, to work, consume, vote and be educated in certain conditioned ways favourable to the state's aims.

Lefebvre is particularly concerned in *Rhythmanalysis* with the notion of the inseparability of time and space. The essay 'Attempt at the Rhythmanalysis of Mediterranean Cities',[4] which he wrote with Catherine Régulier, discusses the special rhythms of Mediterranean cities and their connection with socio-political organization and historical development. One of the problems Lefebvre left for the contemporary urban rhythmanalyst was that of method: does the rhythmanalyst observe the play of rhythms and repetitions within a city from a static position at a distance from the rhythms being observed, as is the case in his 'Seen from the Window' essay,[5] or does she/he move around the city as he seems to suggest in his 'Mediterranean Cities' essay?

The following brief account, referring to selected chapters of the journalist and poet Horace Bertin's 1877 city portrait *Les Heures Marseillaises*,[6] in the light of Lefebvre's work, might illuminate possible methodological approaches regarding these questions, and will ultimately open up possibilities for an expansion of Lefebvre's methodologies. *Les Heures Marseillaises*

---

3 Henri Lefebvre, *Rhythmanalysis: Space, Time and Everyday Life*, trans. Stuart Elden and Gerald Moore (London: Continuum, 2004), 74.

4 Ibid. 85–100.

5 Ibid. 27–37.

6 Horace Bertin, *Les Heures Marseillaises* (Marseille: Éditions Qui Vive, 2004). All following references will refer to this edition; page numbers will be given in the text.

is divided into twenty-four short chapters (of typically between three to five pages each) which describe vividly the everyday activities of the citizens of Marseille. Each chapter relates to one hour of the daily cycle; concerning his own method, Bertin writes in his Foreword that he will

> write down, hour by hour, the occupations, the habits, the pastimes of the city, the changing aspects of its streets, the character of certain places, the physiognomy and the movements of passers-by [...]. (9)

The account is subjectively selective in both spatial and temporal ways. Sometimes the focus of the writing moves from street to street but sometimes it jumps from one part of the city to another. Some 'hours' are described in more detail than others. However, in its reference to the rhythms and repetitions of urban life, Bertin's account is significant for the method of rhythmanalysis in two ways. Firstly, it gives a full and detailed account of one daily cycle in the natural rhythm of night and day, within longer seasonal and annual rhythmic cycles. In this way, it represents a day-long synchronic slice of the everyday life of Marseille; this aspect of Bertin's method could usefully be appropriated by rhythmanalysis. Secondly, it improves on Lefebvre's approach in *Rhythmanalysis* by suggesting a method lacking in the latter: a way of observing and writing about the city whilst being physically involved in its rhythms and flows as the author moves around it and observes its everyday activity.

Bertin's account begins at 5am on a late summer morning in 1877. Pale light is just coming into the deserted streets and most of the city sleeps. The 'philosopher' (11) walking the streets (i.e. Bertin himself) forgets all the strong and mostly bad feelings of the previous day, the 'passions, hatreds, appetites and covetousness' (11). He describes himself as feeling and looking happier. The feelings he alludes to seem to correspond to Lefebvre's emphasis on the public and theatrical quality of social life in Mediterranean cities: 'So what is particular about Mediterranean towns? [...] It seems to us that in them urban, which is to say public, space becomes the site of a vast staging where all these relations with their rhythms show and unfurl themselves.'[7]

7   Lefebvre, *Rhythmanalysis*, 96.

At 5am various people appear opening, up their establishments. Bakeries, *liquoristes* and tobacconists fill up with workers. The day's activities begin quietly. Gradually more and more workers fill the streets and move towards the outer circles of the city. Municipal street-sweepers pass backwards and forwards along streets, moving to a slow, lazy rhythm. Even today such barely noticed daily events as the opening up of shops form parts of a slow, twenty-four hour cycle that most people do not recognize as an element of an overall signature rhythm of a particular place: the same small events of everyday life happen day after day after day, sometimes with little variations at the weekend.[8] They are marked as points on the regular cycle of the day (sunrise, noon, sunset) but they also occur in linear time because regulated working practice is fixed to certain points of a clock-time imposed upon the modern world.

Activities at 5am are as yet slow and low-key. Bertin's narrative moves forward through the city in small jumps in time and space; different parts of the city come to life later, such as the *rue Noailles* in the centre, which is still mostly calm; this slower rhythm is opposed to the quicker rhythms of the *cours Belsunce*, just around the corner, which at the same time is full of labourers and builders waiting to be picked up for work. The narrator moves from street to street. Like the *flâneur* he does not seem to have a planned route. By 6am the air is still fresh but the sun has risen and the day has properly begun.

Urban cyclical rhythms and linear repetitions have become increasingly indistinguishable over the last two centuries.[9] By 1877 the industrial age had begun in Marseille and the movement of pedestrians and traffic throughout the city had become regulated by the linear time that capitalism

8   See Doreen Massey et al., *City Worlds* (London: Routledge, 1999), 57: 'Individual cities combine different kinds of movement to evoke quite distinct senses of rhythm. There is no one overbearing city beat. And yet, there *is* something broadly recognizable about how such rhythms fall into distinct times of the day'.

9   For example, in the realm of work Lefebvre says 'the gestures of labour are organized rhythmically only in forms of work that pre-date industrial labour. The closer industrial activity approximates to industrial production using machines, the more linear repetition becomes, losing its rhythmical character [...] From the very beginning of industrial organization, there is a sudden mutual interference between rhythmical vital processes and linear operations' (Lefebvre, *Critique of Everyday Life, Vol. 3*, 129).

needs to make industry work. The rhythm of what Lefebvre refers to as *dressage* certainly applies here but nature and *its* time and rhythms are evident too on the streets of Marseille. For example, Bertin describes the seasonal fruit and vegetables on sale in a street market's stalls; the produce of a pre-industrial agriculture as a part of the rhythmic cycle of the seasons is described in detail, as in the account of the city's melon sellers (48–9).

Bertin accounts for both the general and the particular movement of people. At 9am he describes employees arriving at the *Préfecture* and the *Hôtel-de-Ville* to start their day of drudgery and boredom. He also notes individuals in a state of poverty and desperation who feel the need to get to the pawnbrokers so early in the morning – 'Such occasional dark and painful dramas!' he says (32). Throughout the text Bertin the journalist gets close to his subject and shows a social conscience as he focuses in on the distress of particular individuals.

The build-up of activity and the movement of workers and commuters (and a few animals) develop over the next hour or so in an uneven way, depending on the area and size of the street. Shops and small industries and individual trades-people of the city open for business and children go by on their route to school. Little by little the streets come to life and the general noise-level increases. Again Bertin moves his cinematic tracking-shot gaze almost at random from the general to a few particular characters in the city-play: he describes the movements of a certain young lawyer who at 9am opens the door of his chambers and puts his brief-case onto his table. This noting of detail in Bertin's text highlights another question of method for rhythmanalysis: how important is it to take account of such detail? How do the small-scale and individual rhythms of everyday life fit in with the larger picture, which might for example deal with large-scale rhythmic movements of large numbers of people?

Lefebvre suggests that the small details of everyday life *are* relevant, and he stresses the importance of the notion of the co-existence of diverse rhythms in what he refers to as *polyrhythmia*. This, when applied to the social realm, can describe a society as being composed of a collection of multiple and varied rhythms, usually in a balanced state of *eurhythmia*.[10]

---

10   For a discussion of polyrhythmia and eurhythmia see Lefebvre, *Rhythmanalysis*, 16.

In his 'Mediterranean Cities' essay, Lefebvre suggests there is a need for distance between the rhythmanalyst and the rhythms he or she analyses by positing that rhythms cannot be analysed while lived, suggesting that one must get outside a rhythm in order to analyse it. And yet the opposite is also true: 'Externality is necessary; yet in order to grasp a rhythm one must have been grasped by it, have abandoned oneself "inwardly" to the time that it rhythmed'.[11] At the heart of rhythmanalysis is a sense of oscillation between being inside experience and its analysis.

In Bertin's Marseille there is an intensely busy hour from 11am until noon, during which the noise and bustle and activity in the city and its traffic reaches their daily peak and during which all the city's financial traders go to the cafés on *La Canabière* to drink vermouth and to do business. At midday, however, everything stops in the city 'as if by enchantment' (47). At this time all is bright and sunlit and cheerful; with just a few merchants advertising their wares by modulating their cries in Provençale to a customary rhythm. Everybody goes home or to a restaurant. People sometimes buy fruit on their way home – strawberries or melons, depending on the month, and young men and women often flirt at the flower market. Soon the streets become deserted as people have their lunch. There are noises and smells of people eating. At this time 'rest has almost everywhere succeeded activity' (50); Bertin says this silence has a certain charm but at 1pm the noise and activity start to build up again and by two o'clock the *sieste* is over and everybody is back at work. Throughout the afternoon many of the streets of Marseille are also occupied by maids, the elderly and retired people, *boules*-players, elegant young women shopping on the *rue Saint-Ferréol* and the *rue de la Darse*. By rhythmic contrast, in the quiet period between three and four o'clock some *quartiers* of Marseille are completely silent. Lefebvre also points out the relevance of this lull in activity to the overall rhythm of a place when he says: 'It is to be noted that a deserted street at four o'clock in the afternoon has as strong a significance as the swarming of a square at market or meeting times'.[12]

---

11   Ibid. 89.
12   Ibid. 96.

At 4pm there is some lively action at the Stock Exchange as the rhythms of international finance and commercial information mark their beat and show the connection of Marseille to other world centres of capital. People stop work between five and eight o'clock and some stroll around the city before heading home, whilst many others go to swim in the sea. Bertin calls 6pm the hour of the absinthe drinkers – as it is throughout the rest of the country's cities, he claims. The cafés of the city centre have a certain variety of exotic clients at this time, especially on *La Canabière*.

At around 6.30pm another popular Provençale cry, this time of a cooked-beet seller, is heard as he roams the streets: '*Bettarabo de Gardanno*' (75). Bertin is keen to report such uses of the Provençale language as a reminder of the roots of the people of Marseille who have become entranced in a negative way by the forces of modernity. He says that it seems like

> these beet-merchants come every year just before the winter to publicly protest against the increasing scorn that Marseille seems to have for their language which is so full of colour and flavour, and for their simple morality of years gone by. (75–6)

This suppression of 'local' language would be understood by Lefebvre as a characteristic of a general homogenizing tendency in everyday modernity: 'All forms of hegemony and homogeneity are refused in the Mediterranean'.[13] Lefebvre, like Bertin, looks back to an idyllic pre-modernity in a way that sometimes seems nostalgic; however, he does not want to take the world backwards in time and negate emancipatory progress.[14] Lefebvre wants to escape from the exploitation and alienation of the worst aspects of modernity and from the destructive collaboration of capitalism and the state. For Lefebvre it was important to reinstate the values of the neglected rhythms of cyclical time within society and to redress the healthy balance between these and linear, social time and its rhythms. (This would be especially important as cyclical and linear rhythms and repetitions increasingly converge over time).

13 Ibid. 98.
14 See the essay 'Revolutionary Romanticism' in Lefebvre's *Introduction to Modernity*, trans. John Moore [1962] (London: Verso, 1995).

At 8pm, when the Marseillais dine, the restaurants fill up and at 8.30, the cafés become busy, as do the *café-concerts* and theatres. Then, in another *en masse* movement, the streets empty as people take trams to the sea-front and to the beach or to the skating-rings away from the summer heat in the city centre.

All through the day there seems to be an ebbing and flowing rhythm in terms of how the city centre fills and empties with people, traffic and noise, stillness and silence. This is part of the daily rhythm of Marseille; each city has its own rhythmic character which is entwined with its relationship to modernity and to its customs of the past.

Every day at 9pm a strange thing happens in Marseille: with lots of noise of whips and bells, herds of she-asses are driven through the streets at a gallop. They are brought to a stop at certain houses; the she-asses are milked on the spot and the milk is sold to the house-holders. Subsequently they take off again at great speed! It happens at the same time every day – cyclical time converging with the regularity of linear time. This seems to have been an almost rural custom of a pre-modern form of agriculture.

Things begin to go quiet between 9pm and 10pm except for certain streets that are lively (all year round) like *La Canabière* and the *cours Belsunce*. In the rest of the city, only a few shops are still open after 10pm, and after 11pm only the small cafés and bars on the quay-side are still lively with laughter and the sound of violins or guitars. From 11pm onwards, only the prostitutes in the 'Ghetto of love', not far from the Old Port, are on the streets together with some of their (potential) clients – sailors and soldiers mostly. This aspect of the economy is simultaneously pre-modern and capitalist. The last wave of activity comes around 12.30pm when the theatres close and some of the streets in the centre, *La Canabière*, and the *rue Noailles* flood with people heading towards nearby cafés. By 1am the city sleeps.

Bertin's account is important in terms of practical method for the rhythmanalyst – does one stay put and observe urban rhythms from one well-chosen vantage point as in Lefebvre's 'Seen from a Window', his rhythmanalytical essay on Paris, or does one move like a *flâneur* from street to street more spontaneously absorbing and noting rhythms? Bertin would certainly have approved more of the latter alternative. In this way his

Les Heures Marseillaises suggests an expansion of rhythmanalytical method beyond Lefebvre's work.

Selected Bibliography

Bertin, Horace, *Les Heures Marseillaises* [1877] (Marseille: Editions Qui Vive, 2004).

Lefebvre, Henri, *Critique of Everyday Life vol. 3*, trans. Gregory Elliott [1981] (London: Verso, 2005).

——, *Introduction to Modernity*, trans. John Moore [1962] (London: Verso, 1995).

——, *Rhythmanalysis: Space, Time and Everyday Life*, trans. Stuart Elden and Gerald Moore [1992] (London: Continuum, 2004).

——, *Writings on Cities*, ed. and trans. Eleonor Kofman and Elizabeth Lebas (Oxford: Blackwell, 1996).

Massey, Doreen, John Allen and Steve Pile, eds, *City Worlds* (London: Routledge, 1999).

JOANNE BRUETON

A Stitch in Time: Temporal Threads in Jean Genet

'A stitch in time saves nine' / 'Un point à temps en vaut cent': English
proverb expressing the benefits of timely prevention, the advantages of
minimal correction; anagram for 'this is meant as incentive'.
—THOMAS FULLER, *Gnomologia, Adagies and Proverbs,*
Wise Sentences and Witty Sayings, Ancient and Modern,
Foreign and British (1732)

In his autobiographical essay on the production of the veil, 'Un Ver à Soie
– points de vue piqués sur l'autre', Derrida explores time as a material construct: lateness, delay, being behind or over time, treated as synthetic problems and dealt with by material solutions. Derrida opens his musings by
insisting that he weave before it is too late, striving to make a stitch in time

avant le verdict, le mien, avant que, tombant sur moi, il ne m'attire avec lui dans la chute,
avant qu'il ne soit trop tard, ne point écrire. Point final, un point c'est tout [...]. Souvenir
d'enfance: en levant les yeux au-dessus de leurs fils de laine, sans en interrompre ni
même ralentir le mouvement de leurs doigts agiles, les femmes de ma famille disaient
parfois, me semble-t-il, qu'il fallait *diminuer* [...] qu'il fallait procéder à la *diminu-*
tion des points ou réduire les mailles d'un ouvrage en cours [...]. Et, par ce maillage
désormais imprenable, laisser encore la rhétorique s'approprier le vrai du verdict.[1]

'A stitch in time saves nine' anticipates the English proverb, and accordingly
Derrida's single stitch promises such prevention; but rather than sewing up
holes to restore full coverage or to repair a broken membrane, his single

1   Jacques Derrida, 'Un Ver à Soie', in Hélène Cixous and Jacques Derrida, *Voiles* (Paris:
     Galilée, 1998), 25–6.

'point c'est tout' achieves the opposite effect and strives to unravel, diminish or hinder such completion. Coverage is already too late for Derrida, belonging to an epistemology governed by veiling and revelation in which truth would have to exist prior to the subject that invokes it. Anathema to his deconstructive approach in which there can be no transcendental outside that determines meaning, Derrida draws on the material metaphor of the veil to critique the temporal finality of an imposed verdict. Rather than perceiving knowledge as a truth first shrouded then exposed, Derrida proposes an alternative process of gleaning 'le vrai du verdict' which directly challenges the immutable, concrete connotations of a die being cast or a judgement made.

'Un point c'est tout': one stitch is all Derrida needs to unravel the cloak of the 'voile derrière lequel une chose est supposé se tenir';[2] one stitch before 'le temps de ce verdict [...] je le sens si paradoxal, tordu, retors, à contretemps',[3] the verdict a material temporality which he perceives as ductile, twisted, *against time*. Derrida's verdict is thus always eager to unravel any finitude, and so he returns to the beginning, using two examples from childhood which challenge the didactic totality of the veil and the verdict: procedurally, he diminishes or slackens the weave so as to glean 'le vrai du verdict'; semantically, he locates in the very term 'verdict', a worm (ver) word (dict), the natural production of the silk threads that have been appropriated into discourses of veiling but whose 'sériciculture [existe] avant le verdict [...] n'était point de l'homme [...] sécrétion de ce qui n'etait ni un voile, ni une toile'.[4] Derrida cultivates the silk thread as an organic, self-governing figure, a thread tied to the time of his childhood and which as a 'fil de soie' subtends matter and time to cultivate a self-sufficient truth in both.

I begin this chapter with Derrida's material reading of the veil and the verdict as I will be exploring time in Genet's work as cast in similar terms. Just as Derrida recasts his loosening verdict as a 'maillage imprenable', a construct which he temporally locates in childhood memory, so too will I be reading Genet's creation of time as an ungraspable, unfurling thread

---

2   Ibid. 26.
3   Ibid. 35.
4   Ibid. 83.

sewn as a wormword, an internal verdict, in his childhood. In examining both how time is materialized as a thread, and how that thread prompts a semantic interplay between *le fil* and *le fils* that catalyses Genet's sacralization of time, I argue that the 'fil' is the privileged signifier of a verdict woven as the weft of Genet's texts. This verdict is constructed as the material ligature that governs Genet's writing, not only a 'fil conducteur' that ties his tomes together, but more specifically a 'fil' that tethers him to a time at birth that he holds sacred. The thread that yokes him to time, this elastic prison which relentlessly entangles him, nonetheless produces the very verdict to which he holds himself captive: Genet endlessly retying the threads of a filiation that might recapture a time once frayed and recast it as a renewed bond. If Genet constructs his own verdict, what veracity is sewn into the wormwords that produce his text? Perhaps his texts are like Derrida's silkworm, their function to reproduce naturally the threads that later become the veil, such that to find the veridiction of Genet's writing we must unpick its *fils* – both its threads and its son – to glean the true matter therein.

Le fil du temps: The Time of the Verdict

Let us first establish time as a thread in Genet's writing. In his literary debut, *Notre Dame des Fleurs*, Genet recounts the verdict given after his conviction of attempted theft:

> Le greffier à enregistré l'aveu, que j'ai signé […] J'ai refait le chemin à travers les corridors souterrains du Palais pour retrouver ma petite cellule noire et glacée de la Souricière. Ariane au labyrinthe. Le monde le plus vivant, les humains à la chair la plus tendre, sont de marbre. – Je sème sur mon passage la dévastation. Les yeux morts je parcours de villes des populations pétrifiées. Mais pas d'issue. Impossible de reprendre l'aveu, de l'annuler, tirer le fil du temps qui l'a tissé et faire qu'il se dévide et se détruise. Fuir? Quelle idée! Le labyrinthe est plus tortueux que les considérants des juges.[5]

---

5   Jean Genet, *Œuvres Complètes II* (Paris: Gallimard, 1952), 69.

Just as Derrida presents the traditional verdict as a permanent and irreversible stitch, so too does Genet present the verdict as a thread which ties him up, its ligature binding him to an ineluctable fate. The undoing of the 'fil du temps' is figured as a process as inflexible as the sculptures around it are implacable: once undone, it can neither wind back into a ball, nor immaterialize itself back into a time which did not exist, which was without materiality. What is striking about Genet's language here is perhaps less that he deploys the cliché of 'le fil du temps', than that he takes it literally, casting himself as Ariane, whose thread classically provided Theseus with a lifeline out of the Minotaur's labyrinth. Genet as Ariane coalesces spatial and temporal terms, his thread not a material rope that offers salvation, but a thread of time which when unravelled leaves him helpless, bound to enter further into a space whose time is atrophied and whose life is petrified as marble sculptures. Time is thus represented as remorseless space: Genet's verdict not conditioned by a forward orientated teleology but downwards, inwards, towards a time in abeyance, a time against time, *à contretemps*, to cite Derrida.

The temporal finality of the verdict is literally a prison to Genet, entrapping him in an immoveable past that his active movement struggles against. Mobility is allied to a devastation that Genet sows as he walks, his passage agitating the temporal fixity of the verdict as he disrupts its closure. We might benefit from the homophony of 'sowing' and 'sewing' here as Genet's movement strives to disperse or break apart the single thread of time that governs him, to make a stitch into that time that might undo its finality. For Geoffrey Bennington reading Derrida's 'Un Ver à Soie', sowing is already too late since it is etymologically tied to lateness: '*sero te amavi*, the epigraph for the whole of JD's text ... *Sero*, "late", "very late", "so late", "too late" [...] *sero, sevi, satum*: to sow, to plant, to bring forth, to produce, to scatter ... to *disseminate*. *Sero sero*: late I disseminate'.[6] Rather than having any impact on time, Bennington's parallels suggest that it is always too late to diffuse or break apart time, its threads cannot be disintegrated or

6   Geoffrey Bennington, *Not Half No End: Militantly Melancholic Essays of Jacques Derrida* (Edinburgh: Edinburgh University Press, 2010), 163.

made productive. In other words, movement can have no impact on the hegemony of time, neither sowing nor sewing can affect the threads that represent it. This corroborates the Kantian formula of a pure time which subordinates movement, reversing traditional conceptions of time as a measure between intervals and instead proposing temporality as a self-governing form, over and above any passing of time. Deleuze formulates this in *Critique et Clinique* as:

> Le temps ne se rapporte plus au mouvement qu'il mesure, mais le mouvement au temps qui le conditionne. Aussi le mouvement n'est-il plus une détermination d'objet, mais la description d'un espace, espace dont nous devons faire abstraction pour découvrir le temps comme condition de l'acte. Le temps devient donc unilinéaire et rectiligne, non plus du tout au sens où il mesurerait un mouvement dérivé, mais en lui-même et par lui-même.[7]

Genet's passage is indeed spatial in its disruption, his movement sows devastation through the space it describes and it is from here that we can abstract an overarching temporality of living, 'le plus vivant', or dead, 'les yeux morts'. Kantian time thus contains movement while remaining itself immutable, and indeed the unyielding nature of Genet's 'fil du temps', this single, linear filament, reinforces the sovereignty of a time which operates independently to the passing of time, or to the time of taking place. There can be no place in this pure time, a form which Deleuze reads as spatially void as 'l'ordre du temps vide. Le labyrinthe a changé d'allure: ce n'est plus un cercle ni une spirale, mais un fil, une pure ligne droite, d'autant plus mystérieuse qu'elle est simple, inexorable.'[8] No longer is Ariadne's thread able to offer emancipation from the labyrinth; instead, the labyrinth becomes the thread itself. This inexorable 'fil du temps', indivisible and incessant, is given form and space as a void not subject to temporal measures, but like Genet's void inside the prison, a torturous timelessness that becomes the prison itself.

In its unbroken linearity, this labyrinthine thread eschews points of reference and is thus deeply disorientating. Rather than a flow or current as

---

7   Gilles Deleuze, *Critiques et Cliniques* (Paris: Editions de Minuit, 1993), 41.
8   Ibid.

it is traditionally conceived in Aristotle's metaphor in the *Physics*, Genet's temporality is indifferent to sequence or succession; neither fast-paced nor progressive, this material 'fil du temps' is entangled, repetitive. Genet describes time in his posthumously published play *Le Bagne* as just such a mercurial construct in which moments overlap or replay themselves, almost forming an a-temporality that abides by its own whims:

> Mon rôle est de confondre le temps, de confondre les nuits [...]. J'oppose la confusion des lianes, on coule, on rampe. Les minutes, les heures se chevauchent. Le temps est élastique. Il s'étire, il s'allonge, il rétrécit. Mic mac. On fume. On bande. On somnole. Le courant électrique circule dans les fils qui ferment l'enceinte.[9]

Despite its ostensible inflexibility in *Notre Dame des Fleurs*, here Genet formalizes time as ductile: a form which stretches, elongates and shrinks, once again all material figurations. Genet's time lacks punctual anchorage, here revelling in its irregularity where the intervals by which it might be measured coincide to produce confusion and sameness. Time in *Le Bagne* is governed according to a principle of non-differentiation: bereft of any teleology, it simply shape-shifts, a 'mishmash' which banalizes the importance of living by temporal markers. Inside the penal colony, time may be irregular but it also regulates. Invoking the 'fils qui ferment l'enceinte', Genet figures his threads once again as the principal structures of governance: literally, the electric current that flows through these wires seals and encloses the prison limiting the space of movement therein; but figurally, these threads house movement, while also being an immutable, eternal form that does not change. The 'fils' that control the prison become the privileged signifiers of the experience of being bound *in* and *to* time. Time is thus stuck, caught on itself, its threads intertwined in a self-repeating permutation of the same, almost a suspension in time following Jean Luc Nancy's description:

> il ne peut pas y avoir de *passage* d'un présent *à* un autre, si ni l'un ni l'autre n'ont lieu. Il y a donc écart, espace. *Spanne*, dit Heidegger. Extension, tension, traction, attraction (*gespannt*: tendu, excité, séduit, captivé). Agitation, spasme, épanouissement.[10]

9   Jean Genet, 'Le Bagne' in *Théâtre Complète* (Paris: Gallimard, 2002), 802.
10   Jean-Luc Nancy, *Le sens du monde* (Paris: Galilée, 1993), 106.

Time is figured in the same ductile terms as Genet's elastic thread, this 'ductus' resonating with s*education*, attraction, captivation, to reveal time as a spatial form that physically grips us. Nancy is critiquing Kant's pure time here, endorsing the Heideggerian form of extension or 'spacing' which suggests that any punctualization, any single moment, negates the possibility of taking place because there is no way of moving on to the next moment. And yet, Nancy describes the punctual moment as itself extendible: 'l'instant comme espacement',[11] the instant imbued with its own spatial stretch that creates the separability of events, experiences, existence. This gap of time is both part of time and a-temporal, an interval that makes room for protracted experience even within the punctual moment.

Nancy's is a time that is literally spun-out: an interstice that enables a single moment to linger and in which we are agitated, touched, a temporal gap wherein we blossom. Time drags in similar spatial intervals in *Le Bagne*, yet Genet claims to eschew the marriage of time and space in an interview in 1981 claiming that:

> Une chose est sacrée pour moi – j'emploie bien le mot sacré – sacré, c'est le temps. L'espace ne compte pas. Un espace peut se réduire ou s'augmenter énormément, ça n'a pas beaucoup d'importance. Mais le temps j'ai eu l'impression, et je l'ai encore qu'un certain temps de vie à ma naissance m'était donné [...]. Il a fallu que je travaille ce temps [...]. J'ai eu comme préoccupation de transformer ce temps en volume, en plusieurs volumes.[12]

Time is often obfuscated in Genet's writing by his own emphasis on spatial modalities, and yet despite the opposition he seems to draw here between time and space, time is still figured *as* space. The terms which he rejects as capricious – 'un espace peut se réduire ou s'augmenter' – are precisely the same as those he uses in *Le Bagne* to describe time as sovereign. As Mairéad Hanrahan has noted, Genet is re-working time as space, trans-*form*ing it as though it were tangible: a subject that 'matters to him *as matter*'.[13] Time

11 Ibid.
12 Genet, *L'ennemi déclaré: textes et entretiens*, ed. Albert Dichy (Paris: Gallimard, 1991), 221.
13 Mairéad Hanrahan, 'Sculpting Time', *Paragraph* 27.2 (2004), 43.

is given body not *within* his corpus but *as* the corpus: he volumizes time, recasting it in material terms as the embodied fabric onto and into which he weaves his text. Neither successive nor progressive, Genet protracts time just as Nancy does, extending it not as a punctual moment but as a span, a 'certain temps' or amount of time which captivates – indeed motivates – Genet's texts.

Tethered to time, Genet's volumes expand it, elongate it, work through the continuous space of this 'temps de vie à ma naissance [qui] [s']était donné'. This stretch of time allotted to him at birth could be read as a generalized lifespan that he states is applicable to 'l'homme le plus anonyme [qui] a le même temps, ou un temps moindre, ou un temps plus grand, peu importe, mais ce temps-là, il est sacré'.[14] But Genet's manner of stretching that time, distending or truncating it, his exaltation of the specific time 'à ma naissance' as the moment that he inherits a time that is given or gifted to him, resonates with Nancy's reading of the spacing of an instant on which we linger. 'Ce temps-là': Genet points out this time at birth and monumentalizes it throughout his writing, protracting this moment as the time that will dictate his life, the stitch in time that produces the weft of his text rather than an entire life-time. It is Genet who actively sacralizes this time, materially constructing it as though it had been ordained, 'donné par un dieu', but which is in fact engineered by 'un dieu que j'invente',[15] Genet thus fashioning the decree that determines all of his texts thereafter. This fabricated given time is catapulted into the hallowed realms of intangibility ('je ne dois pas y toucher')[16] and yet it materializes as this matter with which, for 'soixante-dix ans', Genet had to 'travaille[r] ce temps. Il ne fallait pas qu['il] le laisse en jachère'.[17] He grafts the time given to him at his birth, fosters and cultivates it rather than leaving it as a fallow, and thus works this time into his writing as its productive matter. Following Nancy's *Spanne*, Genet is touched or agitated by this time at his birth, his

14   Genet, *L'ennemi déclaré*, 221.
15   Ibid.
16   Ibid.
17   Ibid.

texts blossom by stretching this stretch of time and as such, I argue that he casts the specific time at his birth as a verdict that he sews into his texts, a Derrridean 'maillage imprenable' that allows us to glean the meaning of his texts thereafter.

Les fils perdus: The Time of Filiation

Having established the primacy of time as a material construct whose threads bind Genet, I want to refine his signifiers as more than abstract vectors that carry time, rather as the filaments whose etymology gestures to a specifically filial time. The time that he is naturally granted at birth is mimetically played out by his own re-gifting of that time back to his texts, the time that he becomes a *fils* rethreaded through the filial signifiers in his texts which eulogize a filiation otherwise absent. The 'fil' reconnects Genet to childhood by making present what he claims in *Un Captif Amoureux* to in fact be absent, Genet the orphan who describes how

> ma vie s'inscrivait en creux, ce creux devint aussi terrible qu'un gouffre. Le travail qu'on nomme damasquinage consiste a creuser à l'acide une plaque d'acier de dessins en creux où doivent s'incruster des fils d'or. En moi les fils d'or manquaient. Mon abandon à l'Assistance Publique fut une naissance certainement différente des autres naissances mais pas plus effrayante qu'elles.[18]

Just as he does not want the time at his birth to be left 'en jachère', as a fallow, neither does he want to leave his life as a 'creux', a hollow, his texts creating a filial imprint that is in fact missing. The 'fil' actively subtends the interstice, materially grafting Genet's childhood here, a signifier that aims to bring an absent filiation into relief: these 'fils d'or', golden threads, or Genet the *fils d'or*, the absent 'golden boy', litotically trying to reclaim and linger on a 'naissance' which sits awkwardly amidst the generalized

---

18   Jean Genet, *Un Captif Amoureux* (Paris: Gallimard, 1986), 205.

experience of filiation he describes. Mirroring the same universality as in the 1981 interview, it is the disparity of Genet's birth, his separation from the normative temporal experience that cuts him off and that seems to catalyse his desire to figure time as a thread that links, a ligature that both ties and unites.

For Nathalie Fredette, this filial rupture marks Genet's whole corpus as she argues 'l'œuvre ne cessera jamais d'être un texte qui s'enchaîne, tissu ou trame, d'où il s'ensuit que l'histoire du "fils" se lit dans la trame secrète du fil (autre filiation)'.[19] Affirming the materiality of Genet's writing, Fredette simultaneously yokes the threads of its fabric not only to time in general, to any 'fil du temps', but to the specific temporality of filiation. Genet's timeless temporal space that we explored in his prisons becomes, in his second novel *Miracle de la Rose*, directly linked to the time of childhood:

> Il me suffit d'évoquer mes amours d'enfant pour que je redescende au fond du temps dans ses plus ténébreuses demeures, dans une région solitaire, où je ne retrouve plus que la Colonie, formidable et seule. Elle me tire à elle de tous ses membres muscles, avec ce geste des matelots qui lèvent de l'eau un filin, une main se portant devant l'autre au fur et à mesure que la corde s'entasse sur le point et je retrouve auprès du Divers regagné, une enfance nauséeuse et magnifiée par l'horreur, que je n'eusse jamais voulu quitter.[20]

Time having been metamorphosed into a 'filin', a life-line, Genet's thread pulls him into the depths of his childhood. Mired in the thick sludge of nostalgia, Genet figures his 'fil' as a sailor's rope, sullied with the dregs and residue collected not when being dragged out of the water, but being dragged in by his childhood memory. Once again Genet's life-line does not provide a route out, but a way in: time once more figured as a cavernous space as magnetic as it is emetic. Time is rendered a shelter of sorts, 'le fil' always paranomastically tied to Genet as a 'fils' looking to return to this 'enfance nauséeuse [...] que je n'eusse jamais voulu quitter'.

---

19   Nathalie Fredette, *Figures Baroques de Jean Genet* (Saint-Denis, Paris: Presses universitaires de Vincennes, 2001), 76.
20   Genet, *Œuvres Complètes II*, 313.

For Genet, 'créer c'est toujours parler de l'enfance. C'est toujours nostalgique'.[21] His writing is always signed by time, by a time signature inscribed through 'le fil' of filiation. Where psychoanalysis may interpret this nostalgic replaying of childhood as constitutive of the writing process, Freud arguing for example that 'imaginative creation, like daydreaming, is a continuation and substitute for the play of childhood',[22] for Genet writing this time, inscribing and unravelling its 'fils' is not a substitute for childhood, but a means of bringing filiation to life through the play of signifiers. Just as he elegizes 'le fil' in his 1957 essay *Le Funambule*, personifying it as matter ('le fil était mort – ou si tu veux muet, aveugle – te voici: il va vivre et parler'),[23] all of his texts also 'exploite[nt] le filon, les fils, les fils, la fliction',[24] as Hélène Cixous remarks. He casts out a line into his texts to bring a filiation to life that was either absent or disconnected, re-inventing the absent fil and threading it into the body of his texts as their writing instrument. In a letter in 1944, he states that 'me donner du papier, c'est comme si dans la rue une boutique de luthier s'ouvrait pour donner à un musicien pauvre qui joue, un jeu de cordes de violon',[25] his simile equating the rudimentary function of the violin strings with the parchment of his texts, these threads metaphorically forming the lines on Genet's page which give voice to his writing. There is an element of both the essential and the gift inherent in these violin strings which the poor player cannot live without and yet of which he is deprived. Such is the relation Genet expresses towards the constitutive but lacking 'fil' in *Notre Dame des Fleurs* when he recounts another violin-orientated childhood memory:

> Culafroy entrait dans sa chambre [...] il arrache un violon grisâtre qu'il a confectionné lui-même [...] avec la couverture cartonnée de l'album d'images, avec le

21 Genet, *L'ennemi déclaré*, 277.
22 Sigmund Freud, 'Creative writers and Day-dreaming', in *Complete Works*, Vol. 9, trans. James Strachey (London: Penguin, 1959), 152.
23 Jean Genet, *Œuvres Complètes V* (Paris: Gallimard, 1978), 9.
24 Hélène Cixous, *L'entretien de la blessure* (Paris: Galilée, 2011), 24.
25 Jean Genet, letter to Maurice Toesca 28 February 1944, in *Lettres à Marc et Olga Barbezat* (Paris: L'Arbalète, 1988), 40.

morceau du manche d'un balai et quatre fils blancs: les cordes. C'était un violon plat et gris, un violon à deux dimensions, avec seulement la table d'harmonie et le manche ou filaient quatre fils blancs, géométriques, rigoureux sur l'extravagance, un spectre de violon [...]. Culafroy ne savait, par ses formes torturées, qu'un violon inquiétait sa sensible mère et qu'il s'en promenait dans ses rêves en compagnie de chat souples, dans des coins de murs, sous des balcon où des filous se partagent le butin de la nuit, ou d'autres apaches s'enroulent autour d'un bec de gaz, dans des escaliers qui grincent comme des violons qu'on écorche vifs. Ernestine pleura de rage de ne pouvoir tuer son fils [...] jamais plus il ne voulut dire le mot commençant par viol.[26]

This make-shift violin, constructed in two-dimensions and thus devoid of any actual musical function, is merely a frame for the 'fils blancs' whose potential vibrations are deeply antagonizing, agitative (to recall the Nancian term). Despite their usual materiality, these strings are disconcertingly ephemeral, spectral, Genet exploiting the play of the signifier rather than their referent and subtending each permutation by friction. The 'fil' moves paronomastically throughout this scene such that the mother's desire to kill her 'fils' slips into the strings that aggravate her: those 'filous' who partition their spoils remind her of the 'fil' which frays her nerves; the 'fils blancs' which prompt the idiom 'cousu de fil blanc' to mean that which is utterly predictable, returning us to the predictive, or verdictive, role of the 'fil' in Genet's texts. The nature of that filial prophecy is anything but transparent, however; the common denominator, negotiated by the 'fil', gestures to a relational violence that severs the connection between mother and son. Genet conditions the 'fil' as a bond engineered by the son but experienced by the mother as a violation: the etymological parity of the violin and *viol* catalysing a drama which sullies any filiation between the two. Rooted in childhood memory, Genet yokes the 'fil' to the failure of filiation and thus posits his text as the machine able to recalibrate the 'fil' into a filature of his own making.

Let us return to Derrida's 'Un Ver à Soie' to determine how Genet's filature reinvents the 'fil' he describes as lacking, reclaiming the 'fils perdu(s)',

---

26   Genet, *Œuvres Complètes II*, 75–6.

those lost threads or sons, that determine so much about the verdict of his texts. Turning from one childhood memory to another, Derrida explains the filature of the silkworm as:

> Un vrai souvenir d'enfance [...]. Dans les quatre coins d'une boite à chaussures, donc, on m'y avait initié, j'hébergeais et nourrissais des vers à soie [...] cette petite vie silencieuse et finie ne faisait rien d'autre, là-bas, si près, sous mes yeux mais à une distance infinie, rien d'autre que cela: se préparer soi-même à se cacher soi-même, aimer à se cacher en vue de se produire au dehors et de s'y perdre, cracher cela même dont le corps reprenait possession pour l'habiter en s'enveloppant de nuit blanche. En vue de revenir à soi, d'avoir à soi ce que l'on est, de s'avoir et de s'être en mûrissant mais en mourant aussi à la naissance [...] pour rester auprès de soi, l'être qu'il avait été en vue de se réengendrer soi-même dans la filature de ses fils ou de ses filles – au delà de toute différence sexuelle ou plutôt de toute dualité des sexes et même de tout accouplement.[27]

Derrida's nostalgia for these silkworms, hatched in his youth and whose 'fils' are emblematic of that childhood, centres on his fascination for their natural, internal production of threads. Derrida hones in on filature as a process devoid of any exteriority, detached from the veil that has been appropriated by discourses of revelation and unveiling: it is instead a natural process that belongs solely to the silkworm that spins them. Secreting this fine thread, Derrida describes the foreign familiarity of the silkworm which gives birth to a 'fil' at the same time as it loses itself within this continuous filament, unable to cut itself off from it. Generated in and by the silkworm, these 'fils' are both sons *and* threads, sons *as* threads, filaments which are never wholly part of or different to the self that produces them. This filature almost enacts a Kristevan abjection in which 'je *m'*expulse, je *me* crache, je *m'*abjecte dans le même mouvement par lequel je prétends *me* poser'.[28] But where Kristeva's subject is defined in opposition to that which is jettisoned, Derrida's silkworm is established within both the process of expulsion and the product of secretion. Derrida's sites of filature are

27 Derrida, 'Un Ver à Soie', 82, 84.
28 Julia Kristeva, *Pouvoirs de l'horreur: essai sur l'abjection* (Paris: Editions du Seuil, 1980), 11.

multiple and defiantly present, the silkworm primed to embody its own secretions in a homophonic play between 'cacher/cracher' such that 'le fil' which is discharged provides a shelter for the self, an abjection which re-engenders the self by never being entirely disconnected from it. This filature generates a filiation that is therefore never wholly other, but whose externalization is necessary to generate a sense of self: 'il projetait au dehors ce qui procédait de lui et restait au fond, au fond *de lui*: hors de soi en soi et près de soi'.[29] This 'fil' is both an inherent part of the self and contiguous to it, the silkworm working to expel that 'soie' which constitutes its own 'soi'. The silkworm is an avatar of a filiation which is thus wrapped up in itself, this 'fil de soie' a cipher for the 'fil' of the self, as a self, such that the filature that spins this thread also externalizes a self giving birth to itself, the line of the 'fil' providing the symbolic conduit through which the 'soi(e)' is engendered.

This silk-thread, or 'fil(s) de soi(e)', whose play of signifiers Derrida literalizes in this text in 1998, is actively dramatized by Genet a decade previously in *Un Captif Amoureux*:

> '*Étrange séparation*', plutôt réprobation glacée m'interdisant l'approche des autres. Au moins cinq ans loin d'eux, comme si, femme musulmane enveloppée d'une mousseline de granit le regard nu, plus vif que profond, je cherchais dans le regard des autres le mince fil de soie qui devait nous relier tous, indiquant une continuité de l'être, repérable par deux regards abandonnés l'un dans l'autre mais sans désir.[30]

His 'fil de soie' strives to materialize a continuum that *ought* to exist between people, that *ought* to enable the self to be established through the eyes of the onlooker, just as one might in the Lacanian Imaginary where the gaze of the other engages me in a relation and both affirms and alienates me in the process. Genet solicits that reflective connection as Hadrien Laroche comments: 'dans ces années, le passage se fait vers la signature de soi dans le regard de l'autre. Autrement dit, la métamorphose des chaînes de la prison – acier, matière fécale, courant d'air – en ce mince fil de soie de l'échange

---

29   Derrida, 'Un Ver à Soie', 83.
30   Genet, *Un Captif Amoureux*, 424.

des regards.'[31] The ties that once fettered Genet are here transposed into the malleable string of connection, of filiation. Genet's 'fil de soie' compliments Derrida's reading of the silkworm which establishes the continuity of being along its silk threads, the threads it produces defining self and son in an unbroken cycle. Perhaps the autobiographical nature of *Un Captif Amoureux* reveals the artifice of Genet's filature, his lived experience never quite in sync with the filial bond he seeks to construct. Always out of line, never on the continuum, Genet compares himself to the veil that prevents mutual interaction, his unilateral engagement only able to survey relations rather than enter into them. The verdict which his texts all unravel and recast here asserts the full poignancy of Genet's disconnection: unable to loosen the weft of this sheer muslin that cordons him off from engagement, he struggles to be part of that continuity that he fetishizes in the signifier of the 'fil' that pervades his writing. The veil depersonalizes him, shrouds him in an impersonal, anonymous detachment that plagues his attempts at self-definition:

> Pendant cinq ans j'avais habité une invisible guérite d'où l'on peut parler et voir n'importe qui et moi-même ou n'importe quoi étant un fragment détaché du reste du monde [...] un lacet de soulier n'indiquaient rien de différent sauf qu'une habitude prise dans l'enfance m'empêchait encore de chausser les Pyramides [...]. Parfaitement noyé dans mon espèce et mon règne, mon existence individuelle avait de moins en moins de surface ni de volume.[32]

Rather than being on the continuum of the 'fil', Genet puts himself in a sentry box alongside it; a discontinuous fragment that has no place along the linearity of connection, slipping from the bonds that enable relation. Detached and unbound, the only tie that grips Genet is the shoe-lace: a temporal ligature that pulls him back to the habits of a childhood already marked by filial rupture. The shoelace is not just any knot but a learned skill acquired in infancy, a cipher for a moment in time when

---

31   Hadrien Laroche, *Le Dernier Genet* (Paris: Editions du Seuil, 1997), 128.
32   Genet, *Un Captif Amoureux*, 424.

we are taught or when there is a connection between parent and child, both mimetically reinforced by the act of tying. This is a nostalgic tie to a filiation that can only materialize in Genet's texts through the signifier, the 'lacet' elicited at the end of this last text a poignant tribute to an imagined economy of connection which Genet can only weave his way into via the text.

Affiliation for Genet is figured not as interpersonal, but as temporal: his affiliations link him to a moment at his birth which then severs connection, a strange separation which he experiences as the exclusionary singularity of an individual existence which 'avait de moins en moins de surface ni de volume'. It seems appropriate to conclude this chapter with the same metaphor of volume that Genet affirmed in 1981 as the vehicle that communicated a time he considered sacred. These last remarks in *Un Captif Amoureux* conflate Genet's final volume with a final foray into a time of filiation that was so constitutive to all the writing that filled the previous tomes. There can be no volumes without this sacred time, it binds his works: time a material ligature that agitates his writing while allowing it to blossom. The temporal stretch of a 'certain temps de ma vie à ma naissance' is reified as a sovereign gap that his works strive to fill, time experienced as a labyrinth which his texts try to navigate but whose guiding thread can only unfurl into this temporal prison which recaptures the time at his birth. Defiantly resistant to being covered over or moving forward, I conceive of such time as a Derridean verdict, a worm-word that Genet stitches as a truth into his texts because his abandonment to the Assistance Publique marks a filial rupture that all his volumes explore. The time of Genet's abandoned childhood is reclaimed as a verdict of his own making: the 'fils perdu(s)' finds new presence in the ubiquitous play of a signifier that recasts filiation as a self-governing, self-producing relation; Genet's worm-words writing a preventative stitch in a time of rupture. Just as we began this paper with Derrida's childhood memory of diminishing in order to let the work's meaning become apparent, so too is it valuable to unfurl the threads of Genet's time as a way of gleaning a truth that he constructs, his shape-shifting time a 'maillage imprenable' woven as a verdict into his texts, and whose material posterity *as* texts serves to preserve a time that really matters.

Selected Bibliography

Aristotle, *Aristotle's Physics*, trans. G. Apostle Hippocrates (Bloomington: Indiana University Press, 1969).

Bennington, Geoffrey, *Not Half No End: Militantly Melancholic Essays of Jacques Derrida* (Edinburgh: Edinburgh University Press, 2010).

Cixous, Hélène, *L'entretien de la blessure* (Paris: Galilée, 2011).

——, and Jacques Derrida, *Voiles* (Paris: Galilée, 1998).

Deleuze, Gilles, *Critiques et Cliniques* (Paris: Editions de Minuit, 1993).

Fredette, Nathalie, *Figures Baroques de Jean Genet* (Saint-Denis: Presses universitaires de Vincennes, 2001).

Freud, Sigmund, 'Creative writers and Day-dreaming', in *Complete Works*, Vol. 9, trans. James Strachey (London: Penguin, 1959), 143–53.

Fuller, Thomas, *Gnomologia, Adagies and Proverbs, Wise Sentences and Witty Sayings, Ancient and Modern, Foreign and British*, collected by T. Fuller, M.D., Queens' College, Cambridge (London, 1732).

Genet, Jean, *L'ennemi déclaré: textes et entretiens*, ed. Albert Dichy (Paris: Gallimard, 1991).

——, *Lettres à Marc et Olga Barbezat* (Paris: L'Arbalète, 1988).

——, *Œuvres Complètes II* (Paris: Gallimard, 1952).

——, *Œuvres Complètes V* (Paris: Gallimard, 1978).

——, *Théâtre Complète* (Paris: Gallimard, 2002).

—— *Un Captif Amoureux* (Paris: Gallimard, 1986).

Hanrahan, Mairéad, 'Sculpting time', *Paragraph* 27.2 (2004), 43–58.

Kristeva, Julia, *Pouvoirs de l'horreur: essai sur l'abjection* (Paris: Editions du Seuil, 1980).

Laroche, Hadrien, *Le Dernier Genet* (Paris: Editions du Seuil, 1997).

Nancy, Jean-Luc, *Le sens du monde* (Paris: Galilée, 1993).

DANIEL A. FINCH-RACE

Fluid Temporality and Identity in Verlaine's 'Ariettes oubliées' I, III, VI, VIII, IX

The Ecopoetics of Time and Identity

The entwinement of time and identity is a prominent feature of ecopoetic works, especially because the environmental concerns that such pieces evoke are deeply engrained in the circumstances of particular protagonists at a given moment. The notion of time is, indeed, an essential part of poetry, whether in terms of how a piece unfolds according to metrical exigencies, or with regard to the status of a specific collection of lines as a historical monument. In *Sustainable Poetry*, Leonard Scigaj offers a wide-ranging definition of ecopoetry, envisioning it as 'poetry that persistently stresses human cooperation with nature conceived as a dynamic, interrelated series of cyclic feedback systems'.[1] Following this notion of recurring processes in nature, poetry (whether explicitly ecological or not) could also be temporally interpreted as a system that ebbs and flows according to the movements of its various parts, ranging from punctuated clauses within individual lines, to whole divisions of a multipartite piece. After all, time becomes linked to precisely demarcated individuality once poetry is given a physical form, not only in terms of the space that a work occupies, but also in the way that it relates to its surroundings, including literary and cultural traditions. Temporal issues thus form the basis of poetic analysis, though they gain special significance in poems with an ecological theme, since such

---

1   Leonard Scigaj, *Sustainable Poetry: Four American Ecopoets* (Lexington: University of Kentucky Press, 1999), 37.

works most often arise from the industrialized era, during which both the non-human world and time increasingly came to be treated as commodities. The nineteenth century beheld, indeed, notable concerns over a lost sense of communion between humanity and the non-human world, leading to increased eco-sensitivity and a desire to recover essentiality; as Scott Bryson aptly identifies in *The West Side of Any Mountain*, poets from the Romantic period onwards looked to reconnect with 'a sense of the world as one organism made up of symbiotic components, both human and nonhuman', embracing 'a sympathy for the nonhuman other that leads to a recognition of kinship between humans and the rest of the natural world, and to an awareness of the human inability ever to understand or articulate the other'.[2] Such difficulties in communication and understanding often express themselves in a language of lack or unease, through which authors attempt to define their own muddled sense of self, as well as their relationship to their surroundings, when explicitly faced with the environment in which they are situated. Nature has long been a mysterious fount of inspiration in discussions of identity, of course, perhaps because the non-human world is at once so fundamental in human affairs, yet provides no easy answers to existential questions. The act of paying heed to the environment is a constructive step towards an understanding of both the self and the wider world, though it is not without danger, as Daniel Grimley suggests in his eco-musical analysis of Sibelius: 'attuning our ears more closely to the often dissonant, unharmonizing sounds of the acoustic environment around us is a risky process, one that renders us vulnerable and that points unerringly to our own contingency, our transient and fleeting presence in the world'.[3] By opening themselves up to ecological concerns, poets initiate a process of enquiry and destabilization that paves the way for challenges to societal preconceptions at the most elemental level, encouraging questions over the values common to anthropocentric hierarchies, especially the unassailability of human proclivities and beliefs with regard to the non-human world.

---

2   Scott Bryson, *The West Side of Any Mountain: Place, Space, and Ecopoetry* (Iowa City: University of Iowa Press, 2005), 121.
3   Daniel Grimley, 'Music, Landscape, Attunement: Listening to Sibelius' *Tapiola*', *Journal of the American Musicological Society* 64.2 (2011), 394–8 (398).

Romances sans paroles, 'Ariettes oubliées' I, III, VI, VIII, IX

Setting the tone for the *Romances sans paroles*, Verlaine's 'Ariettes oubliées'[4] treat the narrator-poet's surroundings as a counterpart to psychosocial musings, with the result that his crepuscular visions come to problematize the blurred relationship between society and the non-human world in tandem with ecopoetic evocations, as a corollary of Yann Frémy's notion in *Verlaine*: 'refusant [un] climat délétère, la section des *Ariettes oubliées* affiche donc une volonté de renouveau poétique'.[5] Temporal and ecological phenomena often serve as touchstones, in fact, for Verlaine's consideration of the musical ephemerality of poetry, in conjunction with the prosodic subversion that Jacques Robichez judiciously foregrounds in *Verlaine entre Rimbaud et Dieu*: 'les *Romances sans paroles* [...] vont cependant assez loin dans le sens des innovations techniques. Elles renient ouvertement l'art parnassien et s'en éloignent jusqu'à une limite que Verlaine ne dépassera pas, ou très rarement'.[6] The 'Ariettes oubliées' thus comprise the essence of a process of maturation, manifest in the evolving role of ecological phenomena as counterparts to Verlaine's exploration of identity and temporality, focalized by Susan Taylor-Horrex in *Verlaine* when she highlights 'Verlaine's [...] art of near-disembodied sensations'.[7] The synaesthetic melancholic musings in each Ariette can be understood as foregrounding nineteenth-century tensions between an eco-sensitive past and the promise of improved relations between society and the non-human world, augmented by the increasing virtuosity with which prosodic rules are subverted.

Building on Benoît de Cornulier's apposite proposal in *Théorie du vers* that 'Rimbaud et Verlaine, qui étaient en réalité affranchis de la mesure

---

4   Paul Verlaine, *Fêtes galantes – La Bonne Chanson – Romances sans paroles – Écrits sur Rimbaud*, ed. J. Gaudon (Paris: Garnier-Flammarion, 1976).

5   Yann Frémy, *Verlaine: la parole ou l'oubli* (Louvain-la-Neuve: Academia, 2013), 118.

6   Jacques Robichez, *Verlaine entre Rimbaud et Dieu* (Paris: Société d'édition d'enseignement supérieur, 1982), 79.

7   Susan Taylor-Horrex, *Verlaine: 'Fêtes galantes' and 'Romances sans paroles'* (London: Grant & Cutler, 1988), 21.

classique de l'alexandrin (vieille servitude dépassée) [...], ont seulement cherché à donner l'impression – graphiquement et sur le papier – qu'ils respectaient les "obligations" classiques',[8] Verlaine can be construed as setting out to destabilize poiesis in a similar way to Rimbaud. The importance of the association between the two men should not go unnoticed, in fact, when considering their output between 1871 and 1873, as Françoise d'Eaubonne recognizes in *Verlaine et Rimbaud, ou la fausse évasion*: 'il est rare de trouver [...] une influence mutuelle allant jusqu'à la compénétration, presque à l'identification à certains moments – sommets d'une liaison – entre deux âmes aussi opposées que le noir et le blanc'.[9] Comparison of the 'Ariettes oubliées' and Rimbaud's verse from the same era suggests that there is a not-insignificant stylistic and ecopoetic commonality between the works of the two poets, further elucidated by Jacques-Henry Bornecque in his contribution to *La Petite Musique de Verlaine*: 'Verlaine, explorateur d'une surréalité dans le réel qui n'appartient qu'à lui, a découvert *l'infrarouge et l'ultraviolet des choses* [en dépassant] l'émulation passionnée de son mauvais ange'.[10] It is thus important to consider the significance of the Rimbaldian conceptualizations that surface in the 'Ariettes oubliées' in light of the preponderance of ecological imagery and subversive versification evident in the works of both poets during the era of their companionship.

Verlaine's preoccupation with temporal and emotional questioning is certainly idiosyncratically striking, particularly on account of the preponderance of *vers impairs* in his work. The uneven number of syllables entailed in the abnormal meter makes his lines unbalanced, implying temporal and definitional upsets that are concerning in both prosodic and personal terms, in keeping with Seth Whidden's claim in *Leaving Parnassus*: 'Verlaine's poems in *Romances sans paroles* are greatly influenced by Rimbaud's poetry,

---

8   Benoît de Cornulier, *Théorie du vers: Rimbaud, Verlaine, Mallarmé* (Paris: Seuil, 1982), 154.

9   Françoise d'Eaubonne, *Verlaine et Rimbaud, ou la fausse évasion* (Paris: Albin Michel, 1960), 12.

10   Jacques-Henry Bornecque, 'L'Œil double et les motivations verlainiennes dans *Romances sans paroles*' in J. Beauverd et al., eds, *La Petite Musique de Verlaine: 'Romances sans paroles', 'Sagesse'* (Paris: Société d'édition d'enseignement supérieur, 1982), 97–113 (113).

and his poetic subject is on the brink of collapse'.[11] A meter common to popular song (and medieval lyric) provides a fitting framework, indeed, for the intimate and enigmatic sketches, strewn with emotional wreckage, that comprise Ariettes I, VIII and the even-numbered lines of IX. Verlaine's positioning of himself as an outsider both in form and content furthermore imbues his work with potency, since it unsettles traditional conceptions of poetry and society, as Arnaud Bernadet emphasizes in *L'Exil et l'utopie*: 'écrire comme *vaincu*, c'est donc instaurer un état d'exception, faire surgir et advenir l'infime et le pluriel du sujet et du sens dans le récit dominant de l'histoire'.[12] The quest for meaning and the narrative of disillusionment that suffuse the 'Ariettes oubliées' thus deserve particular attention, given their potential for illuminating psychosocial and temporal concerns as an adjunct to developments in nineteenth-century ecopoetics, in line with Taylor-Horrex's assertion that the '*Ariettes oubliées* present kaleidoscopic perspectives on the physical, emotional and artistic relationship'.[13] By investigating how the intricacies of these associations are elaborated through the indexation of such concerns against ecological phenomena and prosodic subversion, an ecocritical illumination of the distress and imprecision that permeate Ariettes I, III, VI, VIII and IX will be achieved.

Ariettes I and III: Fluid Identity, Troubled Time, Uncertain Love

The seed of a novel Verlainian poiesis is planted in the first Ariette, beginning with a tripartite anaphora of impersonal assertions that encompasses both a quasi-expiatory offering and an enumeration of sensations in the present tense:

> C'est l'extase langoureuse,
> C'est la fatigue amoureuse,
> C'est tous les frissons des bois. (1–3)

11 Seth Whidden, *Leaving Parnassus: The Lyric Subject in Verlaine and Rimbaud* (Amsterdam: Rodopi, 2007), 15.
12 Arnaud Bernadet, *L'Exil et l'utopie: politiques de Verlaine* (Saint-Etienne: L'université de Saint-Etienne, 2007), 26.
13 Taylor-Horrex, *Verlaine*, 49.

The juxtaposition of monosyllabic repetition and a trisyllabic *rime léonine* in the first two lines sets the tone for the sextet, as well as for the rest of the poem, with its evocation of sensuousness and frailty in relation to an ecological topos, without any obvious human interference. The grammatical detachment of the beginning complements Robichez's idea of naivety on the part of the narrator-poet: 'la tournure impersonnelle suggère une âme dépossédée, spectatrice seulement d'émotions élémentaires, incertaines et gratuites, au bord [...] de l'inconscience'.[14] The contrast between the richness of the opening feminine *rime plate* and the masculine *rime suffisante* in the first pairing of the *rimes embrassées* that complete the stanza suggests a division, in fact, between human experience and the world of nature, especially given the epigraph from Favart: 'Le vent dans la plaine/Suspend son haleine'. It is as if society is pursuing satisfaction at the expense of the non-human world, though the predominance of feminine rhymes in the stanza (F-F-M-F-F-M), as well as elsewhere in the piece, is suggestive of a desire to seek greater complicity with the non-human world, turning away from the domination and exploitation of nature that nineteenth-century androcentric society entailed. The second sextet is emphatically concerned with an ecological theme:

> O le frêle et frais murmure!
> Cela gazouille et susurre,
> Cela ressemble au cri doux
> Que l'herbe agitée expire ... (7–10)

A third party is also introduced in the second instance of *cadence majeure*, which recurs in the same position as in the first stanza, enhancing the link between humanity and its surroundings, since the impersonal 'C'est' (5) preceding an ecological idea has developed to the second-person singular pronoun: 'Tu dirais' (11). The onomatopoeia ('murmure' (7); 'gazouille' (8)) and sibilance ('susurre' (8); 'ressemble' (9)) of the second stanza form a crescendo that evinces the increasingly ephemeral temporality and musicality of the poem, in line with Bernadet's identification of 'une euphorie

14   Robichez, *Verlaine entre Rimbaud et Dieu*, 63.

de la simplicité et de la spontanéité' generating 'une espèce d'authenticité' whereby 'cette naïveté manifeste une autre manière de voir le monde pour le poète, et d'y vivre'.[15] The possibility of contentment in love as a counterpart to the escalating rambunctiousness of the non-human world is muffled, however, at the very end of the sextet by the assonance of the twelfth line, suggestively underscoring the lack of vibrantly noisy nature in human affairs: 'Le roulis sourd des cailloux' (12). The tensions of the poem reach their apogee at the beginning of the final sextet:

> Cette âme qui se lamente
> En cette plainte dormante
> C'est la nôtre, n'est-ce pas?
> La mienne, dis, et la tienne. (13–16)

The introduction of a shared, idealized notion of existence in the fifteenth line is neutered in the sixteenth; a division made all the more emphatic by the quasi-chiasmus and three-one-three balance of the latter, in which the strength of the bond suggested by the *coupe lyrique* of the fifteenth is also parodied, as it precedes the imperative seeking reassurance. Rather than provide a comforting resolution to the dilemma, the last line of the piece further opens up temporal and sentimental questions, seeking comfort about the unexpectedness of the experience at the key moment of transition between day and night: 'Par ce tiède soir, tout bas?' (18). This introductory Ariette thus raises the issues of self-doubt, love and ephemerality in conjunction with ecopoetic expression, while also challenging fixed notions of time and identity.

Ariette III is a poem of tragic melancholy, wherein the narrator-poet cannot comprehend his ceaseless wretchedness: 'Il pleure sans raison/Dans ce cœur qui s'écœure' (9–10). Key terms recur with striking regularity, as introductory phrases ('Il pleure' (1; 9); 'O' (5; 8)), as the second or third syllable of similarly positioned lines in each stanza ('Pour un cœur' (7); 'Dans ce cœur' (10); 'Mon cœur' (16)), or as identical rhymes at the beginning and end of each quatrain ('mon cœur' (1; 4); 'de la pluie' (5; 8); 'sans

15   Bernadet, *L'Exil et l'utopie*, 138.

raison' (9; 12); 'peine' (13; 16)). This unceasing anaphora, combined with
the paronomasia of the two key plosive verbs, is the perfect counterpart to
the image of the steady rainfall on the town: initially, it is a 'bruit doux' (5),
then a symptom of 'la pire peine' (13). The linguistico-poetic artifice that
Verlaine pursues also creates a contrast to the irrigating power of the rain,
in a way that suggests artistic whimsicality, weighed down by dejection,
as Frémy judiciously asserts: 'il s'agirait dans ce poème d'un cas d'écriture
ludique, à l'instar des jubilations zutiques, s'il n'y avait dans le développe-
ment verlainien autant de désespoir'.[16] Emotional uncertainty and definitional fluidity are further channelled through the subversion of rhyming
convention: not only does each stanza alternate between M-F-M-M and
F-M-F-F rhyme, but each differing line does not even fit with any other
rhyming possibility in the poem. The link created amongst 'ville' (2), 'toits'
(6), 's'écœure' (10) and 'pourquoi' (14) is nevertheless suggestive of the
role of urbanization in the unhappiness of the narrator-poet, since he is
trapped in an environment offering no communion with the essentiality
of the non-human world. His despair thus remains unresolved:

> C'est bien la pire peine
> De ne savoir pourquoi
> Sans amour et sans haine
> Mon cœur a tant de peine! (13–16)

Gone is the concept of Verlaine's sardonic nature that Antoine Fongaro foregrounds in his contribution to *Autour du Symbolisme*: the third Ariette lacks
'le scepticisme, voire le sarcasme, qu'il utilise à propos de l'amour'.[17] Ecological
phenomena serve only to demonstrate, perhaps even aggravate, the despair
of the narrator-poet, due to an absence of the reassurance demanded in the
first Ariette. The hexasyllabic meter of the piece underscores, moreover, a
sense of deficiency in Verlaine's experience of love, since eight alexandrines
could almost perfectly be formed from the sixteen lines, yet he rejects such

---

16   Frémy, *Verlaine*, 92.
17   Antoine Fongaro, '"L'Espoir luit …"', in P.G. Castex, ed., *Autour du Symbolisme:*
     Villiers, Mallarmé, Verlaine, Rimbaud (Paris: José Corti, 1955), 227–56 (241).

a harmonious structure. There are not even any instances of internal punctuation, apart from the interjection in the eleventh line that highlights the *cadence majeure* of the third quatrain: 'Quoi! nulle trahison?' (11). The poem encompasses, indeed, the breathless tirade of a lover ceaselessly demanding a satisfying response to the initial question: 'Quelle est cette langueur/Qui pénètre mon cœur?' (3–4). The piece thus develops the empirical, quasi-procedural understanding of love from the first Ariette, substantiating Robichez's proposal that Verlaine's experience is 'comme une analyse, procédant par tâtonnements, par nuances successives.'[18] In this way, Ariette III sets the stage for the juxtaposition of amorous experience against ecological and temporal phenomena at the heart of the remaining pieces; by exposing his poetry to the musicality of his surroundings, in an attempt to commune with something beyond human experience, Verlaine might yet be able to achieve greater complicity with the non-human world and heightened self-understanding.

Ariettes VI, VIII and IX:
Destabilization, Pathetic Fallacy, Disconnectedness

Verlaine is at his most playful and enigmatic in Ariette VI, wherein the octosyllabic metre is practically the only conventional element of versification, as a meter of *vers pairs*. The preponderance of inadmissible masculine-feminine half-rhymes signals that Verlaine is destabilizing poiesis in a manner not dissimilar to that of his younger companion from 1871 to 1873, as Whidden suggests: 'the liberties he takes with respect to versification are inspired by Rimbaud's poetic project.'[19] The subversion of prosodic traditions is neatly established in tripartite fashion: first, by the inversion of rhyming arrangements between stanzas, as F-M-M-F becomes M-F-F-M, apart from in the final two quatrains, in which feminine precedence is maintained; second, by uncertainty over whether the quatrains display *rimes croisées*, implying inadmissible masculine-feminine rhymes, or *rimes embrassées*, following

18   Robichez, *Verlaine entre Rimbaud et Dieu*, 58.
19   Whidden, *Leaving Parnassus*, 77.

the disposition of masculine and feminine pairs, but without achieving any
rhymes; third, through the recurrence of the rhyming phoneme between
'Guet!' (2) and 'égaie' (4) within two stanzas in 'Ramée' (9) and 'famé' (11),
then twice more in the final pair of quatrains, not only in 'abbé' (26) and
'attrapée!' (28), but also in 'fatigué' (30) and 'égaie' (32), where the echo is
made even more prominent by the wholesale repetition of the fourth line as
the conclusion to the piece. This prosodic uncertainty magnificently conveys
the temporal difficulties and disrupted identities of the protagonists in the
piece, though the sixth Ariette differs somewhat from the previous poems
of amorous melancholy, since its overriding concern appears to be a certain
knowing playfulness; Robichez claims that 'Rimbaud est [...] ici, l'initiateur.
On sait son goût pour les "contes de fées, petits livres de l'enfance, opéras
vieux, refrains niais, rythmes naïfs" [*Une Saison en enfer*, 'Alchimie du verbe'].
C'est ce que Verlaine appellera les "Images d'un sou".'[20] The reiteration of
'François-les-bas-bleus s'en égaie' (4; 32) at the end of the poem nonetheless
prefigures the stanzaic repetition of the eighth Ariette; thus the piece represents another stage of maturation in Verlaine's poiesis. The narrator-poet
can be envisioned as concerned with subversively musical versification ('Petit
poète jamais las/De la rime non attrapée!' (28)), as well as with speciesist
humour that places animals below humans as comical objects of spectacle:
'C'est le chien de Jean de Nivelle/Qui mord sous l'œil même du Guet!' (1–2).
Such slapstick at the opening of the poem not only fits with the challenge to
societal and poetic traditions that the 'Ariettes oubliées' express as a whole,
but also with the subversive behaviour of the protagonists in the series as a
whole, of which François-les-bas-bleus is synechdocally evocative:

> Cependant jamais fatigué
> D'être inattentif et naïf
> François-les-bas-bleus s'en égaie. (30–2)

The excess of internal rhyme in the penultimate line, coupled with the striking feminine-masculine *rime pauvre* between 'arrive' (29) and 'naïf' (31),
substantiates Taylor-Horrex's understanding of this Ariette as 'Verlaine's

20   Robichez, *Verlaine entre Rimbaud et Dieu*, 67.

version of Rimbaud's 'Ma Bohème', a half-mocking poem of joyous wandering [...]. It is a poetic adventure'.[21] Verlaine's intent to challenge traditional preconceptions and versification is thus pursued through a continuing destabilization of temporality and identity, as he sketches the contours of a new poiesis in which fluidity and musicality are the defining values.

Nowhere in the nine components of the 'Ariettes oubliées' is there more repetition than in the eighth piece: the first and last quatrains, as well as the second and fourth, are identical, plus all the rhymes are feminine. This prosodic singularity makes the ecopoetic perplexity of the portentous sky, distant forests and scattered organisms even more striking: transcending phantasmagoria, Verlaine evokes an eco-sensitive lament, in line with Robichez's claim that 'chaque [...] vers est un murmure douloureux, suivi d'un long silence. [...] Le sentiment tourne et retourne sur lui-même, chagrin indéfiniment ressassé, qui s'enferme dans une sorte d'hébétude'.[22] The fatalistic, unsettling hopelessness of the piece is highlighted by the pentasyllabic meter in another instance of unbalanced *vers impairs* perpetuating unease and destabilization, as well as by the almost constant enjambement, implying fluctuating temporality and emotions. Practically every quatrain is, in fact, a fluid twenty-syllable unit, since there is no punctuation in the stanzas apart from a concluding mark, foregrounding the unchanging barrenness and 'Ennui' (2; 22) of the 'neige incertaine' (3; 23), as well as the atemporal unnaturalness of the copper-tinged sky (5; 13). These ecological phenomena, coupled with the narrator-poet's pessimistic observation of the lunar cycle, emphasize the crippling stasis and lack of inspirational irrigation in nineteenth-century French society: 'On croirait voir vivre/Et mourir la lune' (7–8; 15–16). Following Antoine Adam's suggestion in *Verlaine* that the post-urbanization world is 'un paysage grelottant [...] qui étreint le cœur'[23] of the protagonist, 'les buées' (12) can be understood as obscuring the way ahead for the narrator-poet, not only distancing him from complicity with his environment, but also compounding his temporal and definitional uncertainties:

21   Taylor-Horrex, *Verlaine*, 53.
22   Robichez, *Verlaine entre Rimbaud et Dieu*, 81–2.
23   Antoine Adam, *Verlaine: l'homme et l'œuvre* (Paris: Hatier-Boivin, 1953), 95.

the vaporous imagery insinuates the extent to which it is difficult for the narrator-poet to define his identity and desires, as well as the way in which industrialization has clouded the value of the non-human world in the eyes of androcentric society. From this perspective, the fifth quatrain becomes even more notable than its differentiation from the other stanzas already dictates: the concluding question mark and two commas in the second line ('Et vous, les loups maigres', (18)) create a remarkable seven-three-ten syllabic division in the stanza that foregrounds the unsettling presence of both the 'Corneille poussive' (17) and the emaciated wolves at the apogee of the piece. The fatalistic distress of the narrator-poet is thus related in terms of another ecopoetic vignette suffused with melancholia and troubling imagery, substantiating Frémy's notion that 'Verlaine [se] tient à un climat d'hésitation objective'.[24] The anxiety of the question with which the Ariette concludes is highlighted by the richness of its rhyme with 'poussive' (17), as well as by its role as the last original member of the *rimes embrassées* before the end of the piece: 'Quoi donc vous arrive?' (20). The poor state of the animals and the wan oak trees in 'Les forêts prochaines/Parmi les buées' (11–12) thus becomes intimately linked to Verlaine's personal and poetic troubles, underscored further by the crescendo to the penultimate stanza before the quasi-capitulatory repetition of the first quatrain as the final stanza of the piece. The cyclical prosody deserves to be envisioned, indeed, as a mirror of the diminishment and difficulties of the wheezing crow, setting up the elevated importance of an ailing avian motif and the inevitability of the decisively detrimental latter phases of industrialization entailed in the lament of the final poem in the series.

Ariette IX is a grave condensation of temporal and ecological concerns in two quatrains, in which Verlaine is preoccupied by a quasi-Rimbaldian ethical and poetic crisis, although he differs from his younger companion's breakaway tendencies by not proposing solutions to the issues raised earlier in the series. Taylor-Horrex focalizes 'Verlaine's use of bird symbolism for distressed states of mind'[25] in this

24   Frémy, *Verlaine*, 97.
25   Taylor-Horrex, *Verlaine*, 48.

reflection on the dilemma of Cyrano de Bergerac's nightingale, also suffused with Baudelairean melancholy, particularly evoked in the first half of the second quatrain, with its sixfold repetition of the occlusive /m/: 'Combien, ô voyageur, ce paysage blême/Te mira blême toi-même' (5–6). Reaching out imploringly to his contemporaries through the apostrophe of the wanderer, Verlaine foregrounds not only the pallor of his degraded environment, but also the misery of fellow organisms, as well as a lack of human understanding with regard to the ecological consequences of industrialization. The piece is, indeed, a dirge of psychosocial and poetic disappointment, directed at the shortcomings of the narrator-poet's time, with both Verlaine's eco-sensitivity and what Pierre Cogny, in his contribution to *La Petite Musique de Verlaine*, calls a 'kyrielle des atténuatifs'[26] reaching their zenith in:

L'ombre des arbres dans la rivière embrumée
Meurt comme de la fumée
Tandis qu'en l'air, parmi les ramures réelles,
Se plaignent les tourterelles. (1–4)

There is also a sense of prosodic dissatisfaction in the employment of *rimes plates* and alexandrines (muddlingly alternated with heptasyllabic lines) for the finale of the 'Ariettes oubliées', deftly sustaining the weary anguish of the narrator-poet. In line with the exclusivity of female rhymes, the slight metamorphosis of the first rhyming phoneme in the singular pairing of 'embrumée' (1) and 'fumée' (2) to the plural couple of 'feuillées' (7) and 'noyées' (8) is suggestive, moreover, of the heightened importance of eco-femininity towards the end of the piece, striking a chord with Jean-Baptiste Morvan's assertion in his psychoanalytical discussion of rhyme that 'les terminaisons "ées" et "elles" possèdent une douceur d'éveil, un appel lent et prévenant à la fixation du sentiment et de l'image.'[27] The prevailing

---

26 Pierre Cogny, 'L'Expression du "rien" dans les *Romances sans paroles*', in J. Beauverd et al., eds, *La Petite Musique de Verlaine: 'Romances sans paroles', 'Sagesse'* (Paris: Société d'édition d'enseignement supérieur, 1982), 75–81 (80).

27 Jean-Baptiste Morvan, 'Psychanalyses de la rime', *Points et contrepoints* 999 (1971), 18–21 (20).

current of non-masculinity in this final Ariette can be envisioned, in fact, not only as a reaction to the androcentric hierarchies of nineteenth-century French society that were the driving force behind the breakneck pace of industrialization, but also as an indication of the importance of valorizing feminized entities, especially the non-human world, for a sustainable future. The last movement of the 'Ariettes oubliées' ultimately emphasizes that the narrator-poet is incapable of finding a solution to the crisis of his age, despite his attempts to plumb the depths of modern experience, so he engages in a cautionary apostrophe ('ô voyageur' (5)) that foregrounds the dangers for human identity arising from a lack of complicity with nature.

Psychosocial Matters

Verlaine is preoccupied with temporal and definitional concerns, searching for meaning in an industrialized era that is psychosocially troubling and ambiguous. In his Paris, factories had sprung up to transform raw materials into objects designed both to increase human mastery of nature and to service the escalating demands of human desires, whilst time-weathered referents were being demolished to make way for Haussmann's boulevards and a new incarnation of the metropolis that left many residents feeling displaced and uneasy. In *Mélancolie et opposition*, Ross Chambers outlines a concept of emotional tumult caused by such circumstances that is particularly applicable to Verlaine, especially in terms of the way in which communication (indeed, versification) becomes muddled under industrialization: 'des brouillards du spleen naît une perception de la réalité des brouillages – identités brouillées, discours brouillés, consciences fausses et/ou hantées d'inconscient'.[28] In this light, the ecological singularities that suffuse the 'Ariettes oubliées' are not only emblematic of the environmental effects of

---

28   Ross Chambers, *Mélancolie et opposition: les débuts du modernisme en France* (Paris: José Corti, 1987), 224.

industrialization and societal rapaciousness, but also of humanity's struggle to comprehend the non-human world when confronted with entities and phenomena that are at once familiar and mysterious. To this end, Friedrich Schelling's emphasis on the nebulous entwinement of the worlds of ecology and poetry in the conclusion to his *System of Transcendental Idealism* is particularly illuminating: 'what we call nature is a poem that lies hidden in a mysterious and marvellous script [...]; for the land of phantasy toward which we aspire gleams through the world of sense only as through a half-transparent mist'.[29] Ariettes I, III, VI, VIII and IX deserve to be understood, indeed, as Verlaine's attempts to fathom the depths of the mysterious worlds of both human and non-human nature, conjoining the two groupings in a manner that lessens the definitional demarcations that were solidifying during the nineteenth-century.

Verlaine's ecopoetic and temporal investigations in the opening section of the *Romances sans paroles* are ultimately subtle and impressionistic, involving synaesthetic and musical concoctions, as well as blurred sentiments and images depicted with a pallid palette. The fluidity that Verlaine infuses into traditional notions of poetry and identity combines with the mounting whimsicality of his verse to exemplify his internal vacillations and uneasy relationship with the values of the society that envelops him, as if in reaction to the modern phenomenon noted by Giorgio Agamben in his *Idea of Prose*: 'the human soul has lost its music – music understood as the scoring in the soul of the inaccessibility of the origin. Deprived of an epoch, worn out and without destiny, we reach the [...] threshold of our unmusical dwelling in time'.[30] The 'Ariettes oubliées' evoke both society's lack of attunement to its surroundings and the extent to which humanity has forgotten its beginnings in the non-human world, as well as the manner in which the unceasing pursuit of progress strips entities not only of an

---

29 Friedrich Schelling, 'Conclusion to *System of Transcendental Idealism*', trans. A. Hofstadter, in D. Simpson, ed., *The Origins of Modern Critical Thought: German Aesthetic and Literary Criticism from Lessing to Hegel* (Cambridge: Cambridge University Press, 1988), 225–31 (228).

30 Giorgio Agamben, *Idea of Prose*, trans. M. Sullivan and S. Whitsitt (Albany, NY: State University of New York Press, 1995), 91.

identity, but also of the ability to dwell peaceably in time and space. The edgy atmosphere of melancholia in Ariettes I, III, VI, VIII and IX should be construed as the result of problematic relationships between beings in the modern age, arising from the difficult dichotomy of neediness and self-sufficiency that the industrialized era entails. In *Reflections on Gender and Science*, Evelyn Keller nonetheless offers a hopeful vision for reconciliation: 'fears of merging, the loss of boundaries, on the one hand, and the fears of loneliness and disconnection, on the other, *can* be balanced [as can] one's contrasting desires for intimacy and independence'.[31] From this perspective, Verlaine's musings about his own identity and the ways in which he is affected both by human notions (especially love) and his environment indicate that he is at the beginning of a journey towards self-knowledge and a novel poiesis: though he still has much turmoil to overcome in order to resolve the conundrums that define human existence, it is only a matter of time before he will find fulfilment.

Selected Bibliography

Adam, Antoine, *Verlaine: l'homme et l'œuvre* (Paris: Hatier-Boivin, 1953).

Agamben, Giorgio, *Idea of Prose*, trans. M. Sullivan and S. Whitsitt (Albany: State University of New York Press, 1995).

Bernadet, Arnaud, *L'Exil et l'utopie: politiques de Verlaine* (Saint-Etienne: L'université de Saint-Etienne, 2007).

Bornecque, Jacques-Henry, 'L'Œil double et les motivations verlainiennes dans *Romances sans paroles*' in J. Beauverd et al., eds, *La Petite Musique de Verlaine: 'Romances sans paroles', 'Sagesse'* (Paris: Société d'édition d'enseignement supérieur, 1982), 97–113.

Bryson, Scott, *The West Side of Any Mountain: Place, Space, and Ecopoetry* (Iowa City: University of Iowa Press, 2005).

---

31   Evelyn Keller, *Reflections on Gender and Science* (New Haven, CT: Yale University Press, 1985), 100.

Chambers, Ross, *Mélancolie et opposition: les débuts du modernisme en France* (Paris: José Corti, 1987).

Cogny, Pierre, 'L'Expression du "rien" dans les *Romances sans paroles*', in J. Beauverd et al., eds, *La Petite Musique de Verlaine: 'Romances sans paroles', 'Sagesse'* (Paris: Société d'édition d'enseignement supérieur, 1982), 75–81.

Cornulier, Benoît de, *Théorie du vers: Rimbaud, Verlaine, Mallarmé* (Paris: Seuil, 1982).

D'Eaubonne, Françoise, *Verlaine et Rimbaud, ou la fausse évasion* (Paris: Albin Michel, 1960).

Debussy, Claude, *Correspondance 1884–1918*, ed. F. Lesure (Paris: Hermann, 1993).

Fongaro, Antoine, '"L'Espoir luit …"', in P.G. Castex, ed., *Autour du Symbolisme: Villiers, Mallarmé, Verlaine, Rimbaud* (Paris: José Corti, 1955), 227–56.

Frémy, Yann, *Verlaine: la parole ou l'oubli* (Louvain-la-Neuve: Academia, 2013).

Grimley, Daniel, 'Music, Landscape, Attunement: Listening to Sibelius' *Tapiola*', *Journal of the American Musicological Society* 64.2 (2011), 394–8.

Keller, Evelyn, *Reflections on Gender and Science* (New Haven, CT: Yale University Press, 1985).

Morvan, Jean-Baptiste, 'Psychanalyses de la rime', *Points et contrepoints* 999 (1971), 18–21.

Robichez, Jacques, *Verlaine entre Rimbaud et Dieu* (Paris: Société d'édition d'enseignement supérieur, 1982).

Schelling, Friedrich, 'Conclusion to *System of Transcendental Idealism*', trans. A. Hofstadter, in D. Simpson, ed., *The Origins of Modern Critical Thought: German Aesthetic and Literary Criticism from Lessing to Hegel* (Cambridge: Cambridge University Press, 1988), 225–31.

Scigaj, Leonard, *Sustainable Poetry: Four American Ecopoets* (Lexington: University of Kentucky Press, 1999).

Taylor-Horrex, Susan, *Verlaine: 'Fêtes galantes' and 'Romances sans paroles'* (London: Grant & Cutler, 1988).

Verlaine, Paul, *Fêtes galantes – La Bonne Chanson – Romances sans paroles – Écrits sur Rimbaud*, ed. J. Gaudon (Paris: Garnier-Flammarion, 1976).

Whidden, Seth, *Leaving Parnassus: The Lyric Subject in Verlaine and Rimbaud* (Amsterdam: Rodopi, 2007).

Notes on Contributors

JOANNE BRUETON read modern and medieval languages at St John's College, Cambridge, and is now completing her PhD at University College London on an AHRC scholarship. Her thesis examines geometries of relation in Jean Genet, drawing on models of ontology in Derrida, Deleuze and Nancy, and spatial aesthetics in Beckett, Cixous and Louise Bourgeois, to explore Genet's interplay between geometry and subjectivity.

CHRISTINA CHALMERS was born in Edinburgh and studied at the University of Cambridge (BA, MPhil). She has written on modernist poetry and politics.

MARTIN CROWLEY works on modern and contemporary thought and culture. His current research examines responses to crisis and catastrophe in the work of modern French thinkers. He is the author of: *L'Homme sans: politiques de la finitude* (with an afterword by Jean-Luc Nancy, 2009); *The New Pornographies: Explicit Sex in Recent French Fiction and Film* (co-authored with Victoria Best, 2007); *Robert Antelme: l'humanité irréductible* (2004); *Robert Antelme: Humanity, Community, Testimony* (2003), and *Duras, Writing, and the Ethical: Making the Broken Whole* (2000); and the editor of *Contact! The Art of Touch/L'Art du toucher* (2007), and *Dying Words: The Last Moments of Writers and Philosophers* (2000).

LOUIS DAUBRESSE is in the third year of a doctoral thesis in the University of Paris III (Sorbonne Nouvelle) in the School of Arts and Media. His thesis explores mute figures in contemporary cinema, to explore the psychological, clinical, sociological and anthropological implications for the relationship between (the lack of) speech in films and the use of exterior sounds.

DANIEL A. FINCH-RACE is a doctoral candidate in modern and medieval languages at the University of Cambridge, specializing in nineteenth-century

French ecopoetics. He is the recipient of an external research studentship from Trinity College.

DAVID GRUNDY is working on a PhD at the University of Cambridge concerning collectivity in African-American poetry. He co-edits the poetry publication series *Materials*, which is based in Cambridge.

RYE HOLMBOE is a third-year doctoral candidate in the history of art at University College London, where his focus is on the relation between figuration and abstraction in contemporary art. He has recently co-authored and edited the book *JocJonJosch: Hand in Foot* (2013), published by the Musée d'art du Valais, Switzerland. He is the co-founder and editor of LOCUS Books. He has published essays and reviews on contemporary art, literature and philosophy.

LISA JESCHKE is a doctoral candidate in the English Faculty at the University of Cambridge, focusing on late modernist poetry and theatricality. She is author of *Dead Cheap* (2014) and co-author of *David Cameron [a theatre of knife songs]* (2014). She co-edits the poetry publication series *Materials*, which is based in Cambridge.

JENNIFER JOHNSON is a doctoral student in the History of Art Department at the University of Oxford. Her thesis, entitled 'Georges Rouault's Modernism and the Question of Materiality', considers questions of meaning and medium in modernist painting between 1900 and 1920. Having begun her academic career studying English literature at Cambridge, she is also interested in the problems shared by modernist art and literature, as well as particular interested in British abstraction and in nineteenth- and early twentieth-century British art and architectural theory.

ADRIAN MAY is a doctoral candidate at the University of Cambridge, studying the contemporary French intellectual revue *Lignes* to explore what happened to the radical philosophical left over the past twenty-five years. He is interested more widely in cultural politics under neo-liberalism, and periodical publications as sites where aesthetics, politics, philosophy and writing coalesce.

ANDREW OTWAY is currently a PhD candidate at Lancaster University. His research focuses on urban rhythmanalysis, referring to the work of Henri Lefebvre, and is supervised by the Department of European Languages and Cultures and the Department of Sociology. He is also interested in cultural geography, Marxism, radical environmental politics and sociology, as they apply to the urban.

ALEXANDRA PAULIN-BOOTH is a PhD candidate in history at the University of Oxford. Her research focuses on conceptualizations of time in the late nineteenth and early twentieth centuries, and their subsequent impact on political ideology and practice.

DANIEL POITRAS completed his PhD in 2013 on the subject of experiences of time and historiography in France and Quebec during the twentieth century. He is now doing a postdoctorate at Sciences Po (Paris) on the student movements in Paris and Berkeley during the 1960s.

JESSICA STACEY is a PhD candidate at King's College London. She is working on a thesis entitled 'Catastrophe and the Anachronic: The *côté sombre* of Pre-Revolutionary France', which examines the manner in which events figured as catastrophic upset linear understandings of time and periodization.

GEORGE TOMLINSON is a PhD candidate at the Centre for Research in Modern European Philosophy at Kingston University. His research focuses on Marx's critique of political economy in relation to philosophies of time and history in the modern European tradition.

Index

Modern French Identities
Edited by Peter Collier

This series aims to publish monographs, editions or collections of papers based on recent research into modern French Literature. It welcomes contributions from academics, researchers and writers in British and Irish universities in particular.

Modern French Identities focuses on the French and Francophone writing of the twentieth century, whose formal experiments and revisions of genre have combined to create an entirely new set of literary forms, from the thematic autobiographies of Michel Leiris and Bernard Noël to the magic realism of French Caribbean writers.

The idea that identities are constructed rather than found, and that the self is an area to explore rather than a given pretext, runs through much of modern French literature, from Proust, Gide and Apollinaire to Kristeva, Barthes, Duras, Germain and Roubaud.

This series reflects a concern to explore the turn-of-the-century turmoil in ideas and values that is expressed in the works of theorists like Lacan, Irigaray and Bourdieu and to follow through the impact of current ideologies such as feminism and postmodernism on the literary and cultural interpretation and presentation of the self, whether in terms of psychoanalytic theory, gender, autobiography, cinema, fiction and poetry, or in newer forms like performance art.

The series publishes studies of individual authors and artists, comparative studies, and interdisciplinary projects, including those where art and cinema intersect with literature.

Volume 1   Victoria Best & Peter Collier (eds): Powerful Bodies.
            Performance in French Cultural Studies.
            220 pages. 1999. ISBN 3-906762-56-4 / US-ISBN 0-8204-4239-9

Volume 2   Julia Waters: Intersexual Rivalry.
            A 'Reading in Pairs' of Marguerite Duras and Alain Robbe-Grillet.
            228 pages. 2000. ISBN 3-906763-74-9 / US-ISBN 0-8204-4626-2